ROUTLEDGE LIBRARY EDITIONS:
GERMAN LITERATURE

Volume 24

GERMAN LYRIC POETRY

GERMAN LYRIC POETRY
A Critical Analysis of Selected Poems from Klopstock to Rilke

S. S. PRAWER

LONDON AND NEW YORK

First published in 1952 by Routledge & Kegan Paul Ltd

This edition first published in 2020
by Routledge
2 Park Square, Milton Park, Abingdon, Oxon OX14 4RN

and by Routledge
52 Vanderbilt Avenue, New York, NY 10017

Routledge is an imprint of the Taylor & Francis Group, an informa business

© 1952 S. S. Prawer

All rights reserved. No part of this book may be reprinted or reproduced or utilised in any form or by any electronic, mechanical, or other means, now known or hereafter invented, including photocopying and recording, or in any information storage or retrieval system, without permission in writing from the publishers.

Trademark notice: Product or corporate names may be trademarks or registered trademarks, and are used only for identification and explanation without intent to infringe.

British Library Cataloguing in Publication Data
A catalogue record for this book is available from the British Library

ISBN: 978-0-367-41588-4 (Set)
ISBN: 978-1-00-301460-7 (Set) (ebk)
ISBN: 978-0-367-85622-9 (Volume 24) (hbk)
ISBN: 978-0-367-85623-6 (Volume 24) (pbk)
ISBN: 978-1-00-301394-5 (Volume 24) (ebk)

Publisher's Note
The publisher has gone to great lengths to ensure the quality of this reprint but points out that some imperfections in the original copies may be apparent.

Disclaimer
The publisher has made every effort to trace copyright holders and would welcome correspondence from those they have been unable to trace.

GERMAN LYRIC POETRY

A CRITICAL ANALYSIS
OF SELECTED POEMS
FROM KLOPSTOCK TO RILKE

by

S. S. PRAWER

ROUTLEDGE & KEGAN PAUL LIMITED
London

*First published in 1952
by Routledge & Kegan Paul Limited
Broadway House, 68-74 Carter Lane
London, E.C.4
Reprinted 1965*

*Printed in Great Britain
by Compton Printing Works Ltd.
London*

for
Professor and Mrs. B. W. Downs

To criticize is to appreciate, to appropriate, to take intellectual possession, to establish in fine a relation with the criticized thing and make it one's own.

HENRY JAMES

Acknowledgements

The following publishers have kindly granted permission to reprint copyright material: Helmut Küpper Verlag, Düsseldorf, quotations from Stefan George; S. Fischer Verlag, Frankfurt am Main, quotations from Hofmannsthal; Insel Verlag, Wiesbaden, quotations from Rilke and Hofmannsthal; Faber and Faber Ltd., passages from Mr. T. S. Eliot's *Four Quartets* and *Selected Essays*; Macmillan and Co., Ltd., passages from Henry James's prefaces and critical works; Hamish Hamilton Ltd., a quotation from Mr. Stephen Spender's *World within World*. I wish also to thank Professor Roy Pascal (Birmingham) and Professor Leonard Forster (University College, London) for valuable help and advice.

Contents

INTRODUCTION	page 1
1. APPROACHING THE GERMAN LYRIC	9
2. THE LYRIC POETRY OF THE AUFKLÄRUNG	26
(a) *Gellert: Epiktet*	26
(b) *Hagedorn: Der Mai*	30
3. KLOPSTOCK AND THE 'GÖTTINGER HAIN'	36
(a) *Klopstock: Der Zürcher See*	36
(b) *Hölty: Die Mainacht*	43
(c) *Claudius: Wiegenlied beim Mondschein zu singen*	47
4. GOETHE	54
(a) *Willkommen und Abschied*	54
(b) *Ganymed*	59
(c) *Auf dem See*	63
(d) *Warum gabst du uns die tiefen Blicke...*	67
(e) *Siebte Römische Elegie*	73
(f) *Selige Sehnsucht*	77
5. SCHILLER	83
Das Ideal und das Leben	83
6. HÖLDERLIN	93
(a) *Der Abschied*	93
(b) *Wie wenn am Feiertage...*	100
7. THE ROMANTICS	112
(a) *Novalis: Sehnsucht nach dem Tode*	112
(b) *Brentano: Der Spinnerin Lied*	121
(c) *Eichendorff: Marias Sehnsucht*	126
(d) *Eichendorff: Zwielicht*	131

CONTENTS

8. HEINE AND PLATEN — page 138
   (a) Heine: Seegespenst — 138
   (b) Heine: Die Weber — 144
   (c) Heine: Zwei Ritter — 150
   (d) Platen: Venedig (Sonnet 5) — 156

9. POETIC REALISM — 161
   (a) Droste-Hülshoff: Mondesaufgang — 161
   (b) Mörike: Mein Fluss — 167
   (c) Keller: Abendlied — 174
   (d) Storm: Hyazinthen — 177

10. MUNICH INTERLUDE AND NATURALIST REACTION — 182
    Heyse: Treueste Liebe — 182

11. CHAOS AND CONTROL — 191
    (a) Meyer: Schwarzschattende Kastanie — 191
    (b) George: Mühle lass die arme still... — 194
    (c) George: Der Herr der Insel — 199
    (d) Hofmannsthal: Manche freilich... and Ballade des äusseren Lebens — 204

12. RILKE — 211
    (a) Die Flamingos — 211
    (b) Ausgesetzt auf den Bergen... — 218
    (c) Sonette an Orpheus, I, xiii — 223

CONCLUSION — 229

BIOGRAPHICAL NOTES — 231

SELECT BIBLIOGRAPHY — 246

GENERAL INDEX — 259

INDEX FIRST LINES — 263

Introduction

It must be the common experience of those whose vocation—or whose fate—it is to teach others the 'appreciation' of literature, to be confronted with some who doubt, not only the efficacy of the teaching in question, but the value of the thing taught. Novel and drama always find a willing audience—but the ominous 'I can't make head or tail of poetry' (with 'What's the *use* of poetry, anyway' lurking unexpressed in the background) is heard all too often, at least at Redbrick universities, when students are frankly discussing their difficulties. All too many still believe, with Peacock in *The Four Ages of Poetry*, that poetry is a kind of 'mental rattle' which the grown man would do well to discard.

Attempting to convince such honest doubters *through abstract arguments* that poetry has something to give them, if they will only allow it to do so, would surely be quixotic. It is only, if at all, through the actual experience of poetry that we can become convinced of its value. We must therefore begin by close reading of actual poems: in order to end, not with mere 'information about' poetry, but with the capacity to respond to it more readily and more intelligently than before.

To this end, we might confront our hypothetical questioner at this stage with an actual lyric: with a work in which a great poet conveys, through the medium of poetry, an experience of *reading*.

DER LESER

Wer kennt ihn, diesen, welcher sein Gesicht
wegsenkte aus dem Sein zu einem zweiten,
das nur das schnelle Wenden voller Seiten
manchmal gewaltsam unterbricht?

Selbst seine Mutter wäre nicht gewiss,
ob er es ist, der da mit seinem Schatten
Getränktes liest. Und wir, die Stunden hatten,
was wissen wir, wieviel ihm hinschwand, bis

INTRODUCTION

> *er mühsam aufsah: alles auf sich hebend,*
> *was unten in dem Buche sich verhielt,*
> *mit Augen, welche, statt zu nehmen, gebend*
> *anstiessen an die fertig-volle Welt:*
> *wie stille Kinder, die allein gespielt,*
> *auf einmal das Vorhandene erfahren;*
> *doch seine Züge, die geordnet waren,*
> *blieben für immer umgestellt.*
>
> R. M. RILKE

The poem begins, characteristically, on a note of puzzled enquiry. The 'Leser' is isolated from his surroundings, held up for inspection as it were, through the grammatical and rhythmic isolation of the word 'diesen'. Who knows him, this man—

> *welcher sein Gesicht*
> *Wegsenkte aus dem Sein zu einem zweiten?*

The enjambement controls stress in such a manner that it falls heaviest on the syllable 'weg'—away. The 'reader' seems to have 'got away', to have escaped from his own life, his own mode of existence, to another: that of the book in which he is immersed. Any reminder of the real world is felt as an unwelcome interruption, rhythmically represented in the next lines, where we actually experience the quick rustling of the leaves in 'das schnélle Wénden vóller Séiten' and the forcible interruption in 'Mánchmal gewáltsam unterbrícht'.

The puzzled inquiry continues. It seems to be a child speaking now: the idea of childhood being implicit in the introduction of the all but omniscient mother. 'Selbst seine Mutter wäre nicht gewiss | ob er es ist...' Has the 'reader' really escaped from himself, from his own mode of being? Is it really he—and not some person made wholly different—

> *der da mit seinem Schatten*
> *Getränktes liest?*

The very question already contains a partial answer. At one level the lines just quoted connote that the 'reader's' shadow is falling on his book—but the stress and the imagery suggest another level of meaning. The line-division makes a heavy stress fall on 'Getränkt': suffused, shot through with, steeped in. The book is steeped in, suffused by, something given off by the 'reader': he gives as well as takes. A considerably more complex conception has replaced the opening, exploratory image of the reader's escape, his 'getting away' from his own being.

> *Und wir, die Stunden hatten,*
> *was wissen wir, wieviel ihm hinschwand ...*

Now at last we are given the precise occasion of the experience Rilke is here evoking. It is a *childhood* experience: the children were at their lessons, watching someone read; and this atmosphere of childhood justifies the air of puzzled, wide-eyed enquiry, of exploration, which we have been noticing throughout the poem and which now manifests itself in the peculiarly hesitant, wondering movement. What do we know ('was wissen wir'—the present tense, after: 'wir, die Stunden *hatten*'! The experience of the past is being re-evoked), how much of his personality, his 'Sein', the 'reader' gave up in his concentrated pursuit—

> *bis*
> *er mühsam aufsah.*

In this superbly modulated phrase, we are made to *feel* the almost painful interruption, the effort required for a return from the world of the book, in the violent disruption of the syntax through line-division, through sectional division; in the glottal stop which begins the second line of the quotation; and in the heavy stresses of the whole phrase. We are not simply *told* that the process is 'mühsam': we are made to experience it in the very effort required of us as with eye and ear we endeavour to respond to the poem.

In the section of the poem which we are now entering something seems to have changed. The rhyme-scheme at any rate is not the same—a line is missing. Hitherto we have had abba cddc; now we begin with ab a c; and if we let our eyes travel further, we see that the 'missing' line has been inserted later, so that instead of abba cddc (in two distinct groups) we now have abac*b*ddc in one closely-knit whole. A 'b' line has been taken out of its 'normal' position (normal, because the previous pattern has

INTRODUCTION

induced a certain expectation) and inserted between the first c and d. The significance of this is not, as yet, clear.

The 'reader', then, looks up, painfully, and brings back with him, into the real world, the whole world of the book he has been reading ('alles auf sich hebend | Was unten in dem Buche sich verhielt'—where the image, 'auf sich hebend', increases the sense of effort already noted). And he brings with him also an attitude, a way of dealing with experience. Instead of passively taking in the world, as most of us do ('statt zu nehmen'), the 'reader' tries to establish with it the kind of relation he has had with the world of the book, a world in which he had to give as well as take. But to do this is to suffer a shock—an effort of re-adjustment is necessary, for the real world, 'fertig-voll', does not require the same sort of collaboration from the reader. This shock Rilke perfectly conveys in enjambement, heavy stress and glottal stop:

> Mit Augen welche, statt zu nehmen, gebend
> Anstiessen ...

The next two lines merge, with an ease characteristic of Rilke, the experience of observed and observer. The whole poem is written from the standpoint of children watching a man read: and now the experience of the 'reader' *becomes* that of his observers, merges with that of growing children suddenly coming up against reality, against 'das Vorhandene', after the solitary games in which they were able to create a world of their own with fragments from their dream of human life.

But what, then, was the use of reading? Has it only unfitted the 'reader' for dealing with life as actually lived? Part of the answer has already been suggested. The reader comes to the world afresh: he experiences it again, as children experience it, instead of merely taking it in, passively, jadedly. He has heeded something of that advice which Rilke gave to a young poet: 'Try, as if you were one of the *first* men, to say what you see and experience and love and lose ... If your everyday life seems poor to you, do not accuse *it*; accuse yourself, tell yourself that you are not poet enough to summon up its riches; since for the creator there is no poverty, and no poor and unimportant place.'[1]

[1] Cf. Coleridge's account of the genesis of the *Lyrical Ballads*: 'Mr. Wordsworth was to propose to himself as his object to give the charm of novelty to

INTRODUCTION

The greatest part of the answer, however, is suggested only by the last two lines of our poem. The children look at the 'reader's' face: and they seem to see there a certain order, an order which was not there before; and Rilke goes on to tell us that the transmutation, the change which had come over the 'reader', was permanent. 'Blieben *für immer* umgestellt.' Reading had wrought a change in the reader's face, indicative of a change in his mind; it had brought a new *order* of emotion, of experience. 'Geordnet', 'umgestellt'—these might be called the key-words of the final, climactic lines. And now at last, when we have come to the last word of the poem, we realize why Rilke altered the pattern of his verse, his rhyme-scheme, in the way we have already indicated. The original pattern was: abba cddc, in two separate groups. Rilke then took a b line out of the first group and inserted it in the second: and through this simple process of 'Ordnung', of 'Umstellung', he integrated the two parts, made them a single indivisible whole.

We thus come to realize, *through the very form of the poem*, that Rilke experienced reading as a mode of ordering and integrating sense-data and emotions.

This brings us, I would suggest, very close indeed to the essential nature and function of poetry. A poet is a man with a supernormal capacity for *ordering* words; for making words fall into simple and complicated pattern, making them modify one another, establishing new relations between them. And this capacity is obviously an index of something else: an equally great capacity for ordering *experiences*, for escaping that 'general mess of imprecision of feeling', those 'undisciplined squads of emotion' of which T. S. Eliot so movingly speaks. What the poet conveys to his readers is not just thoughts, not just abstract ideas—though these may well be present.[1] The poet endeavours to communicate, with maximum immediacy, his *experience* of the world.

> *Mit Augen welche, statt zu nehmen, gebend*
> *Anstiessen ...*

things of every day, and to excite a feeling analogous to the supernatural by awakening the mind's attention from the lethargy of custom, and directing it to the loveliness and wonder of the world before us.'

[1] It would be fatal to degrade poetry into a mere playing with beautiful sounds, to divorce it from thought and intelligence.

INTRODUCTION

Such lines as these, requiring as they do an effort from eye and ear, almost from the whole body, bring the experience home to us with physical impact, and the poet communicates to us, through the ordering of his poem, his very mode of apprehension, his way of—as Hegel called it—devouring the world. A final attitude is only established at the end of the poem: and it is an attitude which includes in itself all that has gone before, becomes full and satisfying only *through* such all-inclusiveness. This process of reaching a final, full, all-inclusive attitude only after passing through doubt and error has been well described by Hölderlin in a letter to his mother of 8 July 1799.
'The poet, if he wishes to depict his little world, must imitate the Creation: there not everything is perfect, and God allows the rain to fall on the good and bad and unjust; he must often say something untrue and contradictory, which must however resolve itself in the whole, in which it is only said in passing, into truth and harmony; and just as the rainbow is beautiful only after the storm, so in poetry truth and harmony appear all the more beautifully and joyously out of untruth and error and suffering.'
This whole process, the process of 'devouring the world', of loving receptivity to life and experience, is more important than any resultant 'idea'. 'The reader should be carried forward'—that is Coleridge's description of a just poem—'not merely or chiefly by the mechanical impulse of curiosity, or a restless desire to arrive at a final solution; but by the pleasurable activity of mind excited by the attractions of the journey itself.'

And so great poetry does not give us information, 'truth' in the scientific sense: it gives us experiences, attitudes. It is the record of rare moments of insight given to the most conscious, most finely organized individuals at a particular time; a record of 'the best and happiest moments in the lives of the happiest and best minds'. As such it has on the one hand—as I. A. Richards has long ago pointed out—a purely historical value. It informs us, not of current opinions, but of current attitudes—how men feel about their world, what they wish for, or dread, or admire. 'It seems to me that no poetry, not even the best, should be judged as if it existed in the absolute, in the vacuum of the absolute. Even the best poetry, when it is at all personal, needs the penum-

INTRODUCTION

bra of its own time and place and circumstance to make it full and whole' (D. H. Lawrence). But the poetry will not be *about* these attitudes, in the sense of 'talking about' them: they will be implicit in it, in ways our analyses will attempt to show (e.g. in the analysis, below, of Mörike's 'Mein Fluss'). Poetry, properly experienced, is our best way of ascertaining how sensitive minds reacted and react to the world as they find it; of coming into immediate contact with those who actually lived out their lives in the country whose language and whose culture we have set out to study.

But great poetry has of course more than merely 'historical' value. 'You have given me praise', writes Wordsworth in his famous letter to John Wilson, 'for having reflected faithfully in my poems the feelings of human nature'—i.e. for having done what we have just discovered the great poet to do habitually. 'I would fain hope that I have done so. But a great poet ought to do more than this; he ought, to a certain degree, to rectify men's feelings, to give them new compositions of feelings, to render their feelings more sane, pure and permanent...' In reliving these moments of insight, we are ourselves living more fully, experiencing more deeply than before. Our emotional life is enriched, stimulated, quickened. Our minds are cleansed of 'the film of familiarity which obscures from us the wonder of our being ... (Poetry) creates anew the universe, after it has been annihilated in our minds by the recurrence of impressions blunted by reiteration' (Shelley: *A Defence of Poetry*).

Poetry enables us, in other words, to have new and deeper experiences; it refines our sensibility, directs it into new and deeper channels. Its study can enrich, beyond any other discipline, our emotional *together with* our intellectual life.

The following pages are intended—through simple, sometimes indeed elementary, analyses of individual lyrics—to help English readers of German poetry towards a fuller response. They do not constitute a complete history of the German lyric: though the close analysis of a single text may often tell us a great deal, not only of the shape of a poet's mind, but also of the literary climate of his time and the society which conditioned it.[1] Poems have

---

[1] 'It would appear', T. S. Eliot reminds us, 'that "literary appreciation" is an abstraction and pure poetry a phantom.'

INTRODUCTION

been chosen, as far as possible, which have both intrinsic and representative value. Analyses of such poems are offered, not of course as *ex cathedra* pronouncements, but as incitements to closer reading, to a fresh response, to ever renewed discussion.

Only thus may poetry be kept alive.

CHAPTER ONE

Approaching the German Lyric

'No, it is impossible', says Marlow in Conrad's *Heart of Darkness*; 'it is impossible to convey the life-sensation of any given epoch of one's existence—that which makes its truth, its meaning —its subtle and penetrating essence. It is impossible. We live as we dream—alone.' But it is just this 'impossible' which the lyric poet in our period at least sets out to accomplish. He does not seek to tell a story, or present conflict of character and opinion: he seeks, within short compass, to annihilate the distance between himself and his reader, to make the reader experience directly the poet's 'life-sensation at a given period of his existence—that which makes its truth, its meaning'.

'The miracle of lyric poetry is this: that individuality, in its essence as individuality, has become experience generally accessible.'[1]

The poet may express his 'life-sensation', his experience, directly, may speak in the first person of his thoughts and aspirations and fears, as does Novalis, for instance, in *Sehnsucht nach dem Tode* (see Chapter Seven, below); or he may express himself through symbols, through objective correlatives, as do—in different ways —Matthias Claudius in *Der Tod und das Mädchen*, Mörike in *Um Mitternacht*, and Platen in the *Venedig* sonnets.

But whether direct or metaphorical, the lyrical poem makes some of its most important effects through its rhythms: through the tension between metrical and syntactical stress. As we read a lyric, we become aware of a pattern, of the metre (however free) in which the work is written. Certain stresses recur at certain intervals; certain breaks (the end of lines, of stanzas) become noticeable at more or less equal distance from one another;

---

[1] Das Wunder lyrischer Dichtung besteht... darin, dass Individualität in ihrer Individualität allgemein erlebbar geworden ist. (Joh. Pfeiffer, *Das lyrische Gedicht als ästhetisches Gebilde*, Halle, 1931.)

certain sounds (especially end-rhymes) are heard more than once. All this imposes a pattern: and this pattern is significantly varied when natural speech-rhythms conflict or coincide with the hypothetical 'regular' metre. Through such tensions as these, through pauses and stresses, the poet is able to convert his experience into generally accessible physical sensation.

A simple example—perhaps excessively simple, for the poem is certainly not a great one—of such tension, such significant variation, is furnished by one of the best known of Heine's 'Lieder':

IM WUNDERSCHÖNEN MONAT MAI

> *Im wunderschönen Monat Mai,*
> *Als alle Knospen sprangen,*
> *Da ist in meinem Herzen*
> *Die Liebe aufgegangen.*
>
> *Im wunderschönen Monat Mai,*
> *Als alle Vögel sangen,*
> *Da hab' ich ihr gestanden*
> *Mein Sehnen und Verlangen.*

Heine here confronts us with four statements. Buds open up—like them, love blossoms in the poet's heart. Birds (begin to) sing—like them, the poet confesses his love. There is obviously progression in this poem (everything leads up to the last, crowning line, the actual confession of a love we have seen blossoming out): but the four elements of comparison have one common factor. Each one denotes something which, hitherto hidden, now bursts forth.

And now we may set ourselves to notice how Heine, by playing natural speech-rhythms across the regular pattern of his stanza, makes his words *do* what they *say*.

At first the movement of the stanza (and the second repeats exactly the first) is comparatively slow and endstopped.

> *Im wúnderschönen Mónat Maí,*
> *Als àlle Knóspen spràngen —*

We notice at the same time that the grammatical construction does not allow us to let our voice sink at the end of the second line[1]: and this combines with the hesitant movement to induce in the reader a feeling of expectancy. Something has yet to come before our voice may come to rest.

The pattern established by the first two lines of each stanza is broken in two significant respects in the last two. Line 3 begins in each case with a heavy stress; and lines 3 and 4 run on, enjambed:

> Dá ist *in meinem Herzen*
> *Die Liebe aufgegangen.*

At the word 'Da' we feel the expectancy to be over: what we have been waiting for has come, bringing with it a great sense of release. 'Da', there it is, the heavy stress at the beginning of the line seems to tell us. And with this release, all hesitancy of movement disappears. The last lines flow unimpeded one into the other.

First expectancy, then fulfilment. Something which has been hidden, bursts forth. The poem *does*, through its movements through significant variation of a regular pattern, what a prose-summary of it would only *say*.[2]

But metre, metrical variation, must not operate in a vacuum. As far as metre acts in and for itself, Coleridge tells us, it tends to 'increase the vivacity and susceptibility both of the general feelings and of the attention'; it acts powerfully, though itself unnoticed, 'as a medicated atmosphere, or as wine during animated conversation':
'Where therefore correspondent food and appropriate matter are not provided for the attention and feelings thus aroused, there must needs be disappointment felt, like that of leaping in the dark from the last step of a staircase, when we had prepared our muscles for a leap of three or four.'

[1] To realize the force of this, we need only imagine Heine to have written:

> *Im wunderschönen Monat Mai*
> *Alle Knospen sprangen.*

[2] An analysis of this poem makes the desired point well enough: but it must be pointed out that the sudden 'Da', the onrush of the last two lines after the hesitancy of the first two, misrepresents the rhythm of the natural phenomenon invoked: the coming of spring. Heine is (as so often) forcing the rhythms of his own experience onto nature.

Metre, like any technical device in poetry, is only an empty shell if the artist has nothing to communicate. Poetic devices are only means to an end.

To see how a great poet uses his medium to communicate an experience, we need only glance at the lyric with which Eduard Mörike ends his Novelle *Mozart auf der Reise nach Prag*.

> *Ein Tännlein grünet wo,*
> *Wer weiss, im Walde,*
> *Ein Rosenstrauch, wer sagt,*
> *In welchem Garten?*
> *Sie sind erlesen schon,*
> *Denk es, o Seele,*
> *Auf deinem Grab zu wurzeln*
> *Und zu wachsen.*
>
> *Zwei schwarze Rösslein weiden*
> *Auf der Wiese,*
> *Sie kehren heim zur Stadt*
> *In muntern Sprüngen.*
> *Sie werden schrittweis gehn*
> *Mit deiner Leiche;*
> *Vielleicht, vielleicht noch eh*
> *An ihren Hufen*
> *Das Eisen los wird,*
> *Das ich blitzen sehe.*

The poem begins with slow, groping lines, made all the more portentous by the 'w' alliteration (wo, wer weiss, im Walde) which both muffles the lines—'but still your finger on your lips, I pray'—and makes heavier stresses fall on the alliterating words. An answer to these portentous, disrupted questionings seems to be coming with the fifth line. But at once the sixth, with its heavy stresses and awed pause, breaks in upon it; harking back, through its dominant vowels and consonants, to the operative 'erlesen'—

> *Sie sind erlesen schon*
> *Denk es, o Seele . . .*

The pauses after 'Denk es' and after 'Seele' seem to be the act of reflection, the act of taking thought, itself. Then, at last comes the outburst, in those two last lines (enjambed!) with their dark vowels (Gr*a*b *zu* w*u*rzeln *u*nd *zu* w*a*chsen) and their terrible import. It is as though until now grief had been kept back, restrained, to break out all the more irresistibly.

The second section begins again on a calmer note: slowly, as though something were being contained, muffled (the 'w' alliteration appears once more—in '*w*eiden auf der *W*iese'). Twice our voice is allowed to come to rest after two lines. But the words 'mit deiner Leiche'—like 'erlesen' in the earlier section—end this restraint. An awed 'Vielleicht' harks back, assonantically, to the 'Leiche' of the previous line; then a pause, for the first time (in this section) in the middle of a line; then, with the repetition of 'Vielleicht', the irresistible outbreak of grief:

> *Vielleicht, vielleicht noch eh*
> *An ihren Hufen*
> *Das Eisen los wird, ;*

and at the last, a terrified brief pause before that vision of light signifying eternal darkness:

> *Das ich blitzen sehe!*

The movement of the poem brings home to us the consciousness of grief, of horror contained for as long as possible, but breaking through with terrible force at the end. There remains only the consolation of the lyric form itself.

The experience which we are here allowed to share, is that of a man who sees his own death approaching nearer and nearer. The consciousness of death moves in upon him—from the wood (wide, unenclosed) to the garden (enclosed) to the grave. The fir-tree and the rose-bush which will draw sustenance from his own body in its grave are unseen, somewhere ('wer weiss?' 'wer sagt?') in the forest, in some garden; the horses which will draw his hearse *are* seen, though at first in the distance; and they come ever nearer, until he can see their iron horse-shoes flashing in the sun. The flash of that last line, with its one dominant stress—

> *Das ich blítzen sehe —*

is that of death. And this experience, of death, or the consciousness of death, ever approaching until it becomes inescapable and all-pervading, is conveyed to perfection by the movement of both stanzas: at first slow, hesitant, contained; then an awed hearking back; and at last the outburst of grief.[1]

'It all depends on the *pause*——', wrote D. H. Lawrence to Edward Marsh on 19 November 1913; 'the natural pause, the natural lingering of the voice according to the feeling—it is the hidden *emotional* pattern that makes the poetry, not the obvious form ... It is the lapse of feeling, something as indefinite as expression in the voice carrying emotion. It doesn't depend on the ear, particularly, but on the sensitive soul ... The ebbing and lifting emotion should be master, and the ear the transmitter.'

A particularly instructive comparison of 'hidden emotional patterns', manifesting themselves in the movement of poetry, is afforded by two lyrics written by men who made their (no doubt genuine) sufferings one of the main themes of their poetry.

HERBSTKLAGE	LEBENSLAUF (Zweite Fassung)
Holder Lenz, du bist dahin!	*Grössers wolltest auch du, aber die*
Nirgends, nirgends darfst du bleiben!	*Liebe zwingt*
Wo ich sah dein frohes Blüh'n,	*All uns nieder, das Leid beuget gwaltiger,*
Braust des Herbstes banges Treiben.	*Doch es kehret umsonst nicht Unser Bogen, woher er kommt!*
Wie der Wind so traurig fuhr	*Aufwärts oder hinab! herrschet in heilger Nacht,*
Durch den Strauch, als ob er weine;	*Wo die stumme Natur werdende Tage sinnt,*
Sterbeseufzer der Natur Schauern durch die welken Haine.	*Herrscht im schiefesten Orkus Nicht ein Grades, ein Recht noch!*

[1] It is most important to notice that the terrible which approaches ever nearer manifests itself in recollections and visions, in objective correlatives, themselves beautiful and joyous. Fir-tree, rose-bush, bounding ponies. Death, the demonic and terrible, is made all the more unbearable through its association with the serene and happy. Is this not very apt for the ending of a work dealing with the later Mozart, whose music has just this surface joy and serenity, which can never obscure the demonic undercurrents? And is it not an apt summary of Mörike's Novelle, which depicts a happy day in the life of its

APPROACHING THE GERMAN LYRIC

Wieder ist, wie bald! wie bald!	*Dies erfuhr ich. Denn nie, sterblichen*
Mir ein Jahr dahinge-	*Meistern gleich,*
schwunden!	*Habt ihr Himmlischen, ihr Alleser-*
Fragend rauscht es aus dem	*haltenden,*
Wald:	*Dass ich wüsste, mit Vorsicht*
'Hat dein Herz sein Glück	*Mich des ebenen Pfads*
gefunden?'	*geführt.*
Waldesrauschen, wunderbar	*Alles prüfe der Mensch, sagen die*
Hast du mir das Herz	*Himmlischen,*
getroffen!	*Dass er, kräftig genährt, danken für*
Treulich bringt ein jedes Jahr	*alles lern,*
Welkes Laub und welkes	*Und verstehe die Freiheit,*
Hoffen.	*Aufzubrechen, wohin er will.*
NIKOLAUS LENAU	HÖLDERLIN

Lenau's poem seems hardly to call for comment at all. It is very easy to read aloud; its melody, helped by the 'au' assonance (braust, traurig, Strauch, schauern, rauscht, Rauschen, Laub) could hardly be simpler. We seem to be driving through a one-way street of emotion: there are no diversions, no hold-ups anywhere along the road. Our voice, like our emotion, needs never to readjust itself.

In this respect, the poem is the exact opposite of *Lebenslauf*, which has to be perused many times before a satisfactory reading may be arrived at. Again and again we are pulled up, diverted; rhythm, modulation, emphasis, direction change continually. We begin with an upward movement: 'Grössers wólltest auch dú', but are immediately checked at the word 'aber':

aber die Líebe zwíngt
Áll uns níeder ...

How perfectly the effect of being dragged down is there achieved by the passage from one line to the next, from one stressed syllable to another! Love

eponymous hero, without allowing us to forget that the fiery soul within is fretting the pigmy body to decay?

APPROACHING THE GERMAN LYRIC

All.   *zwingt*

The falling cadences continue ('Dás Léid béuget gewáltíger') to be checked again at the word 'Doch', at which we begin to rise again. 'Doch es kehret umsonst nicht...' 'Kehret' is indeed a keyword, introducing a sudden turning about in emotion and movement.

The second stanza is simpler, containing after its opening thunderclap, a single passionate statement (characteristically couched, however, in the form of a *question*) of the justice of the gods. Everything leads up to the final line: our voice cannot come to rest until that line comes upon us with a sense of completion, fulfilment, after long withholding.

In stanza three, with its many grammatical pauses and short phrases, its anxious qualification ('Dass ich wüsste...'), the poet seems to be treading carefully, as it were, in the presence of the heavenly powers he has invoked. And the last stanza, with its key-line:

Alles prüfe *der Mensch*

(how appropriate for these turnings and re-directions!) and its profoundly ambiguous ending, reinforces the effect of careful, anxious cogitation after the passionate statement of stanza 2.

The two poems we are comparing are equally successful in their own way. Lenau's represents a simple plangent giving way to grief; Hölderlin's a weighing of the consciousness of grief and pain against consciousness of love, justice and order. And if we prefer—as we surely must—Hölderlin's poem to that of Lenau, it is because the former achieves a poise which the latter lacks. The feelings of a mature mind are seldom as simple, as one-way as *Herbstklage* would suggest—their fluxes and refluxes, their contradictions and co-presences, have been far better caught by Hölderlin. He does not divorce feeling from thinking, emotion from intelligence. Above all, Hölderlin's grief (like Mörike's 'Denk es, o Seele') seems so much the stronger, so much the more genuine than that of Lenau, because he records *resistance* to it, an effort to contain it. The latter seems deliberately to be piling up his agony (the keywords of *Herbstklage* may be said to be: bang, traurig, weine, Sterbeseufzer, schauern, welk, dahingeschwunden); he seems to be wallowing in his sorrow and inciting us to wallow with him.[1]

This judgment may be reinforced by reference to another poem of Hölderlin's; one which shows the poet in his darkest mood.

HÄLFTE DES LEBENS

Mit gelben Birnen hänget
Und voll mit wilden Rosen
Das Land in den See,
Ihr holden Schwäne,
Und trunken von Küssen
Tunkt ihr das Haupt
Ins heilignüchterne Wasser.

Weh mir, wo nehm ich, wenn
Es Winter ist, die Blumen, und wo
Den Sonnenschein,
Und Schatten der Erde?
Die Mauern stehn
Sprachlos und kalt, im Winde
Klirren die Fahnen.

Where Lenau says to us all the time: 'Look: I am moved! You must be moved with me!', Hölderlin merely juxtaposes two clearly visualized scenes (one actual, the other imagined), and allows this juxtaposition—but for a single 'Weh mir!'—to speak for itself. The contrast between the two scenes, and between the two states of mind for which they are objective correlatives, imposes itself without deliberate pointing. Specifically seen things with attributes (Gelbe Birnen, wilde Rosen) contrast with generically seen things without attributes (Blumen, Sonnenschein, Schatten—without attributes because they will be only negatively there, only in the mind which remembers them with regret and contrasts them with actuality); while the beautiful fruits, roses, and swans of the opening make all the more terrible

---

[1] Cf. Rilke:

> *O alter Fluch der Dichter,*
> *Die sich beklagen, wo sie sagen sollten ...*
> Requiem

the ugly sights and sounds of the close, the cold empty walls and creaking weather-vanes.

The contrast thus established is brought home by the movement of the poem. The long period of the first section flows smoothly, the natural speech-pause coinciding with the end of the verse-line; while in the second, speech pause and stress and metrical pause and stress are sharply at variance. Pauses occur in the middle of the lines; it is impossible to let the voice rest at their end:

> *Weh mir, / wo nehm ich, / wenn*
> *Es Winter ist, / die Blumen, / und wo*
> *Den Sonnenschein . . .*

Where the first stanza comes to a beautiful, calm, infinitely legitimate close, the second breaks off harshly, like the snapping of a string. Hölderlin allows this contrast to speak for itself: he does not, as Lenau tends to do, point all the time to his emotion and incite the reader to relish it.

It is a contrast such as this between Hölderlin and Lenau which makes us understand T. S. Eliot's extreme dictum in *The Sacred Wood*: 'The only way of expressing emotion in the form of art is by finding an "objective correlative"; in other words, a set of objects, a situation, a chain of events which shall be the formula of that *particular* emotion; such that when the external facts, which must terminate in sensory experience, are given, the emotion is immediately evoked . . . The artistic "inevitability" lies in this complete adequacy of the external to the emotion.' These are matters of *tone* and *attitude* with which we shall be constantly concerned in our analysis: matters in which we shall be in danger of passing beyond purely literary criticism, to an examination of the quality of the mind to which we are asked to submit ourselves.[1]

To introduce our next topic, we must refer for a moment to a poem by Karl Bröger: a man, himself of working-class stock, who tried to bring poetry again into living relation with the people and their life in this modern age.

---

[1] This, surely, is inevitable. 'Alles, was der Dichter uns geben kann'—wrote Schiller in his famous review of Bürger's poetry—'ist seine Individualität. Diese muss es also wert sein, vor Welt und Nachwelt ausgestellt zu werden.' It goes without saying that this attitude need not—must not—lead to a narrow moralism or a prying into the poet's laundry-bills.

APPROACHING THE GERMAN LYRIC

LIED DER ARBEIT

Ungezählte Hände sind bereit,
stützen, heben, tragen unsre Zeit,
Jeder Arm, der seinen Amboss schlägt
ist ein Atlas, der die Erde trägt.

Was da surrt und schnurrt und klirrt und stampft,
aus den Essen glühend loht und dampft,
Räderrasseln und Maschinenklang
ist der Arbeit mächtiger Gesang.

Tausend Räder müssen sausend gehn,
tausend Spindeln sich im Kreise drehn,
Hämmer dröhnend fallen, Schlag um Schlag,
dass die Welt nur erst bestehen mag.

Tausend Schläfen müssen fiebernd glühn,
abertausend Hirne Funken sprühn,
dass die ewige Flamme sich erhellt,
Licht und Wärme spendend aller Welt.

As we read this, we feel uneasy. Of course, the monotonous rhythm with its stamping alliteration may be intended to convey the rhythm of machinery, the inexorable movement of the piston going up and down: just as those rather obvious onomatopoeic devices of the second stanza paint in words the song of labour for which the title prepares us. But—we uneasily ask ourselves—is not this rhythmic unsubtlety rather a sign that we are here in contact with an essentially insensitive mind?

Bröger's theme is certainly not the *monotony* of labour. He conceives of thousands of willing workmen ('ungezählte Hände sind bereit'—are willing, ready, prepared) performing gladly a vital task: that of maintaining the world. But it must surely give pause that the *nature* of that task is indicated only by the vaguest of clichés. 'Dass die Welt nur erst bestehen mag' (that 'nur erst' is totally redundant—the words are obviously introduced only to fill out the line, without any definite purpose or any definite work to do). 'Abertausend Hirne *Funken sprühn*.' And, worst of all, that pseudo-religious ending:

> *Dass* die ewige Flamme *sich erhellt,*
> *Licht und Wärme spendend aller Welt.*

Bröger is here patently relying on stock-responses; he means nothing definite with his 'ewige Flamme', but trusts that the cliché will raise vague clouds of emotion. He saves himself the trouble of writing a precise poem, and puts his faith (like so many poetasters) in the 'poems' which lie ready-made in the minds of his readers.

But in order to confirm our initial suspicions and convert them to certainty we need only look at the classical image which adorns the first stanza. Every workman (or, more precisely, the arm of every workman beating the anvil) is seen by Bröger as an Atlas bearing the world. The image is, of course, conventional—it has no relation to the life of Bröger or that of the workmen he describes. But it is not the whole point of the Atlas legend that the giant was *compelled to bear the earth against his will*? that he tried, at every opportunity, to rid himself of his burden? Heine realized these implications—

> *Ich unglückseliger Atlas! Eine Welt,*
> *Die ganze Welt von Schmerzen muss ich tragen!*

but Bröger obviously does not. For they run directly counter to his theme: the willing, proud shouldering of a vital task; and the image, when followed out, makes nonsense of the poem.

And so scrutiny of the Atlas image tells us definitely what we had in fact suspected from the beginning: that the whole poem, however sincerely meant, is a sham, the shallow optimism of an insensitive mind. Bröger is not writing modern poetry at all: he deals in half-understood images and clichés taken over from the poetry and prose of an earlier generation, a generation of men with wholly different experiences, a wholly different background from his own and that of his potential audience. *Lied der Arbeit* has no living relation to experience—it is dead, still-born.

The deadness of Bröger's poem was finally demonstrated by reference to a single image. We must however stress at this point that in a great poem, a fully integrated poem, no image can be looked at in isolation. Its effect generally depends on a very wide context—the context, indeed, of the whole work of which it forms part—and can be fully evaluated only if that context is considered; a statement whose truth may be conveniently illustrated by an analysis of one of the best known of German lyrics.

ABSCHIED

O Täler weit, o Höhen,
O schöner, grüner Wald,
Du meiner Lust und Wehen
Andächt'ger Aufenthalt!
Da draussen, stets betrogen,
Saust die geschäft'ge Welt;
Schlag noch einmal die Bogen
Um mich, du grünes Zelt!

Wenn es beginnt zu tagen,
Die Erde dampft und blinkt,
Die Vögel lustig schlagen,
Dass dir dein Herz erklingt:
Da mag vergehn, verwehen
Das trübe Erdenleid,
Da sollst du auferstehen
In junger Herrlichkeit!

Da steht im Wald geschrieben
Ein stilles, ernstes Wort
Von rechtem Tun und Lieben,
Und was des Menschen Hort.
Ich habe treu gelesen
Die Worte schlicht und wahr,
Und durch mein ganzes Wesen
Ward's unaussprechlich klar.

Bald werd' ich dich verlassen,
Fremd in der Fremde gehn
Auf buntbewegten Gassen
Des Lebens Schauspiel sehn;
Und mitten in dem Leben
Wird deines Ernsts Gewalt
Mich Einsamen erheben,
So wird mein Herz nicht alt.

JOSEPH VON EICHENDORFF

One of the most striking features of this poem is the number of terms with distinct religious associations which it contains. '*Andächt'ger* Aufenthalt'. 'Da mag vergehn ... das trübe Erdenleid'. 'Da sollst du auferstehen ...' 'Mich Einsamen *erheben* ...' When therefore we come upon the image

> *Schlag noch einmal die Bogen*
> *Um mich ...*

where Bogen, the usual term for an architectural arch, connotes the arched branches of the trees—we at once associate it with the many religious suggestions, and realize that Eichendorff (like many poets before and after him) is here seeing the forest as a Cathedral built for the worship of God. And obviously, this Cathedral image conveys a great deal of Eichendorff's forest atmosphere: quiet, calm, shelter, awe-inspiring beauty capable of moving to religious devotion. But it also holds suggestions hostile to the poet's purpose—stony rigidity, chill exclusion of nature. Therefore a qualifying image is introduced:

> *Schlag noch einmal die Bogen*
> *Um mich*, du grünes Zelt.

A tent is light and airy, close to nature, not shutting nature out; it counteracts the disturbing aspects of the Cathedral image, without detracting from its religious (Bundeszelt!) and other associations. Neither the 'Bogen' nor the 'Zelt' image can be understood by itself, without reference to the other: or, indeed, to the whole context of religious suggestions which run through the poem.

In the same way, the force of the term 'buntbewegt' in the last stanza—

> *Auf buntbewegten Gassen*
> *Des Lebens Schauspiel sehn —*

can be understood only if we contrast it with earlier intimations of a single restful colour in the forest (*grüner* Wald; *grünes* Zelt) and of the calm and stillness pervading the forest-cathedral in which mankind may read 'ein stilles ernstes Wort'. 'Buntbewegt' conjures up, by contrast, the garishness and (pointless) bustle of the world outside: suggestions which culminate in the image:

'Des Lebens Schauspiel'. From the Cathedral of the forest, where all is 'schlicht und wahr', we pass to the 'theatre' of the workaday world. The force of this theatre image depends on our consciousness of the all-pervading Cathedral image, with which it contrasts.[1]

A striking example of interacting and interdependent imagery is afforded by one of Theodor Storm's lyrics.

SCHLIESSE MIR DIE AUGEN BEIDE

Schliesse mir die Augen beide
Mit den lieben Händen zu!
Geht doch alles, was ich leide,
Unter deiner Hand zur Ruh'.

Und wie leise sich der Schmerz
Well' um Welle schlafen leget,
Wie der letzte Schlag sich reget,
Füllest du mein ganzes Herz.

In plain prose: the poet here asks his beloved to cover his eyes with her hands: for then his sorrow abates, his anguish ceases, and thoughts of her drive out all others.

The first two lines bring the first image: 'Zuschliessen', the locking of a door. Then, following logically: 'Zur Ruhe gehen' —retiring to rest for the night; an idea obviously carried on by 'sich schlafen legen'. With 'sich regen' we have one last movement, corresponding to the last pang of anguish—and then, instead of the expected image of quiescence, of empty calm, one of fullness, completion:

Füllest du mein ganzes Herz.

But the second stanza introduces another complex of images:

---

[1] In the same way, we must consider the whole context of the poem to appreciate fully the force of the term 'saust' in the first stanza:

Da draussen, stets betrogen
Saust die geschäft'ge Welt.

In the forest-cathedral there is shelter (Schlag noch einmal die Bogen Um mich ...), peace, restfulness. 'Saust' suggests the opposite outside the forest: the wind from which the trees shelter; breathless haste; and (in conjunction with 'geschäftig') bustling activity.

'Well um Welle'; 'der letzte Schlag'. The first brings in the sea, which to Storm (a native of Husum, on the Schleswig coast) spelt home—

> *Doch hängt mein ganzes Herz an dir,*
> *Du graue Stadt am Meer;*
> *Der Jugend Zauber für und für*
> *Ruht lächelnd doch auf dir, auf dir*
> *Du graue Stadt am Meer;*

the sea whose waves he could undoubtedly hear from his house in Husum; while the second, carrying on these suggestions (Wellenschlag), merges the last pang of anguish with the last vibrant stroke of the Church-clock (ein Schlag der Dorfuhr, der entfernten).

Storm's poem seeks to reinvoke a recurrent moment in his life: the moment in which his beloved places her hand over his eyes. Its movement conveys to perfection the calming, sheltering effect of this simple action—especially through the long, ebbing period of the second stanza, with its enclosing rhymes (abba instead of, as earlier, abab) after the first stanza divided (grammatically) into two halves. And the imagery, recalling as it does the rhythm, activity and sounds of Storm's everyday life, the simple domestic happiness bestowed by his wife, his home and his homeland, tells us why the simple action described has this calming, sheltering effect. It shows how the 'moment' invoked contains within itself the experience of a whole life-time. 'And all is always now'.

Enough has now been said, in this brief opening chapter, to show that metrical devices, imagery and the rest are only means to an end, must not be considered apart from the function they serve. I would submit, in conclusion, that the same applies to 'vowel-music' and kindred abstractions. Those who count vowels and consonants, and then assign to these a value and significance of their own, apart from their context; those who endeavour, with Adam in Brentano's poem,

> *In dem A den Schall zu suchen,*
> *In dem E der Rede Wonne,*
> *In dem I der Stimme Wurzel,*
> *In dem O des Tones Odem,*
> *In dem U des Mutes Fluchen ...*

are walking on paths very dangerous to the literary critic. 'Word-music' is also a means—though of course an important means—and not an end in itself. The end, as always, is the communication of human experience, significant, ordered and controlled.

CHAPTER TWO

The Lyric Poetry of the Aufklärung

(a)
CHRISTIAN FÜRCHTEGOTT GELLERT
EPIKTET

Verlangst du ein zufriednes Herz:
So lern die Kunst, dich stoisch zu besiegen,
Und glaube fest, dass deine Sinne trügen.
Der Schmerz ist in der Tat kein Schmerz,
Und das Vergnügen kein Vergnügen.
So bald du dieses glaubst: so nimmt kein Glück dich ein,
Und du wirst in der grössten Pein
Noch allemal zufrieden sein.
Das, sprichst du, kann ich schwer verstehn.
Ist auch die stolze Weisheit wahr?
Du sollst es gleich bewiesen sehn;
Denn Epiktet stellt dir ein Beispiel dar.

Ihm, als er noch ein Sklave war,
Schlug einst sein Herr mit einem starken Stabe
Zweimal sehr heftig auf das Bein.
Herr, sprach der Philosoph, ich bitt Ihn, lass Ers sein,
Denn sonst zerschlägt Er mir das Bein.
Gut, weil ich dirs noch nicht zerschlagen habe,
So soll es, rief der Herr, denn gleich zerschlagen sein.
Und drauf zerschlug er ihm das Bein.
Doch Epiktet, anstatt sich zu beklagen,
Fing ruhig an: Da sieht Ers nun!
Hab ichs ihm nicht gesagt, er würde mirs zerschlagen?

Dies, Mensch, kann Zenos Weisheit tun!
Besiege die Natur durch diese starken Gründe,
Und willst du stets zufrieden sein,

> *So bilde dir erhaben ein,*
> *Lust sei nicht Lust, und Pein nicht Pein.*
> *Allein, sprichst du, wenn ich das Gegenteil empfinde,*
> *Wie kann ich dieser Meinung sein?*
> *Das weiss ich selber nicht; indessen klingts doch fein,*
> *Trotz der Natur sich stets gelassen sein.*

Epiktet may be fairly said to represent one of the two dominant trends of *Aufklärung* poetry. Its theme relates it to the poetry of an earlier generation; the generation which remembered the terrors of the Thirty Years War, and inevitably felt that it was dangerous to become too attached to the things of this world. In general, the poets of the *Baroque* era sensed everything in this world to be mutable, transient:

> *Die Blasen in Eile verzischen,*
> *Die Schlangen in Eile hinwischen,*
> *Die Winde mit Eile hinbrausen,*
> *Die Schiffe mit Eile wegsausen:*
> *Wir Menschen auch also bestehen,*
> *In Eile mit Eile vergehen;*

and felt man, faced with this transience, to have the choice of three courses of action. He might, first of all, cry *Carpe diem*, live only for the moment:

> *Drum lasst uns jetzt geniessen*
> *Der Jugend Frucht,*
> *Eh' dann wir folgen müssen*
> *Der Jahre Flucht.*

Or he might endeavour to rise to those mystic heights from which the gulf between time and eternity could no longer be seen:

> *Ich selbst bin Ewigkeit, wenn ich die Zeit verlasse*
> *Und mich in Gott und Gott in mich zusammenfasse.*

Or, lastly, he might oppose to mutability his own inviolable personality:

> *Sei dennoch unverzagt, gib dennoch unverloren,*
> *Weich keinem Glücke nicht, steh' höher als der Neid,*

Vergnüge dich an dir und acht es für kein Leid
Hat sich gleich wider dich Glück, Ort und Zeit verschworen.

It is this last course, the *heroic stoicism* of the Baroque generation, which Epiktet also seems concerned to inculcate.

Gellert, then, takes up one of the great commonplaces of the seventeenth century—in his own formulation: 'die Kunst, sich stoisch zu besiegen'—and tries to make it palatable to his contemporaries. The reader is ostensibly invited to approve of Epictetus' resignation, to accept petty tyranny without a murmur. The German 'Bürger' of Gellert's time, under the sway of princes whose corruption was soon to be pilloried by Lessing and the young Schiller, finds himself asked, not to revolt against oppression, but so to attune his mind that he may disregard it.

There is, however, an important difference in emphasis. For the Baroque poet, heroic stoicism was only a means towards a 'marriage to eternity':

Wer hier beständig steht, trotzt Fleisch, und Fall und Zeit
Vermählt noch in der Zeit sich mit der Ewigkeit;

the eighteenth-century poet wants rather to lead his readers to 'Zufriedenheit', to happiness in *this* world. He is still a moralist, a teacher (Gellert chooses to write *fables*, a genre so highly prized by the Swiss critics Bodmer and Breitinger because it combined the didactic and the 'wondrous', constituted 'ein lehrreiches Wunderbares'); but he no longer points primarily to realms beyond the sky. It is now his task to educate his fellowmen for their lives in the world and the society into which they have been born.

Inevitably, therefore, *Epiktet* ends on a wryly ironical note. Heroic stoicism has meaning only as an end in itself or as a means of attaining eternity—as soon as happiness and contentment in *this* world are the goal, it degenerates into tepid, even cowardly passivity. One cannot, the last lines of *Epiktet* obliquely tell us, deceive oneself: tyranny remains tyranny, pain is felt as pain, however nobly (*erhaben*) we tell ourselves that we ought not to feel it as such.

Indessen klingts doch fein
Trotz der Natur sich stets gelassen sein.

'To be ever calm in face of oppression'—that sounds well in the mouth of the moralist; but when challenged, the moralist is forced to admit that human nature—human weakness perhaps—cannot turn his precept into practice.

The change of attitude we have noted in the last lines of the poem brings with it a change of tone. *Epiktet begins* magisterially, with a moral to be examined and illustrated. Gellert seems determined to turn to account his gift, so highly prized by his contemporaries,

> *Dem, der nicht viel Verstand besitzt*
> *Die Wahrheit durch ein Bild zu sagen.*

The reader (or pupil?) is allowed to question the validity of the initial statement:

> *Das, sprichst du, kann ich schwer verstehn.*
> *Ist auch die stolze Weisheit wahr?;*

and the poet-teacher then counters with an *exemplum* (the story of Epictetus) and a restatement of the moral. But when the reader objects again, appealing to his experience:

> *Allein, sprichst du, wenn ich das Gegenteil empfinde*
> *Wie kann ich dieser Meinung sein?,*

the poet suddenly changes his tone. The magisterial element disappears; the pupil has successfully called the master's bluff. 'Das weiss ich selber nicht.' In the last lines the poet exchanges confidences with his reader, in the tone of one reasonable man talking to another as to his equal.

But though the distance between poet and reader thus diminishes in the course of the poem, it never entirely disappears. Poet and reader never *merge*, as they were to do in later lyric poetry. Gellert addresses himself almost exclusively to his reader's reason, never attempts to communicate an experience directly, in ways we have already examined. This accounts for the total absence of that incommensurable element, those appeals to our emotions through significant distribution of stresses, significant collocations of sounds or of images, which we are accustomed to seek in lyric poetry. The adjectives of *Epiktet*, sparingly used, are colourless to the point of drabness: gross, stolz, erhaben, fein; the interlocked rhyme-scheme, however ingeniously worked out, bears no such living relation to the content as does (for instance) the 'ei' rhyme in Heine's *Nächtliche Fahrt,* or in Theodor Storm's *Die Stadt:*

> *Die Wandergans mit hartem Schrei*
> *Nur fliegt in Winternacht vorbei* ...;

and the movement (statement following statement in strict logical progression—all leading to a surprising 'point' at the end) is as smooth, as even, as little counter to the metrical scheme as the reasonable tone would seem to demand. A mere mention of Gellert's model—Lafontaine—should suffice to show how essentially pedestrian is *Epiktet,* and indeed all Gellert's poetry.

Yet verse such as this performed, at its time, an undoubted function. It created a middle-class audience for poetry: it made adherents of the *Aufklärung* and its sweet reasonableness feel that poetry had something to give them. And the end of *Epiktet,* which retrospectively colours the whole poem,[1] has an urbanity all too rare in German literature, which should endear it to the *homme moyen sensuel,* not only of Gellert's time, but also of our own.

(b)
FRIEDRICH HAGEDORN
DER MAI

> *Der Nachtigall reizende Lieder*
> *Ertönen und locken schon wieder*
> *Die fröhlichsten Stunden ins Jahr.*
> *Nun singet die steigende Lerche,*
> *Nun klappern die reisenden Störche,*
> *Nun schwatzet der gaukelnde Staar.*
>
> *Wie munter sind Schäfer und Herde!*
> *Wie lieblich beblümt sich die Erde!*

---

[1] Once read, the poem is, of course, in our mind *as a whole:*

> Or say that the end precedes the beginning,
> And the end and the beginning were always there
> Before the beginning and after the end,
> And all is always now.

HAGEDORN: DER MAI

Wie lebhaft ist jetzo die Welt!
Die Tauben verdoppeln die Küsse,
Der Entrich besuchet die Flüsse,
Der lustige Sperling sein Feld.

Wie gleichet doch Zephyr der Floren!
Sie haben sich weislich erkoren,
Sie wählen den Wechsel zur Pflicht.
Er flattert um Sprossen und Garben;
Sie liebet unzählige Farben;
Und Eifersucht trennet sie nicht.

Nun heben sich Binsen und Keime,
Nun kleiden die Blätter die Bäume,
Nun schwindet des Winters Gestalt;
Nun rauschen lebendige Quellen
Und tränken mit spielenden Wellen
Die Triften, den Anger, den Wald.

Wie buhlerisch, wie so gelinde
Erwärmen die westlichen Winde
Das Ufer, den Hügel, die Gruft!
Die jugendlich scherzende Liebe
Empfindet die Reizung der Triebe,
Empfindet die schmeichelnde Luft.

Nun stellt sich die Dorfschaft in Reihen,
Nun rufen euch eure Schalmeien,
Ihr stampfenden Tänzer! hervor.
Ihr springet auf grünender Wiese,
Der Bauerknecht hebet die Liese,
In hurtiger Wendung, empor.

Nicht fröhlicher, weidlicher, kühner
Schwang vormals der braune Sabiner
Mit männlicher Freiheit den Hut.
O reizet die Städte zum Neide,
Ihr Dörfer voll hüpfender Freude!
Was gleichet dem Landvolk an Mut?

The Baroque poet hardly ever described, or looked at, natural objects for their own sake: the beauty of nature was but a symbol for or index of the greater beauty of the world to come. Why should the poet lose himself in the transitory, pay tribute to cinders, ashes, dust?

Not so, as a single glance at *Der Mai* will show, the poet of the *Aufklärung*. The work of the Hamburg poet Hagedorn is but the end of a development which may be said to begin with another Hamburg poet: with Barthold Heinrich Brockes. Brockes sought, in his collection significantly entitled *Irdisches Vergnügen in Gott, bestehend in physikalisch und moralischen Gedichten* (1727) 'to describe as far as possible the beauty of nature, in order to inspire myself and others more and more to sing the praises of a wise Creator'.

His poetry therefore alternates between meticulously detailed descriptions of natural phenomena, and moralizing reflections on the goodness of God as revealed in the world, his temple.

> *Der beste Gottesdienst ist sonder Zweifel der*
> *Wenn man vergnüget schmeckt, recht fühlt, riecht, sieht und hört.*

We have come a long way from the Baroque rejection of nature —God is now best worshipped by enjoying his world. This Brockensian tradition, linking natural description with moral comment (a tradition with obvious roots in eighteenth-century England) was carried on, in far less heavy-handed fashion, by such men as Albrecht von Haller and Ewald von Kleist; to be finally secularized in the kind of poem of which *Der Mai* is a representative example.

Hagedorn here catalogues, as Brockes might have catalogued, a number of natural phenomena: the song of nightingale and rising lark, the cry of migrant storks, reeds, springs, and other peaceful and pleasant sights and sounds of the countryside. His observation of nature is not very close, his description conventional rather than first-hand and precise. Such lines as

> *Wie lieblich beblümt sich die Erde*

and

> *Nun heben sich Binsen und Keime*
> *Nun kleiden die Blätter die Bäume*

contrast very obviously with the meticulous and fussy precision of, say, Brockes' description of a snow-flake:

> *Sechs Ecken sieht man insgemein daran*
> *Die spitzig bald, bald rund, von diesen auf das neue*
> *An einer jeglichten in ordentlicher Reihe*
> *Noch andre Spitzen gleich den Zweigen*
> *Sich mit Verwunderung den Augen zeigen;*

while the sober Brockes would hardly have been guilty of the fatuity of 'Die Tauben verdoppeln die Küsse'. But there is about *Der Mai*, despite the rather monotonous tripping measure, despite the monotonous paratactic cataloguing, despite the almost invariably end-stopped lines, a grace and charm wholly absent from *Irdisches Vergnügen*. All the sights and sounds add up to something, combine to produce a light-hearted *Stimmung*, which once, in the last three lines of the fourth stanza, transmutes itself into bewitching melody. Such beautiful continuity of movement as that from 'Nun' to 'Triften', with its gay echoing 'e' sounds (lebendige Quellen; tränken mit spielenden Wellen), followed by the slower, fuller, darker echo of 'den Anger, den Wald', is never equalled in the rest of the poem—or anywhere in eighteenth-century German poetry before Hagedorn.

The light-hearted *Stimmung* which lends authority to the tripping measure of the poem, to the predominance in it of light 'e' and 'i' sounds, and even to the cataloguing technique, the light skipping from one sensation to the next,[1] is obviously connected with Hagedorn's anthropomorphization of nature. The landscape and the seasons assume a gay, light-hearted, irresponsible human personality.[2] They change continually (the winds and flowers 'wählen den Wechsel zur Pflicht'); they make love (the western winds are 'buhlerisch'); they incite to 'jugendlich scherzende Liebe'. Nature teaches man the lesson of easy enjoyment of life: of relaxation after the strained 'Dennoch' of the Baroque.

This links Hagedorn's poem (especially its fifth stanza) with that trend of German poetry which may be regarded as the obverse of the trend represented by Gellert, and which may be fairly said to dominate German poetry before the emergence of

---

[1] 'Hüpfende Freude' (in the penultimate line of the poem) perfectly characterizes this movement.

[2] As always in the *Aufklärung*, man is the measure, nature only exists for him It is significant that the poem ends with the contemplation, not of natural beauty, but of country-folk in holiday mood.

Klopstock.[1] In 1554, Henri Estienne had published a collection of late Greek poems attributed to the poet Anacreon. These were translated into German by Gottsched, and later (in 1746) J. P. Uz and N. Götz; and as earlier in France, they exerted a great influence on the themes selected for treatment by German poets.

> *Anakreon mein Lehrer*
> *Singt nur von Wein und Liebe ...*
> *Soll denn sein treuer Schüler*
> *Von Hass und Wasser singen?*
> (J. W. L. GLEIM)

But German anacreontic poets obviously could not realize, among the stolid or vulgar bourgeoisie and the haughty aristocracy of their time, the kind of elegant, easy, hedonistic living they celebrated in their poetry.[2] They therefore elevated to a principle the complete divorce of literature from life (jocund their *muse* was, but their *life* was chaste):
'Never draw conclusions from an author's works about his manners and morals ... For poets write only to show their wit, even if in so doing they should make men doubt their virtue.' (GLEIM, preface to *Scherzhafte Lieder*, 1744.)
The anacreontic poets provided a wishdream world of playful irresponsibility into which the German *Bürger* might escape after his daily and dutiful labours.

Poetry as an escape into irresponsibility, but for that reason carefully divorced from life: that obviously tallies with the Horatian ending of *Der Mai*, with the implied: 'O rus, quando ego to aspiciam?' of the last lines.

> *O reizet die Städte zum Neide*
> *Ihr Dörfer voll hüpfender Freude!*

The city-dweller Hagedorn looks longingly at the imagined joys

[1] Both Lessing and Goethe began as anacreontic poets.
[2] Gleim's complaint, in a letter to Uz about a masked ball he attended in 1746, is characteristic: 'Es geht in der Tat bei dieser Lustbarkeit ein bischen zu unordentlich her, als dass sie mir gefallen sollte. Auf dem adeligen Platz ist man zu blöde, auf dem bürgerlichen findet man kein sprödes Mädchen. *Anakreons Maskeraden sind artiger gewesen.* Es sind wenig Erfindungen und fast gar keine Scherze bei den hiesigen. Die grobe Wollust hat überall die Oberhand.' (*My italics*.)

of a stylized country-life. As Gessner fled into a pastoral golden age ('aus unseren Sitten weg in ein goldenes Zeitalter'), Ewald von Kleist to the deserted fields:

Ihr blühenden Schönen, flieht jetzt den atemraubenden Aushauch
Von güldenen Kerkern der Städte! Kommt, kommt in winkende
  Felder!,

Haller to a domain of pristine innocence among the simple peasants of the Swiss alps:

> *Seht ein verachtet Volk zur Müh und Arbeit lachen,*
> *Die mässige Natur allein kann glücklich machen —*

so Hagedorn seeks to take refuge in his Horatian bucolic world, in an idealized country-side.

The anthropomorphization of nature we have noted has however a yet greater significance. The playful, irresponsible personality which Hagedorn confers on the landscape is in many respects *his own*: and thus the gulf between literature and life is lessened instead of (as with the anacreontics) widened. Hagedorn, in other words, points forward—though he cannot be said to do more than point—to that fusion of natural phenomena and human experience which was to be finally achieved by Goethe.

CHAPTER THREE

Klopstock and the 'Göttinger Hain'

(a)
FRIEDRICH GOTTLIEB KLOPSTOCK
DER ZÜRCHER SEE

Schön ist, Mutter Natur, deiner Erfindung Pracht
Auf die Fluren verstreut, schöner ein froh Gesicht,
Das den grossen Gedanken
Deiner Schöpfung noch einmal denkt.

Von des schimmernden Sees Traubengestaden her,
Oder flohest du schon wieder zum Himmel auf,
Komm in rötendem Strahle
Auf dem Flügel der Abendluft,

Komm und lehre mein Lied jugendlich heiter sein,
Süsse Freude, wie du! gleich dem beseelteren
Schnellen Jauchzen des Jünglings,
Sanft, der fühlenden Fanny gleich.

Schon lag hinter uns weit Uto, an dessen Fuss
Zürch im ruhigen Tal freie Bewohner nährt;
Schon war manches Gebirge,
Voll von Reben, vorbeigeflohn.

Jetzt entwölkte sich fern silberner Alpen Höh',
Und der Jünglinge Herz schlug schon empfindender,
Schon verriet es beredter
Sich der schönen Begleiterin.

Hallers 'Doris', die sang, selber des Liedes wert,
Hirzels Daphne, den Kleist innig wie Gleimen liebt;
Und wir Jünglinge sangen
Und empfanden, wie Hagedorn.

KLOPSTOCK: DER ZÜRCHER SEE

*Jetzo nahm uns die Au in die beschattenden
Kühlen Arme des Walds, welcher die Insel krönt;
Da, da kamest du, Freude!
Volles Masses auf uns herab!*

*Göttin Freude, du selbst! dich, wir empfanden dich!
Ja, du warest es selbst, Schwester der Menschlichkeit,
Deiner Unschuld Gespielin,
Die sich über uns ganz ergoss!*

*Süss ist, fröhlicher Lenz, deiner Begeistrung Hauch,
Wenn die Flur dich gebiert, wenn sich dein Odem sanft
In der Jünglinge Herzen
Und die Herzen der Mädchen giesst.*

*Ach, du machst das Gefühl siegend, es steigt durch dich
Jede blühende Brust schöner und bebender,
Lauter redet der Liebe
Nun entzauberter Mund durch dich!*

*Lieblich winket der Wein, wenn er Empfindungen,
Bessre sanftere Lust, wenn er Gedanken winkt,
Im sokratischen Becher
Von der tauenden Ros' umkränzt;*

*Wenn er dringt bis ins Herz und zu Entschliessungen,
Die der Säufer verkennt, jeden Gedanken weckt,
Wenn er lehret verachten,
Was nicht würdig des Weisen ist.*

*Reizvoll klinget des Ruhms lockender Silberton
In das schlagende Herz, und die Unsterblichkeit
Ist ein grosser Gedanke,
Ist des Schweisses der Edlen wert!*

*Durch der Lieder Gewalt bei der Urenkelin
Sohn und Tochter noch sein; mit der Entzückung Ton
Oft beim Namen genennet,
Oft gerufen vom Grabe her,*

*Dann ihr sanfteres Herz bilden und, Liebe, dich,
Fromme Tugend, dich auch giessen ins sanfte Herz,*

> *Ist, beim Himmel! nicht wenig!*
> *Ist des Schweisses der Edlen wert!*
>
> *Aber süsser ist noch, schöner und reizender,*
> *In dem Arme des Freunds wissen ein Freund zu sein!*
> *So das Leben geniessen*
> *Nicht unwürdig der Ewigkeit!*
>
> *Treuer Zärtlichkeit voll, in den Umschattungen,*
> *In den Lüften des Walds und mit gesenktem Blick*
> *Auf die silberne Welle*
> *Tat ich schweigend den frommen Wunsch:*
>
> *Wäret ihr auch bei uns, die ihr mich ferne liebt,*
> *In des Vaterlands Schoss einsam von mir verstreut,*
> *Die in seligen Stunden*
> *Meine suchende Seele fand;*
>
> *O so bauten wir hier Hütten der Freundschaft uns!*
> *Ewig wohnten wir hier, ewig! Der Schattenwald*
> *Wandelt' uns sich in Tempe,*
> *Jenes Tal in Elysium!*

We have now seen Hagedorn concerned to break down the impersonality of Baroque as well as of early *Aufklärung* poetry, by infusing into nature something of his own. With Klopstock such impersonality disappears altogether: the individual, often in conscious opposition to society, to the *profanum vulgus*, asserts himself uncompromisingly. Klopstock conceives himself as a poet-prophet, who has the mission of inspiring others to share his own high thoughts and feelings. Not for him the *niedrige Tändeleien* of the anacreontics—already in his farewell speech at Schulpforta, at the age of twenty-one, he had lamented the fate of German poetry:
'Why is it the misfortune only of poetry, that divine art, to be soiled by unconsecrated hands, and evermore to crawl upon the ground?'
After the crawling of the anacreontics, the ambling of Gellert, the light skipping of Hagedorn, we are now invited to soar with Klopstock.

Der Zürcher See is a poem of recollection, the recollection of a happy day (30 July 1750) spent by the poet and his friends in boating on the beautiful lake at the foot of Mount Ütli. But Klopstock does not recollect in tranquillity. He does not, as Brockes, as even Kleist and Haller would have done, calmly describe the sights and sounds encountered on the occasion of which he speaks. Klopstock invokes Joy, who came from heaven on that occasion upon him and his friends, to inspire his song, and he does this in stanzas—stanzas 2 and 3 of the poem—whose power and melody are unmatched in earlier German poetry. Not for Klopstock the reasonable parataxis of Gellert and Hagedorn, the sentence-structure which allows statement to follow, or be subordinated to, statement in strictly logical sequence. While the poet plays his soaring rhythms across his strict asclepiad stanza, while he achieves a magnificent incantatory effect by so controlling his stress that it falls heaviest on the twice-repeated *komm*, he communicates his own expectancy and excitement through the complex structure of his sentences. Beginning with an adverbial phrase ('Von des schimmernden Sees Traubengestaden her'), he withholds the main verb for two lines by interposing a qualifying clause: 'Oder flohest du schon wieder zum Himmel auf'. But even then our voice cannot come to rest until, in the middle of the second line of stanza 3, we are at last told who it is that is being addressed; until we have been given the subject of the sentence (süsse Freude) and the comparative clause (wie du). And then, after a briefer upward surge, comes the broad downward sweep, so well suited to the last line of an asclepiad stanza:

> *gleich dem beseelteren*
> *Schnellen Jauchzen des Jünglings,*
> *Sanft, der fühlenden Fanny gleich.*

Here the keyword is *sanft*; the many hushing fricatives enforce it, and the rhythm falls in harmony.

This masterly use of the possibilities of the asclepiad stanza, its rising opening and falling close, we may notice again and again. In stanza 7, for instance:

> *Da, da kamest du, Freude,*
> *Volles Masses auf uns herab!,*

or again in stanzas 8 and 9; while Klopstock avoids, in stanza 14, the natural downward sweep of the close of the asclepiad by carrying on his complex sentence to the next stanza. In this last passage we have again a magnificent upward surge, achieved through the withholding of the main verb (ist ... nicht wenig), and through constant interpositions and interjections; until we are set down, gently, without losing our feeling of elation, in the last two lines of stanza 15. Such poetry as this must be read with the ear rather than the eye. It was not for nothing that Klopstock himself constantly stressed the necessity of reading poetry aloud, or hearing it read; the ancient Greeks, he declared, 'loved their poets and their pleasure too much to do as we tend to do: to sit in a corner, *see* the sound, and therefore experience no more than half of the poem'.

We cannot do justice to Klopstock unless we *listen* to him.

The rapturous soaring movement we have seen to be characteristic of Klopstock is in fact announced, and explained, in the very first lines of our poem. Nature, we are told, is beautiful; but the mind of man, occupied with lofty thoughts suggested by nature (contemplated or recollected), is more beautiful still. Klopstock only begins by looking at nature; nature is only his running-board or jumping-off point; from there he takes us, higher and higher, into realms of thought and feeling; into the mind of man stimulated by Joy, by Wine, by the thoughts of Fame, and—above all—by Friendship. Hence the ever-rising movement of the verse; hence the constant comparatives.(schöner, beseelter, empfindender, bebender, sanfter, süsser, reizender); hence the many dynamic verbs; and hence the paucity of visual and aural impressions of the outing on the lake. From contemplation of the landscape, Klopstock soars at once into the realm of man's mind, the haunt and the main region of his song. Hence also the nature of the adjectives Klopstock employs: they suggest relations and feelings (heiter, frei, empfindend) and only the vaguest sense-impressions (gross, rötend, ruhig). Man and his mind are conceived as the supreme masterpieces of the Creator.[1]

And it is surely not fanciful to see in Klopstock's characteristic preoccupation with great (and correspondingly vague) thoughts

[1] Significantly enough, Klopstock indulges freely in *personification*: in lending human qualities to abstractions (Freude ... Schwester der Menschlichkeit, Deiner Unschuld Gespielin) and to natural phenomena (Süss ist, fröhlicher Lenz, deiner Begeistrung Hauch ... wenn sich dein Odem sanft In der Jünglinge Herzen ... giesst). Man, as always, is the measure.

and emotions, in this ecstatic soaring away from actuality into regions of the mind, an attempt to transcend the narrowness of his actual German environment. Gellert had accepted that actuality, though viewing it now and then with urbane irony; Hagedorn, and to a greater degree the anacreontics, had tried to escape into playful irresponsibility; Klopstock builds a paradise of the mind for himself and his friends.

> *Wäret ihr auch bei uns, die ihr mich ferne liebt,*
> *In des Vaterlands Schoss einsam von mir verstreut ...*
>
> *O so bauten wir hier Hütten der Freudschaft uns!*
> *Ewig wohnten wir hier, ewig! der Schattenwald*
> *Wandelt uns sich in Tempe,*
> *Jenes Tal in Elysium!*

'In des Vaterlands Schoss einsam von mir verstreut.' Klopstock does not adress himself, as Gellert undoubtedly did, to any actual community; he addresses a few chosen spirits dispersed throughout his atomized fatherland; men united only by common literary allegiances, allegiance to Haller's *Doris*-ode, to Kleist's *Frühling*, to the nature-poetry of Hagedorn. And even in his relations with these we notice the characteristic soaring away from actuality. The honest but mediocre *Bürger* whom Klopstock thought worthy of his friendship were neither Tempean nor Elysian; we find them consistently overrated, or rather transformed by the poet's imagination (notably in the *Wingolf* ode: *An seine Freunde*). *Der Zürcher See* celebrates, not friends, but that abstracted 'friendship' which we see, at the supreme climax of stanza 16,[1] to hold more delight than all the joys of Spring, of Wine, and of Fame.

In this poem, then, reflected in its very movement, we find for the first time that flight from nature into man's mind, from actuality into the ideal, which the atomization of Germany, the narrowness of German society, was to force upon so many poets

[1] In an as yet unpublished lecture on this poem, Professor Friedrich Beissner (Tübingen) has analysed its structure: it begins with an isolated stanza; then follow seven connected stanzas rising to the climax of stanza 8; then again seven connected stanzas of rising intensity; then the sixteenth stanza shown by its three comparatives to be the real climax of the whole poem; and at last an 'Abgesang' of three stanzas. The ode may thus be seen to be constructed with great art: 1:7; 7:1 (like an image in a mirror!) and three closing stanzas.

—notably upon Schiller. No one was more painfully aware of this process than Hölderlin, who wrote to Schiller on 4 September 1795:
'It is the dislike of myself and my surroundings which has driven me into abstraction,'
and to his friend Neuffer on 12 November 1798:
'Alas! Since my earliest youth the world has driven my spirit back upon itself, and that still causes me pain. There is one hospital to which a poet can crawl who has come to grief in the way I have—and that is Philosophy.'
But for Klopstock, writing nearly half a century earlier, this flight back into the mind was a matter for rejoicing, not pain. He has still the simple optimism of the early *Aufklärung*, and sees no gulf between reality and the ideal. It is joy to be alive in God's world—'Göttin Freude, du selbst! dich, wir empfanden dich!'; it is joy to dwell in regions of the mind, and transform actual beauty into even greater beauty, into Tempe and Elysium. With him, what was later to become a 'retreat' to the mind becomes a widening of experience.

For we must not allow the upward surge of Klopstock's poetry to blind us to the other, the downward movement we have already noted, a movement made explicit in that twice-repeated image of *pouring*: 'Die sich über uns ganz ergoss', 'Und die Herzen der Mädchen giesst'. Man, so Klopstock feels, does not strive upwards in vain. There is some divine principle, of which Joy, Spring and Wine are manifestations, which descends upon man and satisfies his striving. Man's ecstasy, his upward flight inspired by thoughts of fame and friendship, allow him to meet halfway those divine influences which rain down upon him.

In *Der Zürcher See*, as elsewhere, Klopstock is secularizing the heritage of German Pietism. Emotions hitherto reserved for the soul's intercourse with God are now transferred to man's intercourse with his own mind and with his fellow-man.[1]

> *Aber süsser ist noch, schöner und reizender,*
> *In dem Arme des Freunds wissen ein Freund zu sein!*
> *So das Leben geniessen,*
> *Nicht unwürdig der Ewigkeit!*

[1] The phrase 'Hütten der Freundschaft' in the last stanza of the poem has obvious religious associations—associations with the 'tabernacles' of *Exodus*.

Reservoirs of feeling are thus opened which had long lain blocked up: a new kind of relation between man and man is mirrored in poetry. Not for Klopstock the reasonable, urbane conversation which Gellert cultivated with his readers; not for him ('unberufen zum Scherz' he calls himself) the playful tone of Hagedorn. Klopstock seeks to make an emotional assault upon his reader, communicate to the reader his own joy, his own enthusiasm. And for this assault he creates a superb instrument: a verse-form in which emotional replaces logical order in ways already examined. No wonder then at the force of Klopstock's impact upon the generation of the 70's.

'Klopstock has called into being, as it were, a new language for our most individual, our purest feelings; and he has thereby formed our sensibility, led us to self-knowledge, given a voice to our heart, and bestowed upon our language a delicacy, fullness and melody undreamt of before his time.'

Herder's tribute cannot be gainsaid—Klopstock's dominating position in the history of the German lyric is assured; though many of us would doubtless feel that his severance from real vulgar living, and consequently from the German language as actually spoken, was all too rigid, his enthusiastic tone and revelling in emotion too self-conscious, and his optimism a little too facile, to make his poetry a living force in our own lives.

(b)
LUDWIG CHRISTOPH HEINRICH HÖLTY
DIE MAINACHT

Wenn der silberne Mond durch die Gesträuche blickt,
Und sein schlummerndes Licht über den Rasen geusst,
   Und die Nachtigall flötet,
      Wandl' ich traurig von Busch zu Busch.

Selig preis' ich dich dann, flötende Nachtigall,
Weil dein Weibchen mit dir wohnet in einem Nest,
   Ihrem singenden Gatten
      Tausend trauliche Küsse gibt.

Ueberschattet von Laub, girret ein Taubenpaar
Sein Entzücken mir vor; aber ich wende mich,

> *Suche dunkle Gesträuche,*
> *Und die einsame Träne rinnt.*
>
> *Wann, o lächelndes Bild, welches wie Morgenrot*
> *Durch die Seele mir strahlt, find' ich auf Erden dich?*
> *Und die einsame Träne*
> *Bebt mir heisser die Wang herab!*

For Klopstock's withdrawal from actuality into regions of the mind a moonlit landscape was the ideal setting.

> *Willkommen, o silberner Mond,*
> *Schöner, stiller Gefährt' der Nacht!*
> *Du entfliehst? Eile nicht, bleib, Gedankenfreund!*
> *Sehet, er bleibt, das Gewölk wallte nur hin.*

Moonlight blurs the clear outlines of things, makes it easier to disregard their actuality, to idealize them, and to escape from them into realms of pure thought. The moon is a *Gedankenfreund*, like the twilight which accompanies the first awakening of a May morning:

> *Des Maies Erwachen ist nur*
> *Schöner noch wie die Sommernacht,*
> *Wenn ihm Tau, hell wie Licht, aus der Locke träuft,*
> *Und zu dem Hügel herauf rötlich er kommt.*

And in such twilight there arise melancholy thoughts, thoughts of a happiness which has gone or can never be ours; and these are transmuted into a sorrow which is yet subtly luxurious.

> *Ihr Edleren, ach es bewächst*
> *Eure Male schon ernstes Moos!*
> *O wie war glücklich ich, als ich noch mit euch*
> *Sahe sich röten den Tag, schimmern die Nacht!*

From here, from Klopstock's *Die frühen Gräber*, a direct line leads to Goethe's *Jägers Abendlied* and *An den Mond*. As a point somewhere along that line we may see the Hölty of *Die Mainacht*.

Hölty adhered to a group of enthusiastic Göttingen students who tried to transform into actuality those metaphorical huts of friendship ('O so bauten wir hier Hütten der Freundschaft uns!') for which Klopstock yearned. Far away from the courts, which they regarded with moral abhorrence, but equally far from that middle-class public which had taken Wieland ('den Sittenverderber Wieland') and the anacreontic poets to its capacious bosom, these young men sought to write only for the kind of circle Klopstock too had addressed: a circle of friends and kindred souls scattered throughout Germany,

> *Die, von Fürsten unangefeuert*
> *Hasser goldenen Lohns, Hasser weitstrahlender*
> *Pöbelehren, mit hohem Schwur*
> *Alles Leben nur dir, Tugendgesang, geweiht!*
>
> (J. H. VOSS)

Among these kindred souls there arose a fantastic cult of friendship, a cult of emotion for its own sake, which may be seen at its purest in the letter in which J. H. Voss describes to his friend Ernestine the leave-taking of the two Counts Stolberg.[1]

And yet, despite these almost hysterical gestures of friendship, the most valuable, the most obviously 'experienced' poems of Ludwig Hölty can in no way be described as gregarious. Even in the poems of surface gaiety (*Aufmunterung zur Freude* is perhaps the best known) we sense that the poet is deliberately goading himself to joy and to the company of his fellows: the *krankes Herz*, the *zerrissene Seele* of which he speaks, are his own.

Die Mainacht very obviously derives from the poet whom Hölty so deeply admired, and whose admiration he craved in turn:
'The man whose work finds favour in Klopstock's eyes has already entered the forecourts of the temple of Immortality and will surely enter its All-holiest. The voice of Posterity will be identical with that of Klopstock.'
But it is only the gentle, melancholy Klopstock of *Die frühen Gräber*, not the tempestuous singer of Joy, who finds his way into Hölty's work. Klopstock had succeeded in creating a German equivalent of the Spenserian mode[2]; and it is this mode, 'most musical, most melancholy', which Hölty carries on.

---

[1] Sept. 1773. The letter is reprinted in *Der Göttinger Dichterbund*, ed. Sauer (Kürschners Deutsche Nationalliteratur, Berlin-Stuttgart, n.d.), p. xxiv.

[2] Characterized by '...The slow movement and melody, the use of imagery predominantly... decorative, the Romantic glamour, the tendency towards

The first stanza of *Mainacht* establishes the moonlight atmosphere. We experience the hushed silence in the *sch* consonants (Ge*sch*räuche, *sch*lummern, Bu*sch*), the soft light in the 'li' and 'il' groupings (si*l*bern, b*l*ickt, *L*icht), the sadness in those dark vowels of: Nachtig*a*ll, W*a*ndl', tr*au*rig von B*u*sch z*u* B*u*sch. The conventional landscape described in this stanza—with its obligatory bushes, meadow and nightingale, all of which had already formed the stock-in-trade of the anacreontic poets—seems conducive enough to melancholy, seems to provide a fitting background for the poet's sadness. But a contrast is already implied. The sounds and sights of nature are so beautiful—and yet the poet is downcast. This contrast is made explicit in stanzas 2 and 3. The nightingales and doves are ecstatically happy in one another's company; the poet is alone, and has to turn away from the birds' delight. 'Suche dunkle Gesträuche'—again the dark vowels (Hölty later emended this line to: 'Suche dunklere Schatten'), this time all the darker because of the *ü* and *e* sounds of the preceding lines.

If we have seen the poet's grief becoming stronger and more explicit in stanzas 2 and 3, we reach the climax in stanza 4: an agonized question to which there can be no answer. The movement, hitherto so smooth, is broken, almost jerky, while the withholding of the main verb ensures rising tension:

> *Wann, o lächelndes Bild, welches wie Morgenrot*
> *Durch die Seele mir strahlt, find' ich auf Erden dich?*

The poet desires to find happiness *on earth*, to realize on earth the ideal (an ideal of simple, domestic happiness) which is in his soul, radiant as the dawn: but though the real dawn will come, the poet's happiness will not. 'Und die einsame Träne | Bebt mir heisser die Wang' herab!'

This thin sweet moonlight poem, with its tone of gentle indulgence of grief, presents a most interesting contrast to the moonlight poetry of the Romantics. Hölty, like the Klopstock of *Die frühen Gräber*, obviously does not wish to escape into some transcendental or faerie world, into the 'mondbeglänzte Zaubernacht' of Ludwig Tieck. *Die Mainacht* is the work of a man who feels strongly (like most of his contemporaries) that loneliness is *not* man's

a gently elegiac note. In the Spenserian mode no object is sharply focussed on the consciousness.' (L. C. Knights, *Explorations*, pp. 48–9.)

natural state, but one who has obviously failed to find the happiness he sought in the forced gregariousness of the *Göttinger Hain*. As the contrast between the happiness of those slightly absurd birds and the poet's own 'einsame Träne' suggests, Hölty is seeking a shared happiness—in vain. And so, instead, he luxuriates in his sorrow. But it is still *to the earth* that he looks for a realization of his ideals ('Wann ... find ich auf Erden dich'); there is not as yet any of that deliberate search of escape from the present, from this vale of tears, which was to be the mark of German Romanticism.

(c)
MATTHIAS CLAUDIUS
WIEGENLIED BEIM MONDSCHEIN ZU SINGEN

So schlafe nun du Kleine!
Was weinest du?
Sanft ist im Mondenscheine
Und süss die Ruh.

Auch kommt der Schlaf geschwinder,
Und sonder Müh,
Der Mond freut sich der Kinder,
Und liebet sie.

Er liebt zwar auch die Knaben,
Doch Mädchen mehr,
Schenkt ihnen schöne Gaben,
Von oben her.

Und glänzt auf sie herunter
Hoch übern Wald,
Scheint jugendlich und munter;
Und ist schon alt.

Schon älter als ein Rabe,
Sieht manches Land,
Mein Vater hat als Knabe
Ihn schon gekannt.

Der hat mir viel Geschichten
Vom Mond erzählt,

Von Muhmen und von Nichten,
    Die er gequält.

Von Mädchen und von Freiern,
    Von Feenreih'n,
Und andern Ebenteuern,
    In Mondenschein.

Von allen diesen Dingen —
    Wer wollte schrei'n?
Eins will ich dir noch singen,
    Denn schlaf auch ein.

Das Lied von meiner Mutter,
    Als sie im Tal
Zum Monde für mich flehte.
    Sie sass einmal

In einer Abendstunde
    Den Busen bloss,
Ich lag mit offnem Munde
    In ihrem Schoss;

Sie blickte sanfte Freude
    Und seufzte tief.
Der Mond beschien uns beide,
    Ich lag und schlief.

Dann sah sie auf: 'Mond scheine —
    Ich hab' sie lieb,
Schein' Glück für diese Kleine!
    Ich hab' sie lieb.'

Nun denkt er immer wieder
    An diesen Blick,
Und scheint von hoch hernieder
    Mir lauter Glück.

Er schien in meiner Laube
    Mir ins Gesicht
In meiner Hochzeitslaube —
    Du warst noch nicht.

CLAUDIUS: WIEGENLIED BEIM MONDSCHEIN ZU SINGEN

Matthias Claudius, journalist and private tutor at the little village of Wandsbeck near Hamburg, did not belong to the *Hain*, though he numbered some of its members among his friends. Nor, characteristically, did he share the unconditional admiration of Klopstock in which the *Hain* tended to indulge. 'Here and there', he declared in a—largely favourable—review of Klopstock's Odes,
'I hit upon passages which made me quite dizzy; and I felt as though an eagle wanted to fly up to the heavens and soared so high that there seemed to be nothing but movement—that no-one could tell whether it was the eagle flying or only a freak of the atmosphere. Then I used to put the book down and whistle a tune, like (Sterne's) Uncle Toby.'
Klopstock, then, in attempting to rise above the flatness of contemporary verse, rejecting much of the vocabulary of earlier poets, resurrecting older terms and coining new ones, tended to soar into regions too rarefied, too remote from human experience, to be entirely to Claudius's taste. For Claudius, in his patriarchal village life where he achieved that family happiness of which Hölty could only dream, had discovered another stream from which to nourish his poetry. In his work, the academic culture of the *Göttinger Hain* blends with the simplicity and power of a popular tradition: with elements from folk-song and folk-lore, so long absent from German literature. Claudius is thus able to provide the ideal counterweight against the often 'Babylonish' diction of Klopstock.

The simple rhymed stanzas[1] of *Wiegenlied beim Mondschein zu singen* alternate between lines of three and lines of two stresses, to which metrical pattern the speech-rhythms deliberately conform. The longer lines with their feminine endings suggest to perfection the musings of the mother—a looking inward, into the mind; while the shorter (with masculine endings) take us to

---

[1] Klopstock was later (1784) to express his pride at having freed German poetry from the 'bondage' of rhyme and iambics:

> ... ein böser Geist mit plumpem
> Wörtergepolter, der Reim ...
>
> ... und die Sprache war
> Durch unsern Jambus halb in Acht erklärt.

(Cf. A. Closs, *Die freien Rhythmen in der deutschen Lyrik*, Bern, 1947, p. 62.)

the rocking cradle, to the baby—outwards, into the world. This relationship becomes explicit in stanza 8, in which the longer lines speak of the mother's intention, the shorter—interrupting—of the baby's need to be soothed:

> *Von allen diesen Dingen —*
> *Wer wollte schrei'n?*
> *Eins will ich dir noch singen,*
> *Denn schlaf auch ein.*

The quietening, reassuring effect of the whole, with its rocking cradle movement, is enhanced by the spirants and fricatives (*schlafe, was weinest, sanft, süss, Schlaf, geschwinde,* etc.) which pervade the poem.

Gently rocking movement, coincidence of speech stress and metrical stress, hushing consonants—all so appropriate to a cradle-song—inevitably bring to mind a passage from Yeats.
'The purpose of rhythm is to prolong the moment of contemplation, the moment when we are both asleep and awake, by hushing us with an alluring sense of monotony, while it holds us waking by variety, to keep us in that state of trance in which the mind, liberated from the pressure of the will, is unfolded in symbols.' (*Essays*, pp. 195–6.)
It is just this 'state of trance', a condition in which 'we are both asleep and awake', into which the reader is 'hushed with an alluring sense of monotony' by Claudius's *Wiegenlied*.

Only when this condition has been induced can we share the central experience of the poem. With a sense of revelation, of sudden illumination, we come to the ninth stanza: the stanza in which the mother selects one moment of special significance (von allen diesen Dingen . . . eins) from the mass of her experiences of the moon. Her own mother, she tells the baby, once was sitting

> *In einer Abendstunde*
> *Den Busen bloss,*
> *Ich lag mit offnem Munde*
> *In ihrem Schoss;*
>
> *Sie blickte sanfte Freude*
> *Und seufzte tief.*
> *Der Mond beschien uns beide,*
> *Ich lag und schlief.*

CLAUDIUS: WIEGENLIED BEIM MONDSCHEIN ZU SINGEN

The child is asleep in her mother's lap; yet she knows intuitively what her mother is doing and saying. She is both asleep and awake. She is 'in that state of trance in which the mind, liberated from the pressure of the will, is unfolded in symbols'. And this state—making for intuitive sharing of experience—is identical with that which the rhythm of the poem has induced in the reader. The reader is enabled to share immediately, intuitively, the experience of mother and child.

And that brings us to the very heart of the poem. Where Klopstock yearned towards his friends scattered throughout Germany, where Hölty's 'lonely tear' was made the more bitter by the companionship of doves and nightingales, Claudius has come to know an existence of undisturbed harmony. Men are bound to one another at a deeper than conscious level: by family ties, by shared experience, by tradition, by love of God. For these insoluble ties the all-pervading Moonlight is an ideal symbol. The harsh contours of the world are obscured, and it becomes easy (as we have seen the very rhythm of the *Wiegenlied* to do) to merge inward and outward, memory and present joy:

> *Er schien in meiner Laube*
> *Mir ins Gesicht,*
> *In meiner Hochzeitslaube —*
> *Du warst noch nicht.*

The moon is permanent, where the world changes (Scheint jugendlich und munter | Und ist schon alt); she can therefore bind together past and present. She played the same part in the life of grandmother, mother and child, recalling for each of them the great recurrent moments of life: generation, and birth, and motherhood. Legends have accumulated about her, which are handed down from father to son, and thus form a continuous oral tradition. And just as moonlight binds together past and present, so it unites far and near (sieht manches Land), unites the whole world; for it represents that blessing from above—von oben her, auf sie herunter, von hoch hernieder—towards which the whole world, towards which the community, towards which the family looks.

This, then, is the experience which the reader of *Wiegenlied beim Mondschein zu singen* can so immediately share: the happiness to be found in the family circle bound by tradition and shared experience to nature, to the community, to God. This happiness, personally experienced, Claudius *presents* in his 'pure, manly and unaffected' diction. There is no moralizing, no abstraction. The poet allows the juxtaposition of clearly visualized scenes to make its own impact. The mother rocking the cradle; the moon's pranks as related by her father; the baby in its mother's lap, its mouth open, half in sleep, half in yearning for the mother's breast; the young wife in her arbour—changing scenes, in which yet there is permanence, for upon all of them shines the moon, and in all of them there is love. And just as the moonlight, just as love, bind together these varied scenes, memory and actuality, the dead and the living, man and God, so the soothing, rocking rhythm—

Sanft ist im Mondenscheine
Und süss die Ruh'—

binds together the whole poem and enables Claudius to communicate directly, physically almost, his own experience and that of the community of which he felt himself a part.

We have travelled a long way from Gellert and the 'reasonable' moralizing of the *Aufklärung*. After the otherworldliness of the Baroque era, Gellert showed us German poetry looking habitually towards this world rather than the next; while in the work of Hagedorn, the poet's personality began to impose itself on a nature looked at, once again, for its own sake. Klopstock furthered this process: uncompromisingly individual, he transcended nature, not in favour of the next world, but in favour of his own high thoughts and feelings. With Hölty, the human personality seems to be at variance with nature; but a reconciliation is ever sought. And Claudius, no less personal than the rest, brought poetry once again into contact with folk-song and folklore,[1] and thus gave his own experience a greater validity. The German lyric had become, largely thanks to Klopstock, far more efficient a medium for the communication of individual human experience than it had ever been; and its writers seemed to be

[1] And, of course, the Lutheran hymn, whose praises Claudius never tired of singing.

CLAUDIUS: WIEGENLIED BEIM MONDSCHEIN ZU SINGEN

groping towards that fusion of the personal and the general, of man's mind and the nature it perceived, which was to be finally achieved by Goethe.

To his work we must now turn.

CHAPTER FOUR

Goethe

(a)

WILLKOMMEN UND ABSCHIED

Es schlug mein Herz. Geschwind, zu Pferde!
Und fort, wild wie ein Held zur Schlacht.
Der Abend wiegte schon die Erde,
Und an den Bergen hing die Nacht.
Schon stund im Nebelkleid die Eiche
Wie ein getürmter Riese da,
Wo Finsternis aus dem Gesträuche
Mit hundert schwarzen Augen sah.

Der Mond von einem Wolkenhügel
Sah schläfrig aus dem Duft hervor,
Die Winde schwangen leise Flügel,
Umsausten schauerlich mein Ohr.
Die Nacht schuf tausend Ungeheuer,
Doch tausendfacher war mein Mut,
Mein Geist war ein verzehrend Feuer,
Mein ganzes Herz zerfloss in Glut.

Ich sah dich, und die milde Freude
Floss aus dem süssen Blick auf mich.
Ganz war mein Herz an deiner Seite,
Und jeder Atemzug für dich.
Ein rosenfarbes Frühlingswetter
Lag auf dem lieblichen Gesicht
Und Zärtlichkeit für mich, ihr Götter,
Ich hofft' es, ich verdient' es nicht.

Der Abschied, wie bedrängt, wie trübe!
Aus deinen Blicken sprach dein Herz.
In deinen Küssen welche Liebe,
O welche Wonne, welcher Schmerz!

WILLKOMMEN UND ABSCHIED

Du gingst, ich stund und sah zur Erden
Und sah dir nach mit nassem Blick.
Und doch, welch Glück, geliebt zu werden,
Und lieben, Götter, welch ein Glück!

Like so many of his contemporaries, Goethe had begun as a camp-follower of the anacreontics, writing, in his student days at Leipzig, elegantly turned verses in the manner of Gleim and Götz. But during his stay at Strassburg (1770-2), Goethe may be said to have found his true manner as a lyric poet; aided no doubt by his three great experiences of that time: the Sesenheim idyll (his love for Friederike Brion), recognition of the beauty of Gothic architecture (which he found to be, not formless, but a 'characteristic' art, fashioned according to organic, inner laws), and contact with J. G. Herder, the most powerful and original[1] mind of his generation. The first great example of this new manner is *Willkommen und Abschied*, which may be said to initiate a new phase, the great phase, of the modern German lyric.

Herder deprecated the laborious excogitations of the *Aufklärung*:

'Poetry, which ought to be the most impulsive child of the human spirit, the most sure of itself, has become the most uncertain, lame and vaccillating; poems have turned into much corrected school-exercises' (*Über Ossian und die Lieder alter Völker*). He emphasized anew the sense-perceptions of natural man, and opposed them to the mere ratiocination of his contemporaries: 'We hardly see and feel at all: we only ponder and cogitate' (ibid.). Goethe was in this at one with Herder: 'He is poor indeed, who lives by the head alone'; and it is therefore significant that *Willkommen und Abschied* opens with *physical sensation*. 'Es schlug mein Herz.' A blind urge, at once obeyed with that leap on to horseback so perfectly rendered by the second half of the line 'Geschwind zu Pférde'—a swift decision, a leap (accomplished at 'Pfér ...'), and the settling in the saddle.

---

[1] Not, of course, 'original' in the manner of the spider in the *Battle of the Books*. Herder's work focused the ideas of many of his contemporaries and immediate predecessors: notably those of Edward Young (*Conjectures on Original Composition*) and of Hamann.

The image of the second line (eschewed in the later version) exactly conveys the life-sensation of the poet during that ride through the night: the blind rushing of the blood, the youthful recklessness, the sense of danger disregarded; while the slight grammatical pause after 'fort' gives the rest of the line an impetus, a sudden spurt, a wildness, which is sacrificed in the more colourless 'Es war getan fast eh gedacht' of the second version. Only then, after the first two disrupted lines, begins the steady gallop of the horse, reflected in the grammatically and rhythmically unbroken lines that follow. It is, at first, an almost gently rocking movement, despite all speed, all wildness, all impetus: a movement which gives rise to the comforting vision of the Evening as a mother, cradling her babe the Earth, while Night curtains the mountains. But suddenly the comforting vision changes, with one of those sudden leaps from image to image, sense-perception to sense-perception, which Herder had praised in primitive poetry: it changes to one of terror.

> *Schon stund im Nebelkleid die Eiche*
> *Wie ein getürmter Riese da.*

The rhythm itself seems to 'tower' as we pass from the unstressed 'wie ein ge . . .' to the increasingly heavier stresses of '. . . türmter Riese da'; while the verb 'stund . . . da' seems to pull us up, as it were, suggesting the towering solidity of this giant. It is the only *static* verb in the whole of these dynamic opening stanzas.

The visions, the images, become more and more threatening. From the bushes, darkness already lowers, a monster with a hundred eyes; the moon peers drowsily, half hidden behind her cloudy veil; the wind brushes past the rider with silent, bat-like wings which we too can hear and feel:

> *Die Winde schwangen leise Flügel*
> *Umsausten schauerlich mein Ohr;*
> *Die Nacht schuf tausend Ungeheuer . . .*

There is no mere cataloguing here of natural phenomena: no 'ornamentation' with rococo gods, the knick-knacks of an outworn mythology. Goethe looks at nature with the eyes of earliest man, of those who created the original myths. He has made himself once again, in his poetry, the *sensuous man* whom Herder wished to revive:

'Since there is sound everywhere in nature, nothing is more natural to a man who uses his senses than to suppose that nature lives, talks, and acts. The savage saw the lofty tree with its majestic foliage and marvelled at it: the leaves stirred and rustled! A god was speaking through them!... Whatever stirs, lives, whatever makes sound, speaks.'

Yet in giving life to nature, Goethe does no violence to it, as we have seen Heine, for instance, to do (see page 11). The natural phenomenon is there, closely observed: the bushes in the moonlight, with light leaves, but round black interstices between them; and it is this closely observed phenomenon which is anthropomorphized, made to see instead of being seen, to glower with a hundred black eyes. Goethe takes from nature and gives to nature, doing violence neither to nature nor to himself.

This first section of the poem ends, as it began, with physical sensation—but this time including in it something spiritual, as the rider opposes his own fearlessness, his own determination, to the horrors of the night.

Only then, at the third stanza, do we reach the *Ave* for which the title prepares us. 'Ich sah dích' (or, even stronger, more effective, in the later version: 'Dích sah ich'). At the word 'dich' we are finally pulled up. The ride is over. We now know that the object of the blind urge depicted at the opening was contact with another, a beloved human being; and the pent-up expectations give way (with that keyword: 'Floss' in line 18) to flooding release. The visions, the images, now disappear, for the poet is wholly with his beloved, and has no part of his mind free for peopling the world around him with myths.

> *Ganz war mein Herz an deiner Seite*
> *Und jeder Atemzug für dich.*

Again there is taking and giving ('Und Zärtlichkeit für mich...'!), but this time entirely on the human plane. The poet receives from his beloved the love he gives to her.

Another leap (like one of those 'Sprünge und Würfe' of which Herder speaks in *Über Ossian*) to the *Vale*, the 'Farewell' of the title. In this first version of the poem, it is the beloved who goes away, and the poet who stands and looks after her: and I cannot but feel that the later version (*Ich ging, du standst und sahst zur Erde ...*) alters for the worse. After the significant pause which follows 'du gingst' (how well this renders the pang of parting!), we have the poet standing still, for the first time, to reflect; and this pause, this standing still, makes all the more effective the joyous, vigorous conclusion, in which the poet tears himself away from sorrow. In these simple, crowning lines active and passive, giving and taking, unite in a single glance toward the divine. Perfect harmony between subject and object, man and the world he perceives:[1] that is Goethe's experience of the world, and here it finds expression. No wonder that the Romantics, who knew no such harmony, failed to see the significance of this ending.

'We have noticed (writes Friedrich Schlegel) that the author's poems begin emotively and romantically, but descend into prose towards the end; that is true also, in our opinion, of the older, beautiful songs *Willkommen und Abschied, Neue Liebe, neues Leben*.' Nothing, surely, could more misrepresent the movement of Goethe's poem than to speak of a 'decline into prose'.

Yet Schlegel's dictum does point to something important in *Willkommen und Abschied*: not a 'decline', but a progression. From crowding imagery the poem passes to simple statement; from blind physical sensation to joyous, conscious recognition of happiness and harmony; from darkness to light; from loneliness to society. Just as the poem begins at night and ends with the coming of morning,[2] so the last lines bring to consciousness, to clear daylight, what had been unconsciously, blindly there before. They tell us of the harmony of lover and beloved, subject and object, man and nature. And this rise into daylight and clarity is

[1] How closely the beloved is bound to nature in the most conspicuous metaphor of the final stanzas:

> *Ein rosenfarbes Frühlingswetter*
> *Umgab das liebliche Gesicht.*

It is but a step from here to the *Mailied*, with its identification of love of a human being with love of all nature.

[2] The second version makes this clearer:

> *Doch ach, schon mit der Morgensonne*
> *Verengt der Abschied mir das Herz ...*

characteristic even of the *early* Goethe who never—despite all his emphasis on the world of the senses—declined into primitivism, into mere 'thinking with the blood'.

It has been often observed, with some justice, that something new and important enters German literature with the Sesenheim lyrics: a startling youthful vigour. Even the *young* poets of Hamburg and Göttingen and Leipzig has seemed old men in their anacreontic poses, their *Hain* melancholy, their devout ecstasies. Now at last a young man has the courage to speak as a young man, to record faithfully his own experiences.

'He is truly young; and that is a great deal in a world in which men are *born* old.'

Yet for all this, it must be stressed that there is nothing immature or clodhopping about the Sesenheim Goethe. *Willkommen und Abschied*, for all its vigour, has its own complexity. It is a poem of *Doch*, of 'Yet in spite of this...' The night holds terrors, yet the rider is courageous and gay; the parting holds sorrow, yet the poet ends with a paean to the goodness and delight of love reciprocated. Man sees the terror and sorrow of life, and yet affirms life—not blindly, but joyously and energetically.

(b)
GANYMED

Wie im Morgenrot
Du rings mich anglühst,
Frühling, Geliebter!
Mit tausendfacher Liebeswonne
Sich an mein Herz drängt
Deiner ewigen Wärme
Heilig Gefühl,
Unendliche Schöne!

Dass ich dich fassen möcht'
In diesen Arm!

Ach, an deinem Busen
Lieg' ich, schmachte,
Und deine Blumen, dein Gras
Drängen sich an mein Herz.

Du kühlst den brennenden
Durst meines Busens,
Lieblicher Morgenwind,
Ruft drein die Nachtigall
Liebend nach mir aus dem Nebeltal.

Ich komme! ich komme!
Wohin? Ach, wohin?

Hinauf, hinauf strebt's.
Es schweben die Wolken
Abwärts, die Wolken
Neigen sich der sehnenden Liebe.
Mir, mir!
In eurem Schosse
Aufwärts,
Umfangend umfangen!
Aufwärts,
An deinem Busen,
Alliebender Vater!

In *Willkommen und Abschied* we saw Goethe discard the rococo gods of his youth, pale allegories of a poet without faith, in favour of what might be called 'home-made' myths. *Ganymed* takes us a stage further: it shows us a German poet using classical mythology as a symbol to express some real feeling or aspiration. The myth of Ganymede, the beautiful boy snatched up to heaven by Zeus to be his cup-bearer, becomes a symbol for delighted, passionate, pantheistic yearning toward union with nature. The myths of classical Greece are remoulded, as Herder declared they should be, 'in a new, creative, fruitful and artistic way'.

It is not perhaps surprising that in the doubly atomized society of eighteenth-century Germany—atomized both by its division into petty states and by that beginning division of labour which Schiller deplored so much in his *Ästhetische Briefe*—a desire for greater unity, closer union, should arise. Union of human faculty with human faculty, of man with man, of man with nature. This desire often took a pantheistic form: the form of yearning towards the Spinozist ἓν καὶ πᾶν (the one united to the all), one of the most frequently quoted tags in the last quarter of the eighteenth century. And it is this yearning, this pantheist desire, which powerfully and distinctively finds voice in *Ganymed*.

The poem is characteristic of Goethe's *Sturm und Drang* period in throwing strongest emphasis on, concentrating its meaning in, the verbs. 'The life', Hamann had said, 'which strikes us in the very sound of the verbs, show that they are the oldest part of language.' And the very verbs the poet uses convey the impulsion of nature towards man, man towards nature. They are nearly all *dynamic*, expressing direction. Spring 'glüht an'; its warmth and beauty, like the flowers and the grass, 'drängt sich an das Herz'; the poet desires to seize nature in his arms (dass ich dich fassen möcht...); the clouds 'schweben abwärts', the poet yearns 'aufwärts'. The world and the poet, like Aristophanes' lovers in the *Symposium*, strive to be ever more closely united. Like the great mystics, Goethe uses love-imagery to express his yearning towards the divine: Spring is the 'Geliebter', the poet 'schmachtet' at his bosom, the nightingale calls 'liebend', the clouds 'neigen sich der sehnenden Liebe'. Nature impelled towards man, man towards nature, until a union is achieved ('an dein*em* Busen'— the dative of the possessive pronoun shows that the poet's wish has at last been granted, that he is no longer striving towards, but actually *at*, the bosom of the God): that surely links *Ganymed* with *Willkommen und Abschied*.

> ...*Welch Glück, geliebt zu werden,*
> *Und lieben, Götter, welch ein Glück.*

The 'Umfangend umfangen' of *Ganymed* is only a more ecstatic expression of this same harmony of active and passive, giving and receiving. Even the love-imagery is the same in both poems.

In keeping with the ecstatic tone of *Ganymed* is the grammatical structure of its sentences. Klopstock already, and after him—with greater emphasis—Herder had pointed out the importance of *inversion* in poetry: the device whereby an impressionistic, emotional word-order is substituted for the logical order of prose. The poet becomes conscious first of the call of the nightingale and its direction, and only then of the nightingale itself:

> *Ruft drein die Nachtigall*
> *Liebend nach mir aus dem Nebeltal;*

first of a feeling of delight, of love, and only then of its cause

> *Mit tausendfacher Liebeswonne*
> *Sich an mein Herz drängt*
> *Deiner ewigen Wärme*
> *Heilig Gefühl ...*

As his ecstasy increases, the sentences disintegrate almost entirely into joyous exclamation, vocatives and jubilant fragments.

This ecstasy justifies also Goethe's choice of free verse for this and other *Sturm und Drang* odes. *Ganymed* represents an ecstatic surrender to the beauty and divinity of nature—an active of course, not a purely passive surrender, a delighted seizing of experience; and no metrical scheme could express this better than a free verse moulded at every moment and in every detail by that particular experience. At first, in falling cadences and longer lines, the slow but irresistible motion of nature towards man:

> *Es schweben die Wolken*
> *Abwärts, die Wolken*
> *Neigen sich der sehnenden Liebe.*

Then, in the sprung rhythm of shorter lines (contrasting with the unusually long line just quoted) the eager, energetic rising of man's response to nature, his beloved:

> *Mir! Mir!*
> *In eurem Schosse*
> *Aufwärts!*

Here indeed we have what Goethe had already admired in the Gothic cathedral at Strassburg, and what he was later to call 'innere Form': a work of art, not formless, not chaotic, but obeying its own laws, moulded at every moment by an experience; moulded, to use a term much loved in the *Sturm und Drang* period, by the artist's *genius*.

And here, in this closeness to experience, we may see Goethe already true to a principle he was to formulate again and again throughout his life: 'Look at the real world and try to give it expression: for that is what the ancients did, when they were alive.' The end of the poem, as Albert Köster has long ago pointed out, describes a real, a common experience. The poet is lying in the grass, looking upwards, and (dazzled perhaps by the sun) seems to see the clouds wafting downwards and to feel himself floating towards them, as though the power of his yearning had achieved the desired union.[1] And this correctly observed, correctly rendered process becomes a symbol, merges with the myth of Ganymede. Goethe never *transcends* the real world, as Klopstock tended to do; he makes it transparent, mythical, symbolical, without doing violence to it.

(c)
AUF DEM SEE

Und frische Nahrung, neues Blut
Saug'ich aus freier Welt;
Wie ist Natur so hold und gut,
Die mich am Busen hält!
Die Welle wieget unsern Kahn
Im Rudertakt hinauf,
Und Berge, wolkig himmelan,
Begegnen unserm Lauf.

Aug', mein Aug', was sinkst du nieder?
Goldne Träume, kommt ihr wieder?
Weg, du Traum, so gold du bist:
Hier auch Lieb' und Leben ist.

Auf der Welle blinken
Tausend schwebende Sterne,
Weiche Nebel trinken
Rings die türmende Ferne;

---

[1] Cf. Richard Jefferies, *The Story of My Heart*: 'Sometimes on lying down on the sward I first looked up at the sky, gazing for a long time till I could see deep into the azure and my eyes were full of colour; then I turned my face to the grass and thyme, placing my hands at each side of my face so as to shut out everything and hide myself. *Having drunk deeply of the heaven above and felt the most glorious beauty of the day ... I now became lost, and absorbed into the being or existence of the universe*' (my italics). The whole of Jefferies' first chaper is the very stuff of Goethe's *Ganymed*.

Morgenwind umflügelt
Die beschattete Bucht,
Und im See bespiegelt
Sich die reifende Frucht.

For perfection of 'innere Form', for complete harmony, indeed unity, of physical movement, thought-movement and verse-movement, for plasticity and—at the same time—suggestive symbolism, this little poem has few equals among Goethe's works.

Auf dem See begins, vigorously, with strong stresses recurring regularly: an obvious reflection of that 'Rudertakt' which is made explicit in line 6. The reader experiences an almost muscular tension as he passes from the stressed monosyllable which ends line 1 to that which begins line 2. To this exhilarating physical movement, the rowing reproduced by the rhythm, correspond the cheerful thoughts of the goodness, friendliness, motherliness[1] of nature, which are recorded in the first section.

The opening of the second section brings a change.

Aug, mein Aug, was sinkst du nieder?
Goldne Träume, kommt ihr wieder?

Trochees replace the earlier iambs; falling cadences replace the rising; slow, broken lines replace the uninterrupted lines to which our ear has now become accustomed. The implications of this on the physical plane are obvious: they are indeed suggested by the verb 'sinkst', so appropriate to the falling, 'sinking' rhythm. The rower is resting on his oars. And on the mental plane the cheerful thoughts of the opening have now given way to thoughts of the past, of a happiness that lies behind. But then, by an effort of the will, we are pulled back, or rather forwards into the present:

Weg, du Traum, so gold du bist:
Hier auch Lieb und Leben ist.

---

[1] This comes out more elementally in the original version of 1775:

Ich saug an meiner Nabelschnur
Nun Nahrung aus der Welt.

AUF DEM SEE

The rower is plying his oars again, more vigorously than before. The past is put behind, and the claim of the present energetically reasserted.

And after the vigorous strokes of the oar comes the smooth gliding into harbour, wonderfully suggested by the many *s*, *sch*, *w* and *f* sounds, the absence of all harsh consonantal collocations:

> *Auf der Welle blinken*
> *Tausend schwebende Sterne,*
> *Weiche Nebel trinken*
> *Rings die türmende Ferne;*
> *Morgenwind umflügelt*
> *Die beschattete Bucht*
> *Und im See bespiegelt*
> *Sich die reifende Frucht.*

Rhythm and physical movement again correspond closely: and again the thought-movement too—quiet contemplation of nature—is entirely in harmony.

We have now seen the evolution of the rhythm of *Auf dem See*: from vigorous iambs to falling cadences, then to energetic rising rhythms, and to the smooth gliding of the close. This corresponded to the physical movement of the rower on the lake: at first rowing energetically, then resting on his oars, then pulling again with vigorous strokes, and finally gliding into harbour; and also to the thought-movement of the poem: from cheerful thoughts of the goodness of nature to remembrance of things past, thence to a jerk forwards into the present and a new contemplation of nature. But to all this corresponds another development. The rowers seem at first to be rowing at *night* (illumined by the lake-reflected stars[1]); night which gives place to morning at the end of the poem. *Auf dem See*, like *Willkommen und Abschied*, passes from night to morning: and it is therefore appropriate that the first section gives no precise description of nature (nothing but the mountains cloudy against the heavens vaguely discerned in the darkness) while the last ends with that 'ripening fruit' which is clearly seen, reflected (though not in unrelieved brightness) in the morning lake.

---

[1] ll. 13–14 subtly merge an image of actual stars with another image: little points of light dancing on the wave as the sun rises.

This passage from night to morning, from the darkly discerned to the distinctly seen and contemplated, clearly suggests yet another plane at which *Auf dem See* has to be considered. This plane, the symbolical, will become obvious after a scrutiny of the imagery of the poem.

In its first version, *Auf dem See* began 'Ich saug an meiner Nabelschnur | Nun Nahrung aus der Welt'. This bold image, identifying man's relation to nature with that of a baby to its mother, is clearly present even in the more subtle version we are considering. One need only point to such phrases as 'saug ich' in the second line, 'die mich am Busen hält' in the fourth, 'wieget' in the fifth. If we contrast with this the vision which ends the poem: 'die *reifende* Frucht', there can be little doubt that the passage from lake to harbour, from night to day, from vague subjective impressions of nature to precise, objective impressions, from unquestioning well-being at the bosom of nature through questionings to contemplation—that all this symbolizes the passage from youth, from childhood, to beginning maturity. The rower on the lake is not simply (as the place of this poem in *Dichtung und Wahrheit* would seem to indicate) Goethe between Frankfurt and Weimar, but every man at a certain period in his life.

'From youth to manhood, from emotion to reason, from the realm of fancy to that of freedom.'
This is the path along which Hölderlin wanted to lead his Hyperion: it is the path along which Goethe's *Auf dem See* leads the reader. And it is surely not without its significance that man does not make this journey alone, but in the company of his fellows:

> *Die Welle wieget* unsern *Kahn*
> *Im Rudertakt hinauf.*

A deceptively simple poem about a nocturnal journey on Lake Zürich becomes naturally and unforcedly a symbol for the course of a whole life, of Goethe's life and of our own. Yet the central physical experience of the rower is never lost sight of: it informs the rhythm and controls the thought-movement. Man need not transcend his sense-impressions, soar away from nature, as Klopstock did in *Der Zürcher See:*

'Look within yourself, and you will find everything you seek, and rejoice when outside yourself... you find Nature assenting to all you have found within.' (*Sprüche in Prosa*, 720.)

(d)
WARUM GABST DU UNS DIE TIEFEN BLICKE...

Warum gabst du uns die tiefen Blicke,
Unsre Zukunft ahndungsvoll zu schaun,
Unsrer Liebe, unserm Erdenglücke
Wähnend selig nimmer hinzutraun?
Warum gabst uns, Schicksal, die Gefühle,
Uns einander in das Herz zu sehn,
Um durch all die seltenen Gewühle
Unser wahr Verhältnis auszuspähn!

Ach, so viele tausend Menschen kennen,
Dumpf sich treibend, kaum ihr eigen Herz,
Schweben zwecklos hin und her und rennen
Hoffnungslos in unversehnem Schmerz;
Jauchzen wieder, wenn der schnellen Freuden
Unerwart'te Morgenröte tagt.
Nur uns armen liebevollen beiden
Ist das wechselseit'ge Glück versagt,
Uns zu lieben, ohn' uns zu verstehen,
In dem andern sehn, was er nie war,
Immer frisch auf Traumglück auszugehen,
Und zu schwanken auch in Traumgefahr.

Glücklich, den ein leerer Traum beschäftigt!
Glücklich, dem die Ahndung eitel wär!
Jede Gegenwart und jeder Blick bekräftigt
Traum und Ahndung leider uns noch mehr.
Sag', was will das Schicksal uns bereiten?
Sag', wie band es uns so rein genau?
Ach, du warst in abgelebten Zeiten
Meine Schwester oder meine Frau.

Kanntest jeden Zug in meinem Wesen,
Spähtest, wie die reinste Nerve klingt,
Konntest mich mit Einem Blicke lesen,
Den so schwer ein sterblich Aug' durchdringt.

Tropftest Mässigung dem heissen Blute,
Richtetest den wilden irren Lauf,
Und in deinen Engelsarmen ruhte
Die zerstörte Brust sich wieder auf;

Hieltest zauberleicht ihn angebunden
Und vergaukeltest ihm manchen Tag.
Welche Seligkeit glich jenen Wonnestunden,
Da er dankbar dir zu Füssen lag,
Fühlt' sein Herz an deinem Herzen schwellen,
Fühlte sich in deinem Auge gut,
Alle seine Sinnen sich erhellen
Und beruhigen sein brausend Blut.

Und von allem dem schwebt ein Erinnern
Nur noch um das ungewisse Herz,
Fühlt die alte Wahrheit ewig gleich im Innern,
Und der neue Zustand wird ihm Schmerz.
Und wir scheinen uns nur halb beseelet,
Dämmernd ist um uns der hellste Tag.
Glücklich, dass das Schicksal, das uns quälet,
Uns doch nicht verändern mag!

The reader comes to this poem with something of a shock. Is this the Goethe of *Willkommen und Abschied*, of *Ganymed*, of *Auf dem See*? The earlier poems had all begun subjectively, in an individual way: with the poet, face to face with nature. 'Es schlug *mein* Herz.' 'Wie im Morgenrot | Du rings *mich* anglühst...' 'Und frisches Leben, neues Blut | Saug *ich* aus freier Welt.' Here, in this letter written at Weimar, on 14 April 1776, to Frau von Stein, the *Lida* of his poetry, Goethe speaks for both the lovers at once. Warum gabst du *uns* die tiefen Blicke...? The earlier poems had begun vigorously, with exclamations: this one opens with a question, slowly, mysteriously, weightily, reflectively. The former had all begun with physical sensation: the beat of the heart, the rapturously experienced glow of a spring morning, vigorous rowing in the night; the latter begins with reflection on the relationship of two human beings. The three earlier poems had recorded a delighted abandon to all the moment had to give. Not that Goethe had closed his eyes to all that was *not* happy and joyous:

he could conceive of nothing without its polar opposite, of no joy without sorrow. 'Freud muss Leid, Leid muss Freude haben', says Mephisto, with more truth than the context would lead us to expect. But *Willkommen und Abschied* overcame the consciousness of terror ('Doch frisch und fröhlich war mein Mut') and of sorrow ('Und doch, welch Glück, geliebt zu werden ...'), *Ganymed* that of incomplete union and fusion,[1] *Auf dem See* that of a happiness which lies in the past.

> *Weg, du Traum, so gold du bist:*
> *Hier auch Lieb und Leben ist.*

Love and life are here, in the present; the past (and the future) are a dream if they are not assimilated into the present, into the moment of experience. This truth, the claims of the moment which Goethe was later to proclaim so magically in Suleika's words:

> *Der Spiegel sagt mir, ich bin schön!*
> *Ihr sagt: zu altern sei mein Geschick.*
> *Vor Gott muss alles ewig stehn,*
> *In mir liebt ihn für diesen Augenblick*

seems emphatically denied by *Warum gabst du uns die tiefen Blicke*.

The poem begins with a question so urgent, so insistent for all its deliberation and weightiness, that the poet cannot even find leisure, until the fifth line, to *name* the power he is invoking. The question concerns a human relationship: a relationship which the very form of the question (one lover speaking for both) shows to be close and intimate. But this relationship is not a normal, human one. The deep insight the lovers have into their future and into one another's heart is not the effect of long acquaintance, steady possession, long cohabitation. It has been conferred upon them by fate—but to what end? Such insight renders them incapable of achieving the happiness of those who, 'wähnend selig', give only the present moment its due. After such knowledge—what forgiveness? The lovers cannot now live what is characterized, half in yearning and half in contempt, as a *dream*-life:

---

[1] That precisely is the difference between *Ganymed* and *Werther*. There are many links between the two (cf. especially Werther's letter of 10 May); but Werther cannot overcome the dualism of man and nature, cannot affirm the ἓν καὶ πᾶν proclaimed by his lyric counterpart.

> *Immer frisch auf Traumglück auszugehen*
> *Und zu schwanken auch in Traumgefahr.*
> *Glücklich, den ein leerer Traum beschäftigt!*

They are precluded from the empty contentment of ordinary mortals.

The image through which Goethe first expresses this feeling is that of a jostling crowd in which others are blindly caught up, but in which the lovers never lose themselves (ll. 7 ff.); an image which merges, in the following lines, with another. The new image, which characterizes, not the lovers, but ordinary mortals living their dream-life in and for the moment, is that of an uncertain floating along, of suspension. Schweben zwecklos hin und her ... Und zu schwanken auch in Traumgefahr ... But as has already been seen—and this is the central paradox of the poem—the very clarity with which the lovers apprehend one another is itself unclear; this lack of mystery is itself the greatest mystery. For there is not, in their present relationship, anything to explain such insight. Lida is not the poet's sister, as Iphigenie was the sister of Orest,[1] neither is she his wife. The relationship which alone can confer on human beings such deep insight must therefore lie in the past. Only metempsychosis can account for it.

> *Ach, du warst in abgelebten Zeiten*
> *Meine Schwester oder meine Frau.*

The attitude of *Auf dem See* has been completely reversed. Reality (Lieb und Leben) lies all in the past.

How, then, is such 'reality' to be apprehended? Not through sense-experience, of course: only through introspection, delving among submerged memories. This process begins at line 27, and it brings with it something uncanny. A disintegration of the personality! At first the 'we' of the opening lines disintegrates into 'you' and 'I'; and then the 'I' itself disintegrates (in the manner of *Ilmenau*) into 'I' and 'he'. The Goethe of the present confronts a Goethe of the past, an Orest-Goethe calmed by an Iphigenie-Lida. And then, as we emerge from these uncertain memories—are they memories of the past at all? is not Goethe actually de-

---

[1] ll. 29–44 reproduce almost exactly the theme of Goethe's *Iphigenie auf Tauris*.

scribing (ll. 29–44) Lida's *present* effect on him, transferred to an imagined past?—we come upon a familiar image:

> *Und von allem dem schwebt ein Erinnern*
> *Nur noch um das ungewisse Herz.*

The image of uncertain floating, of suspension: this time applied not to the life of the crowd, but to that of the lovers. Their very clarity of apprehension entails an uncertainty, a 'dumpfes Treiben' which is more confused even than that of the thousands who hardly know their own heart: for it entails introspection, a gaze into a changeless past—so weightily rendered in the long, heavily-stressed line 47—which makes the everchanging present joyless and drab. The result is a life divided against itself:

> *Und wir scheinen uns nur halb beseelet* . . . ,

and a consequent inability to enjoy the moment as it passes. 'Dämmernd ist um uns der hellste Tag.'

Here we have reached the key-line of the poem. Clarity, insight ('der hellste Tag'): yet obfuscation, mystery ('dämmernd'). And *dämmernd* would seem to characterize exactly the mood, the tone of the whole poem. Its dreamy monologuizing; its slow unchanging movement; its failure—for all the concreteness of the verbs—to 'focus objects sharply on the consciousness'; its predominantly musical quality, asserting itself from the very beginning, with those long, predominantly dark vowels of the opening lines; and that avoidance of harsh consonantal collocations which makes the German language sound almost like Italian. We have met all this before: in Klopstock's *Die frühen Gräber*, in Hölty's *Mainacht*. This is the German equivalent of the Spenserian mode; and the images already noted—uncertain suspension (schweben) and twilight (dämmert)—most aptly characterize it.

Yet suddenly the last two lines of the poem break in upon us: wholly unexpected, and yet so right, so inevitable. To them might be applied the words in which Goethe described to Eckermann the ending of his *Novelle*:

'To find an image for the course of this work, picture yourself a green plant shooting up from its root, thrusting forth strong green leaves from the sides of its sturdy stem, and at last terminating in a flower.—The flower is unexpected and startling, but

come it must; in fact, the whole foliage existed only for the sake of that flower, and would be worthless without it.'
This moment too has its value and its happiness. To sorrow and pain man can oppose his own consistent personality, the sensibility which receives and shapes experience: and Goethe does this for both the lovers in lines which, though they do not abandon the smooth musicality of the rest of the poem, nevertheless stand out in vigour and energy:

> *Glücklich, dass das Schicksal, das uns quälet,*
> *Uns doch nicht verändern mag.*

Here is Goethe's 'doch' again. The human personality, the self —'Geprägte Form, die lebend sich entwickelt'—does not really disintegrate.

The last word of the poem introduces, however, a profound ambiguity.[1] At one level, the last two lines connote that fate, though it may torture the lovers, *cannot* alter their δαίμων, their innate developing personality, or indeed their love for one another. But the word 'mag' suggests also that fate does not *want* to alter this: that it is, in fact, not a malignant power at all, though the insight it has conferred may cause pain. The experience here recorded is recognized, despite all its pain and anxiety, as necessary and good. Goethe, the *Augenmensch*, the man of sense-experience, *had* to merge with Lida, his polar opposite; for without contraries, as Blake said, is no progression. After disintegration, after schizophrenia almost, Goethe has reasserted himself, a fuller man for the new experience. He has found, to use Blake's terminology just once again, his western path right *through* the Gates of Wrath.

---

[1] We may here recall that Goethe has anticipated Professor Empson in stressing the value, indeed the necessity, of such ambiguity in poetry:

> *Denn, dass ein Wort nicht einfach gelte*
> *Das müsste sich von selbst verstehn.*
>   (*West-östlicher Divan.*)

(e)
SIEBTE RÖMISCHE ELEGIE

O wie fühl' ich in Rom mich so froh! gedenk' ich der Zeiten,
　Da mich ein graulicher Tag hinten im Norden umfing,
Trübe der Himmel und schwer auf meine Scheitel sich senkte,
　Farb- und gestaltlos die Welt um den Ermatteten lag,
Und ich über mein Ich, des unbefriedigten Geistes
　Düstre Wege zu spähn, still in Betrachtung versank.
Nun umleuchtet der Glanz des helleren Äthers die Stirne;
　Phöbus rufet, der Gott, Formen und Farben hervor.
Sternhell glänzet die Nacht, sie klingt von weichen Gesängen,
　Und mir leuchtet der Mond heller als nordischer Tag.
Welche Seligkeit ward mir Sterblichem! Träum' ich? Empfänget
　Dein ambrosisches Haus, Jupiter Vater, den Gast?
Ach! hier lieg' ich und strecke nach deinen Knieen die Hände
　Flehend aus. O vernimm, Jupiter Xenius, mich!
Wie ich hereingekommen, ich kann's nicht sagen: es fasste
　Hebe den Wandrer und zog mich in die Hallen heran.
Hast du ihr einen Heroen herauf zu führen geboten?
　Irrte die Schöne? Vergib! Lass mir des Irrtums Gewinn!
Deine Tochter Fortuna, sie auch! Die herrlichsten Gaben
　Teilt als ein Mädchen sie aus, wie es die Laune gebeut.
Bist du der wirtliche Gott? O dann so verstosse den Gastfreund
　Nicht von deinem Olymp wieder zur Erde hinab!
'Dichter! wohin versteigest du dich?'—Vergib mir: der hohe
　Kapitolinische Berg ist dir ein zweiter Olymp.
Dulde mich, Jupiter, hier, und Hermes führe mich später,
　Cestius' Mal vorbei, leise zum Orkus hinab.

With the *Roman Elegies*, Goethe is once again on his 'western path'. The balance of the *Lida* lyrics is being redressed: redressed through frank sensuality. These *Erotica Romana* record the Rome experience of a German artist, who apprehends a whole culture, not through book-learning, not through intellectual conversation with others, but through physical sensation. Fondling the living body of his beloved, the poet feels better able to understand the works of art with which Rome surrounds him:

> *Dann versteh' ich den Marmor erst recht: ich denk und vergleiche,*
> *Sehe mit fühlendem Aug', fühle mit sehender Hand,*

and physical love enjoyed without remorse or recrimination leads to a fresh understanding of classical mythology:

> *In der heroischen Zeit, da Götter und Göttinnen liebten*
> *Folgte Begierde dem Blick, folgte Genuss der Begier.*

The *Roman Elegies* do not tell us (as so many have thought) that a German poet would have derived no benefit from his stay in Rome had he not indulged in a love-affair there: they show us rather that an alien culture can be apprehended passionately as well as intellectually; and that the past must be re-created in present experience.

> *War das Antike doch neu, da jene Glücklichen liebten.*[1]

The love-affair is real enough at one level: but at another it is an image, a symbol, for a whole way of life. The general is being apprehended, as Goethe was beginning at this time to demand in his theoretical utterances and writings, *through* the particular. The poet's experience is normative.

The *Seventh Elegy* constitutes therefore a paean to an entirely happy *present*: a present on which shines the light of the Roman sun illuminating forms and calling forth colours. Even the night, 'sternhell', fails to obscure these forms. The poet is entirely content in his love,[2] in his presence in Rome, in his contact with classical culture and mythology. The very style of lines 7–10 of the Elegy brings home to us this contentment with, this resting in, the present. Gone are the dynamic, active verbs of the *Sturm und Drang*—anglühen, andrängen, dreinrufen, hinaufstreben; instead the static, contemplative, 'umleuchtet', 'glänzet', 'klingt',

---

[1] Or as the Princess puts it in *Tasso*:

> *Und soll ich dir gestehen, wie ich denke:*
> *Die goldne Zeit, womit der Dichter uns*
> *Zu schmeicheln pflegt, die schöne Zeit, sie war*
> *So scheint es mir, so wenig als sie ist;*
> *Und war sie je, so war sie nur gewiss*
> *Wie sie uns immer wieder werden kann.*

[2] The elegy originally began: 'O wie machst du mich, Römerin, glücklich'...

'leuchtet'. Altogether, it is not verbs (dynamic), but nouns (static) which now dominate the syntax. Balanced, alliterating nouns:

> Phöbus rufet, der Gott, Formen und Farben hervor,

or later:

>   es fasste
> Hebe den Wandrer und zog mich in die Hallen heran.
> Hast du ihr einen Heroen herauf zu führen geboten?

and again:

> Bist du der wirtliche Gott? O dann so verstosse den Gastfreund
> Nicht von deinem Olymp wieder zur Erde hinab!

The adjectives too have changed in character: the striving, dynamic 'unendlich Schöne', 'brennender Durst', 'sehnende Liebe' of *Ganymed* have been replaced by simple sense-impressions: '*sternhelle* Nacht', '*weichste* Gesänge', '*ambrosisches* Haus'. All this makes for stillness, harmony, contemplation. And in keeping with it all are the hexameters, the classical distichs, self-contained, at rest in themselves. This metre serves at the same time to link the experience of the German poet with that of the poets of Rome, of Tibullus, Catullus and Propertius:

> *Amor schüret die Lamp indes und denket der Zeiten*
>   *Da er den nämlichen Dienst seinen Triumvirn getan;*

and it lends a peculiar sanction even to the boldest descriptions of the delights of love. 'The different poetic forms', said Goethe to Eckermann, 'have in themselves great and mysterious effects. If the content of the *Roman Elegies* were propounded in the tone and the verse-form of Byron's *Don Juan*, what I have said there would sound quite depraved.'

But the quiet, self-contained distichs of lines 7–10 are preceded by lines in which the Roman verse-form breaks down: in which the sense overflows hexameter and distich in unaccustomed agitation. For here the present is invaded by the consciousness of an unhappy past, by the recollection of a darkling northern world without form or colour. In this world there was no delight of the senses, and the poet felt therefore (as the dragging rhythms—with 'senkte' as the keyword—immediately tell us) dragged down into the depth of his own mind.

> *Und ich über mein Ich, des unbefriedigten Geistes*
> *Düstre Wege zu spähn still in Betrachtung versank.*

That is how the introspective *Lida* experience looks now, from its polar opposite. In *Warum gabst du uns die tiefen Blicke* the present, for all its insight and delight, had seemed dark when held against an imagined past: in the *Roman Elegies* the present (recreating a happy antiquity) is made all the happier by the recollection of what lies behind.

But with line 11 another agitation enters the verse. Though the distichs remain intact, the hexameters and pentameters begin to break up within themselves, to overflow one into the other. This time the cause of an agitation which the rhythms allow us to share directly is not remembrance of time past: it is rather apprehension, fears for the future. Could such happiness last? Could pagan Rome really be built in Weimar? Could one be a whole man in a divided world?

> *Bist du der wirtliche Gott? O dann so verstosse den Gastfreund*
> *Nicht von deinem Olymp wieder zur Erde hinab.*

The world of the *Roman Elegies*, so Goethe feels, is precariously placed: he could live in it only for one happy moment, between a discontented past and an uncertain future.

And so we have in the *Elegies*, for all their weight, all their firmness, a sense of poise, of precarious balance achieved and held with difficulty, which lends them their peculiar charm and even poignancy. They represent no facile escape into a dream-world, but rather an attempt, with full recognition of all difficulties and obstacles, to live the life of a full man, the life of sense and passion as well as intellect and reason, in a much-divided society. The Seventh Elegy begins confidently, as the *Sturm und Drang* Goethe might have begun: 'O wie fühl ich in Rom mich so froh!' but it ends with the wary step suggested by hesitant movement, soft consonants, alliteration on 'h', and the key-word 'leise':

> *Dulde mich, Jupiter, hier, und Hermes führe mich später,*
> *Cestius' Mal vorbei, leise zum Orkus hinab.*

These are not the accents of a classical poet, of a classical literature. 'A living, healthy classical literature and art', writes Sir Herbert

SELIGE SEHNSUCHT

Grierson, 'reflects the spirit of a self-confident society seeking in art and literature the expression of its ideals and convictions, and requiring of art the same attention to form, to correctness, which it seeks in manners and all the gestures of life.' Since there was no such society in Weimar, in Germany ('nirgends ein Zentrum', Goethe complained) a self-confident classical literature could not arise. Calm contemplation of the present was not for Goethe: the *Elegies* could be no more than a phase.

(*f*)
SELIGE SEHNSUCHT

Sagt es niemand, nur den Weisen,
Weil die Menge gleich verhöhnet,
Das Lebendge will ich preisen
Das nach Flammentod sich sehnet.

In der Liebesnächte Kühlung,
Die dich zeugte, wo du zeugtest,
Überfällt dich fremde Fühlung
Wenn die stille Kerze leuchtet.

Nicht mehr bleibest du umfangen
In der Finsternis Beschattung,
Und dich reisset neu Verlangen
Auf zu höherer Begattung.

Keine Ferne macht dich schwierig,
Kommst geflogen und gebannt,
Und zuletzt, des Lichts begierig,
Bist du Schmetterling verbrannt.

Und so lang du das nicht hast,
Dieses: Stirb und werde!
Bist du nur ein trüber Gast
Auf der dunklen Erde.

Not the least successful feature of the *Römische Elegien* had been the balance there achieved between natural German speech-rhythms—the voice of an urbane modern—and classical metres. This balance in itself reflected the poise which we have seen to be characteristic of the whole work. Goethe moved with perfect freedom within self-imposed limitations. In the long run, however, such limitations were felt as irksome, for they removed Goethe too far from what Hopkins called 'the naked thew and sinew' of his own language. Some of the commonest German words would never fit into hexameters: the word 'Eidechse', for instance, which the poet was constrained, in *Venetianische Epigramme*, to replace by its Latin equivalent:

> *Wollt ihr mirs künftig erlauben, so nenn ich die Tierchen* Lacerten
> *Denn ich brauche sie noch oft als gefälliges Bild.*

No wonder, then, that Goethe soon returned, in his lyrical poetry, to more native metres,[1] not abandoning these even when he conquered another world of poetry—that of the Persian poets, of Saadi and Hafiz—in the *West-östlicher Divan*.

In the work of Hafiz, Goethe found a reflection not only of some of his most cherished ideas, but also of his own fate, his own life in turbulent times. Like Hafiz, he turned away from the turmoil of his own political world, in which wars of conquest and liberation were being fought out—

> *Nord und West und Süd zersplittern,*
> *Throne bersten, Reiche zittern,*
> *Flüchte du, im reinen Osten*
> *Patriarchenluft zu kosten;*

not, however, into a dream-world, but into a realm of eternal truth apprehended in and through the senses as well as the intellect:

> *Dort im Reinen und im Rechten*
> *Will ich menschlichen Geschlechten*
> *In des Ursprungs Tiefe dringen,*
> *Wo sie noch von Gott empfingen*
> *Himmelslehr in Erdensprachen*
> *Und sich nicht den Kopf zerbrachen.*

[1] In later life, Goethe explicitly commented on the dangers inherent in the use of classical metres:

> *Zugemessne Rhythmen reizen freilich*
> *Das Talent erfreut sich wohl darin;*
> *Doch wie schnelle widern sie abscheulich,*
> *Hohle Masken ohne Blut und Sinn.*

'Himmelslehr in Erdensprachen', that is, intimations of first and last things, of the laws of nature, obtained through experience of this world. Nothing could better characterize Goethe's later poetry.

Selige Sehnsucht begins softly, with two short, insistent phrases whispered (as the consonants tell us) into the ear. 'Sagt es niemand, nur den *W*eisen.' This is to be a statement of deepest beliefs, not fit for the loveless mocking crowd.

> *Die wenigen, die was davon erkannt*
> *Die töricht g'nug ihr volles Herz nicht wahrten,*
> *Dem Pöbel ihr Gefühl, ihr Schauen offenbarten,*
> *Hat man von je gekreuzigt und verbrannt.*[1]

The poem is to praise (so, at least, we have to take lines 3 and 4 at this point) the living being which yearns for death by fire.

From the group of elect addressed in the first stanza (second person plural) the poet seems to turn, at the beginning of the second, to the individual, the reader (second person singular). He speaks of 'Liebesnächte'—far apart in time it would seem, for the night of being begotten and that of engendering appear together. Past and present coalesce in the recurrent moment. But it is not, here, the moment of delight, of perfect satisfaction, celebrated in the *Römische Elegien*. 'In der Liebesnächte *Kühlung*.' The word 'Kühlung' implies an impression that this was, and yet was not, a consummation. In such moments of mingled delight and dissatisfaction

> *Überfällt dich fremde Fühlung*
> *Wenn die stille Kerze leuchtet.*

Not 'Gefühl', but 'Fühlung'—a Goethean coinage, perfectly expressing a strange but sweet sensation of groping response to something outside. The groping is there in the consonants, as is the sweetness in the vowels:

> *Überfällt dich fremde Fühlung.*

The feeling comes, of course, from within—but there is something outside which inspires, which answers to it. Is it perhaps

---

[1] The passage quoted comes, of course, from *Faust*: but Goethe found the same injunction in the Persian poets.

the still candle? An actual candle shining in the darkness, but one which sends out ray after ray of meaning. It is the object of desire (we recall the *Flammentod* of the first stanza); it is also the light which shines in all darkness; it is also the joyous unwavering soul burning with a clear flame in the midst of strange sensations.

The third stanza strives away from present embrace, away from present darkness, towards the light. The actual love-relationship no longer satisfies: from merging with our kind we long to merge with, to lose ourselves in, something higher:

> *Und dich reisset neu Verlangen*
> *Auf zu höherer Begattung.*

This verse, in which the stress is so controlled that it falls heaviest on *auf*, really seems to sweep us to higher regions. We are not here in the world of the *Römische Elegien*, with their eternal delightful sameness of love, their steady possession:

> *Herzliche Liebe verbindet uns stets und treues Verlangen,*
> *Und den Wechsel behält nur die Begierde sich vor;*

but here too it is only in and through *human* love that we can conceive higher longings, that we can find an image, a simile, a symbol for them.

The upward flight begun in the third stanza continues in the fourth. No distance can appal us, clog us, complicate us (all these meanings, and more, are present in the characteristic coinage —'macht dich schwierig'). Impulsion and attraction combine; line 14 tells us this through its bold construction, successfully merging active ('kommst geflogen') and passive ('wirst gebannt' or 'bist gebannt'). Kommst geflogen und gebannt—here we have the whole *Ganymed* experience in a single bold ellipsis. And then, made the more impressive by the masculine verse-ending, comes the climax:

> *Und zuletzt, des Lichts begierig,*
> *Bist du Schmetterling verbrannt.*

Only now, just before the sentence is completed, do we realize that the *du* of the poem was not a human being at all: that Goethe has been making us share, without our realizing it, the experience of a moth attracted by the candle. That was the significance of line 6 (the moth is born and begets in the same night); that was the significance, the attraction, of the candle in line 8.

But this realization is at once superseded by another. We were *right* in applying to ourselves, as human beings, the 'du' of the poem: for there is something which links Goethe's experience and our own to that of the moth. The longing of the moth is our longing. Life cannot remain at rest, but must ever strive to lose itself in something higher, to die in order to live:

> *Und so lang du das nicht hast,*
> *Dieses: stirb und werde!*
> *Bist du nur ein trüber Gast*
> *Auf der dunklen Erde.*

The earth too would be but dark and colourless if light and darkness did not always strive to merge,[1] if the inanimate did not feel the same *selige Sehnsucht* as man and the animal world. For the yearning of which the opening stanza spoke—and this again we do not realize until we have reached the end of the poem— was not a yearning for death at all (not at all, that is, what we usually associate with a moth consumed by the candle-flame), but a yearning for life, for the constant renewal which is the condition of life. 'It is so delightful', wrote Goethe to Nees von Esenbeck four years before his death, 'to contemplate life from the standpoint of death; not from the night-side, however, but from the side of eternal day, where death is continually being swallowed up by life.' It is precisely this which distinguishes the yearning of *Selige Sehnsucht* from Novalis's longing for oblivion in eternal night, and which gives such peculiar sanction to Goethe's interpretation—one might almost say, recreation—of the traditional symbols of moth and candle-flame.

Selige Sehnsucht reinduces, in this way, an experience which was—as Goethe never tires of telling us—the deepest, the most constantly recurrent experience of his later life. It is an experience of that unity towards which *Ganymed* had once striven: the unity of all life from the inanimate earth through the lower forms of life to man. All these are bound together by a common law and a common destiny. What Goethe was later to write to Boisserée—

[1] This is the theme of *Wiederfinden* in the same collection, the *West-östlicher Divan*.

'Everything in life is metamorphosis, from plants and animals to man, and man too ... It is all so simple and eternally the same; to be our Lord God is really very easy, for it needs but a single concept, once the creation has been accomplished'—
that he makes the reader experience directly in the *Divan* poem, by making him share for a moment, without his knowledge, the life of a moth, and then leading him suddenly to the realization that moth and man and the whole earth obey the same simple law.

Goethe may thus be said to lead the reader, in *Selige Sehnsucht*, the way he had travelled himself, and the way which the Lord promised to lead Faust:

> *Wenn er mir jetzt auch nur verworren dient*
> *So werd' ich ihn bald in die Klarheit führen.*

The poem moves from whispered injunction to clear statement; from confusion (what is the theme of the poem? Who is being addressed) to clarity; from darkness (der Finsternis Beschattung) to light. That is the characteristic Goethean spiral, common to *Willkommen und Abschied, Auf dem See*, and *Selige Sehnsucht*. It is the basic, the recurrent pattern of Goethe's experience. As Goethe said himself in a review of Schlosser's *History of the Ancient World* (1826): he belonged to a generation 'die aus dem Dunklen ins Helle strebt', which strove out of darkness into light.

CHAPTER FIVE

Schiller

DAS IDEAL UND DAS LEBEN

Ewigklar und spiegelrein und eben
Fliesst das zephyrleichte Leben
Im Olymp den Seligen dahin.
Monde wechseln, und Geschlechter fliehen,
Ihrer Götterjugend Rosen blühen
Wandellos im ewigen Ruin.
Zwischen Sinnenglück und Seelenfrieden
Bleibt dem Menschen nur die bange Wahl;
Auf der Stirn des hohen Uraniden
Leuchtet ihr vermählter Strahl.

Wollt ihr schon auf Erden Göttern gleichen,
Frei sein in des Todes Reichen,
Brechet nicht von seines Gartens Frucht.
An dem Scheine mag der Blick sich weiden,
Des Genusses wandelbare Freuden
Rächet schleunig der Begierde Flucht.
Selbst der Styx, der neunfach sie umwindet,
Wehrt die Rückkehr Ceres' Tochter nicht;
Nach dem Apfel greift sie, und es bindet
Ewig sie des Orkus Pflicht.

Nur der Körper eignet jenen Mächten,
Die das dunkle Schicksal flechten;
Aber frei von jeder Zeitgewalt,
Die Gespielin seliger Naturen,
Wandelt oben in des Lichtes Fluren
Göttlich unter Göttern die Gestalt.
Wollt ihr hoch auf ihren Flügeln schweben,
Werft die Angst des Irdischen von euch,
Fliehet aus dem engen dumpfen Leben
In des Ideales Reich!

Jugendlich, von allen Erdenmalen
Frei, in der Vollendung Strahlen
Schwebet hier der Menschheit Götterbild,
Wie des Lebens schweigende Phantome
Glänzend wandeln an dem styg'schen Strome,
Wie sie stand im himmlischen Gefild,
Ehe noch zum traur'gen Sarkophage
Die Unsterbliche heruntersteig.
Wenn im Leben noch des Kampfes Wage
Schwankt, erscheinet hier der Sieg.

Nicht vom Kampf die Glieder zu entstricken,
Den Erschöpften zu erquicken,
Wehet hier des Sieges duft'ger Kranz.
Mächtig, selbst wenn eure Sehnen ruhten,
Reisst das Leben euch in seine Fluten,
Euch die Zeit in ihren Wirbeltanz.
Aber sinkt des Mutes kühner Flügel
Bei der Schranken peinlichem Gefühl,
Dann erblicket von der Schönheit Hügel
Freudig das erflogne Ziel.

Wenn es gilt, zu herrschen und zu schirmen,
Kämpfer gegen Kämpfer stürmen
Auf des Glückes, auf des Ruhmes Bahn,
Da mag Kühnheit sich an Kraft zerschlagen
Und mit krachendem Getös die Wagen
Sich vermengen auf bestäubtem Plan.
Mut allein kann hier den Dank erringen,
Der am Ziel des Hippodromes winkt;
Nur der Starke wird das Schicksal zwingen,
Wenn der Schwächling untersinkt.

Aber der, von Klippen eingeschlossen,
Wild und schäumend sich ergossen,
Sanft und eben rinnt des Lebens Fluss
Durch der Schönheit stille Schattenlande,
Und auf seiner Wellen Silberrande
Malt Aurora sich und Hesperus.
Aufgelöst in zarter Wechselliebe,

*In der Anmut freiem Bund vereint,
Ruhen hier die ausgesöhnten Triebe,
Und verschwunden ist der Feind.*

*Wenn, das Tote bildend zu beseelen,
Mit dem Stoff sich zu vermählen,
Tatenvoll der Genius entbrennt,
Da, da spanne sich des Fleisses Nerve,
Und beharrlich ringend unterwerfe
Der Gedanke sich das Element.
Nur dem Ernst, den keine Mühe bleichet,
Rauscht der Wahrheit tief versteckter Born;
Nur des Meissels schwerem Schlag erweichet·
Sich des Marmors sprödes Korn.*

*Aber dringt bis in der Schönheit Sphäre,
Und im Staube bleibt die Schwere
Mit dem Stoff, den sie beherrscht, zurück.
Nicht der Masse qualvoll abgerungen,
Schlank und leicht, wie aus dem Nichts gesprungen,
Steht das Bild vor dem entzückten Blick.
Alle Zweifel, alle Kämpfe schweigen
In des Sieges hoher Sicherheit;
Ausgestossen hat es jeden Zeugen
Menschlicher Bedürftigkeit.*

*Wenn ihr in der Menschheit traur'ger Blösse
Steht vor des Gesetzes Grösse,
Wenn dem Heiligen die Schuld sich naht,
Da erblasse vor der Wahrheit Strahle
Eure Tugend, vor dem Ideale
Fliehe mutlos die beschämte Tat.
Kein Erschaffner hat dies Ziel erflogen,
Ueber diesen grauenvollen Schlund
Trägt kein Nachen, keiner Brücke Bogen,
Und kein Anker findet Grund.*

*Aber flüchtet aus der Sinne Schranken
In die Freiheit der Gedanken,
Und die Furchterscheinung ist entflohn,
Und der ew'ge Abgrund wird sich füllen;*

Nehmt die Gottheit auf in euren Willen,
Und sie steigt von ihrem Weltenthron.
Des Gesetzes strenge Fessel bindet
Nur den Sklavensinn, der es verschmäht;
Mit des Menschen Widerstand verschwindet
Auch des Gottes Majestät.

 Wenn der Menschheit Leiden euch umfangen,
Wenn Laokoon der Schlangen
Sich erwehrt mit namenlosem Schmerz,
Da empöre sich der Mensch! Es schlage
An des Himmels Wölbung seine Klage
Und zerreisse euer fühlend Herz!
Der Natur furchtbare Stimme siege,
Und der Freude Wange werde bleich,
Und der heil'gen Sympathie erliege
Das Unsterbliche in euch!

 Aber in den heitern Regionen,
Wo die reinen Formen wohnen,
Rauscht des Jammers trüber Sturm nicht mehr.
Hier darf Schmerz die Seele nicht durchschneiden,
Keine Träne fliesst hier mehr dem Leiden,
Nur des Geistes tapfrer Gegenwehr.
Lieblich wie der Iris Farbenfeuer
Auf der Donnerwolke duft'gem Tau,
Schimmert durch der Wehmuth düstern Schleier
Hier der Ruhe heitres Blau.

 Tief erniedrigt zu des Feigen Knechte,
Ging in ewigem Gefechte
Einst Alcid des Lebens schwere Bahn,
Rang mit Hydern und umarmt' den Leuen,
Stürzte sich, die Freunde zu befreien,
Lebend in des Totenschiffers Kahn.
Alle Plagen, alle Erdenlasten
Wälzt der unversöhnten Göttin List
Auf die will'gen Schultern des Verhassten —
Bis sein Lauf geendigt ist —

> *Bis der Gott, des Irdischen entkleidet,*
> *Flammend sich vom Menschen scheidet*
> *Und des Aethers leichte Lüfte trinkt.*
> *Froh des neuen ungewohnten Schwebens,*
> *Fliesst er aufwärts, und des Erdenlebens*
> *Schweres Traumbild sinkt und sinkt und sinkt.*
> *Des Olympus Harmonien empfangen*
> *Den Verklärten in Kronions Saal,*
> *Und die Göttin mit den Rosenwangen*
> *Reicht ihm lächelnd den Pokal.*

As a theoretician and critic of literature, and above all as a dramatist, Schiller (1759–1805) is of unequalled importance: but his place in a history of the German lyric (especially one which excludes the ballad) is not, despite his popularity, an eminent one. Schiller's most characteristic 'lyrics' are but abstract thought clothed in rhetoric. A few remarks on what is generally recognized as Schiller's greatest poem[1] may indicate both the nature of his achievement and his peculiar limitations.

Das Ideal und das Leben begins with a description of the ideal life, the life of the Greek gods. There is no struggle, no striving, no mutability; desire and enjoyment are perfectly balanced. On earth, however, no such harmony is possible, except through self-abnegation, through pure disinterested contemplation. While the body is subject to cloying and decay, the mind of man has power to find true enjoyment in the contemplation of the ideal.

> *Fliehet aus dem engen dumpfen Leben*
> *In des Ideales Reich.*

That is the characteristic flight of a man dissatisfied with his own age and his own time.

But characteristically Schiller does not exhort us to live in passive contemplation of the ideal. While on this earth, man must never cease to strive, so that he may remould nearer to the heart's desire the sorry scheme of things. As constant encouragement he has, in *Beauty*, a reflex of the unity and harmony of the ideal: especially in the beauty of *Art*, achieved by the artist with infinite

---

[1] That was certainly Schiller's own estimate—v. his letter to Wilhelm von Humboldt, 9 August 1795.

toil, yet retaining in its ultimate perfection no vestige of such toil.

> *Nicht der Masse qualvoll abgerungen*
> *Schlank und leicht, wie aus dem Nichts gesprungen*
> *Steht das Bild vor dem entzückten Blick.*

Heaven can never wholly be built on earth, the ideal never be fully realized in the actual: but in Beauty, in Art, we have at least a reflection of the harmony and unity towards which all men must strive.

What is true of aesthetics holds good in ethics also. We can never obey to the full the demands of the categorical imperative, of the ethical *Thou shalt*. Our deeds will always fall short of the ideal. But the willing spirit may perform what weak flesh cannot. We may so inform our mind that it is in perfect harmony with the moral law: so that we *will* what we *ought* to do.

> *Nehmt die Gottheit auf in euren Willen*
> *Und sie steigt von ihrem Weltenthron.*

Inclination and duty may, and should, become one.

And now the aesthetic and the ethical merge, as Schiller broaches the problem which touches him most: the problem of Tragedy. In real life our reaction to human suffering must of necessity be inharmonious. We must feel pain, indignation born of pity for human misery.

> *Und der heil'gen Sympathie erliege*
> *Das Unsterbliche in euch.*

In art, however, the depiction of human suffering should not cause grief or pain or indignation—all should be harmonized by admiration for human courage, human greatness.

> *Keine Träne fliesst hier mehr dem Leiden,*
> *Nur des Geistes tapfrer Gegenwehr.*

In art the most disharmonious is made harmonious and beautiful. Tragedy is the highest reflection of the Ideal in Life.

Das Ideal und das Leben began with a vision of divine harmony. It continued, with the strict logic of abstract thought, to present the disharmony, disunity of life, of our existence on this earth, indicating both the stern features of our physical and the compensative features of our moral being. In contemplating the Ideal and working towards its realization the poet found encouragement and hope. And so he ends the poem with the myth of Heracles, the man who never ceased to battle with the monstrous forces of this world, undismayed by the tyranny of Eurystheus and the persecutions of Hera, and who at last achieved an apotheosis, realized the harmonious life of the gods. With his soaring to and reception on Olympos the poem comes to a noble, if still rhetorical, close. The Ideal and Life may one day coincide.

This summary of the intellectual content of *Das Ideal und das Leben* (which followed exactly the course of the poem) will have sufficiently indicated the nature of Schiller's experience of life. Life on this earth was to Schiller a recalcitrant material which had to be fashioned, through unremitting labour, into something other than it is: something more approaching the ideal in the human mind. Only in pure disinterested contemplation of beauty could man find respite from this constant struggle. The poet who feels this cannot delightedly surrender himself to experience, embrace experience, as we have seen Goethe to do; nor can he accept experience, keep himself open to it, in the manner of Hölderlin. He must, instead, oppose his personality to life, must struggle against its temptations, must work upon it. Since this was Schiller's attitude to life, he had to endeavour to communicate it in ways which differed from those of other lyric poets, poets who felt better able to surrender themselves to the world and all it had to give. We must beware, therefore, of judging him purely by standards abstracted from the work of Goethe, Hölderlin or the German Romantics.

What strikes the reader first when he comes to *Das Ideal und das Leben* is its lucid logical construction and its inexorable verse-movement. The poem is constructed like a well-thought-out oration. First an introductory statement; then four antitheses (four pairs of stanzas, of which one stanza begins with 'Wenn' and describes the stern labours of life, while the other begins with 'Aber' and brings consolation from the realm of the Ideal); and finally the peroration, harking back to the opening. The whole is punctuated by alliterating epigrammatic formulae:

> *Zwischen Sinnenglück und Seelenfrieden*
> *Bleibt dem Menschen nur die bange Wahl,*

or again:

> *Nehmt die Gottheit auf in euren Willen*
> *Und sie steigt von ihrem Weltenthron,*

and even by such resounding platitudes as

> *Nur der Starke wird das Schicksal zwingen*
> *Wenn der Schwache untersinkt.*

A platitude—as Schiller himself realized—is twice a platitude in poetry. 'Never is a platitude as obvious as when it is expressed in poetry' (letter to Körner, 24 November 1797). 'What oft was thought, but ne'er so well expressed' cannot apply to Schiller: for his poetry is consciously divorced from society, from its speech as from its manners, so that for him old truths do not become new in a new social setting.

As inexorable as the over-all construction is the verse-movement of the poem. Again and again the main stress thunders down in the same place, all the heavier (and—many would feel—more unbearable) because of the constant alliteration.

> *Da mag Kühnheit sich an Kraft zerschlagen*
>
> *Und mit krachendem Getös die Wagen ...*
>
> *Nur der Starke wird das Schicksal zwingen*
>
> *Wenn der Schwache untersinkt.*
>
> *Und im Staube bleibt die Schwere*
>
> *Mit dem Stoff, der sie beherrscht, zurück.*

The divorce from speech-rhythm, from any German that was ever spoken, is complete.

But this construction, this movement, are both adapted to convey Schiller's experience of life. He could not surrender himself to the world, to the fluxes and refluxes of feeling it inspired: he had to force it into a pattern, to approximate it to the Ideal. The violence done to the natural sequence of experience and to the German language reflect exactly the violence Schiller habitually did, in his mind, to the world he saw and heard and felt.

This characteristic attitude to the world—a fundamentally hostile attitude—explains also the lack of sense-perceived detail in Schiller's poems. His imagery is mainly conventional and allegorical: Proserpina plucking the fruits of Hades, a chariot-race, Laocoon struggling with the serpents, Heracles ascending Olympos—all are but pale allegories, counters for ideas.

> *Aber sinkt des Mutes kühner Flügel*
> *Bei der Schranken peinlichem Gefühl,*
> *Dann erblicket von der Schönheit Hügel*
> *Freudig das erflogne Ziel.*

The physical detail of such lines is of no account. Wings and hills are introduced only to trick out the abstractions. And throughout the poem adjectives are used which are intellectual rather than visual, oral or tactile. Hoch, duftig, ewig, traurig, kühn, mächtig, freudig, fühlend. All these have but the vaguest physical connotations, if they have any at all.

For the world is not to be contemplated for its own sake. Schiller would rather escape from it, as Klopstock did before him, into the human mind.

> *Aber flüchtet aus der Sinne Schranken*
> *In die Freiheit der Gedanken . . .*

A flight into the mind, into the Ideal, should help to reunite the divided human personality and thus lead to a regeneration of mankind in the ugly, cramping modern world which Schiller knew. It was not to be an escape in the usual sense:

'How ill-advised man would be if he were to chose the way towards the Ideal in order to save himself the way to Reality!'; it was to lead to regeneration of life in this world, in ways which Schiller's *Briefe über ästhetische Erziehung* sufficiently demonstrate.

The poet is not, as we have seen, interested in the physical details of the external world: he seems fascinated rather, in *Das Ideal und das Leben*, by relations. The relations between man and the world, between contrasting ideas, contrasting desires.

> *Ihrer Götterjugend Rosen blühen*
> *Wandellos im ewigen Ruin.*

The roses, the eternal ruin, do not matter—they are not in any way precisely seen: what matters, is the relation between the two, the clash of their juxtaposition. This sense of contrast and clash (fundamental to the whole poem, announced even in its title) sharply distinguishes Schiller from Klopstock. It is the mark of the dramatist rather than the lyrical poet: of the dramatist, who pits his characters against one another, against fate, against the gods, and pursues to their logical end the conflicts arising from that contraposition. In just the same way, Schiller allows *Wenn* to clash with *Aber*, Life with Ideal, throughout his poem, until a final solution, a synthesis, is reached.

If, therefore, Schiller does succeed in conveying his experience, it is an experience which makes for drama, for tragedy, rather than lyric poetry. The poet himself was fully aware of this. 'The lyric genre to which you would direct me', he wrote to his friend Körner six years before the composition of *Das Ideal und das Leben*, 'I regard as a place of exile rather than as a province I have conquered.' And the modern reader too, coming to Schiller's lyrics from those of Goethe, of Hölderlin, or of Mörike, feels himself exiled from the country he loves. He cannot but be repelled by the lack of every incommensurable element, of all singing notes in Schiller's poetry; by the violence it does to the natural rhythms of the spoken language; and not least by its hortatory tone:

> *Wollt ihr schon auf Erden Göttern gleichen,*
> *Frei sein in des Todes Reichen,*
> *Brechet nicht von seines Gartens Frucht.*

The musical 'effects' of *Das Ideal und das Leben* have always had their admirers; the passage, for instance, which evokes the course of the river, wild among cliffs but ineffably calm in the shaded plains:

> *Aber der, von Klippen eingeschlossen,*
> *Wild und schäumend sich ergossen,*
> *Sanft und eben rinnt des Lebens Fluss*
> *Durch der Schönheit stille Schattenlande,*
> *Und auf seiner Wellen Silberrande*
> *Malt Aurora sich und Hesperus;*

but even such passages as these are too obviously worked out, excogitated, to compensate for the general lack of lyric grace.

CHAPTER SIX

Hölderlin

(a)
DER ABSCHIED

Trennen wollten wir uns? wähnten es gut und klug?
  Da wirs taten, warum schröckte, wie Mord, die Tat?
    Ach! wir kennen uns wenig,
      Denn es waltet ein Gott in uns.

Den verraten? ach ihn, welcher uns alles erst
  Sinn und Leben erschuf, ihn, den beseelenden
    Schutzgott unserer Liebe,
      Dies, dies Eine vermag ich nicht.

Aber anderen Fehl denket der Weltsinn sich
  Andern ehernen Dienst übt er und anders Recht
    Und es listet die Seele
      Tag für Tag der Gebrauch uns ab.

Wohl ich wusst es zuvor, seit die gewurzelte
  Ungestalte die Furcht Götter und Menschen trennt,
    Muss, mit Blut sie zu sühnen,
      Muss der Liebenden Herz vergehn.

Lass mich schweigen! o lass nimmer von nun an mich
  Dieses Tödliche sehn, dass ich im Frieden doch
    Hin ins Einsame ziehe,
      Und noch unser der Abschied sei!

Reich die Schale mir selbst, dass ich des rettenden
  Heilgen Giftes genug, dass ich des Lethetranks
    Mit dir trinke, dass alles
      Hass und Liebe vergessen sei!

Hingehn will ich. Vielleicht seh ich in langer Zeit
  Diotima! dich einst. Aber verblutet ist

Dann das Wünschen und friedlich
Gleich den Seligen, fremde gehn

Wir umher, ein Gespräch führet uns ab und auf,
Sinnend zögernd, doch itzt mahnt die Vergessenen
Hier die Stelle des Abschieds,
Es erwarmet ein Herz in uns,

Staunend seh ich dich an, Stimmen und süssen Sang
Wie aus voriger Zeit, hör ich und Saitenspiel,
Und die Lilie duftet
Golden über dem Bach uns auf.

Goethe and Schiller had both been able, despite their plaints, to create for themselves a substitute for a truly national public, for the public of Homer and Sophocles and Shakespeare. They were able, at least, to make their voice heard, and to hope that their plea for aesthetic education might result in the creation of the kind of cultured élite which Tasso (the Tasso of Goethe's play) found at Ferrara.

Zur Nation euch zu bilden, ihr hofft es, Deutsche, vergebens;
Bildet, ihr könnt es, dafür freier zu Menschen euch aus.

It was this kind of supra-national élite which Goethe addressed in such poems as *Selige Sehnsucht*. 'Sagt es niemand, nur den Weisen...' At Weimar he found at least sufficient 'Weise', sufficient understanding admirers, not to feel too strongly the inevitable isolation of the artist in the modern world.

Not so Friedrich Hölderlin (1770–1843). Neglected and scarcely known among his contemporaries, he was conscious of a terrible loneliness, feeling that he stood alone in his aspirations towards the *complete* man, towards the harmonious deployment of all human faculties in a regenerated society. He lived, so it seemed to him, in a godless and divided age in which true communal life was impossible.

Aber weh! es wandelt in Nacht, es wohnt wie im Orkus
Ohne Göttliches unser Geschlecht. Ans eigene Treiben
Sind sie geschmiedet allein, und sich in der tosenden Werkstatt
Höret jeglicher nur, und viel arbeiten die Wilden

DER ABSCHIED

> *Mit gewaltigem Arm, rastlos, doch immer und immer*
> *Unfruchtbar, wie die Furien, bleibt die Mühe der Armen;*

in an age, moreover, which did not even feel the *need* for regeneration and which refused therefore to listen to the poet's voice. Among contemporaries such as these, among the plutocratic clique of the Gontards at Frankfurt, he felt lost and forsaken.

> *Ich verstand die Stille des Äthers*
> *Der Menschen Stimme verstand ich nie.*

Only in Susette Gontard, the *Diotima* of his poetry, did he find a human being who valued and shared his aspirations, who seemed to him a reincarnation of a happier humanity and therefore (like himself) misunderstood in the 'age of darkness' in which she was condemned to live.

> *Du schweigst und duldest, denn sie verstehn dich nicht*
> *Du edles Leben! Siehest zur Erd und schweigst*
> *Am schönen Tag, denn ach! umsonst nur*
> *Suchst du die Deinen im Sonnenlichte ...*
>
> *Die zärtlichgrossen Seelen, die nimmer sind.*

With her he could create, in isolation from the rest of mankind, his own better world:

> *Es schufen sich einst die Einsamen liebend*
> *Nur von Göttern gekannt, ihre geheimere Welt;*

in her company he could hope that the great storms of the time (the time, it must be remembered, of the French Revolution) would usher in a happier era for the whole of humanity, an era comparable to that of Themistoclean Greece.

> *Ja! noch siehet mein sterblich Lied*
> *Den Tag der, Diotima! nächst den*
> *Göttern mit Helden dich nennt, und dir gleicht.*

But from Diotima too the world, with its notions of probity and decorum, forced him to part. In *Der Abschied*, the poem we are now to consider, this final separation, this thrust into a deeper darkness and more absolute solitude, most movingly find its voice.

The harsh consonants and the heavy stress of the very first

syllable of the poem convey at once, physically, the wrench of parting; and anxious questions, breaking up the lines, add to this a feeling of uncertainty, of doubt of the lovers' own probity and wisdom. The second line, with its anxious jerking movement, throws up (through grammatical and rhythmic isolation) one terrifying phrase. 'Wie Mord.' That is the phrase which seems, with its suggestions of some fearful, unnatural act, to dominate the whole stanza, explaining the wrench of the opening and the anxious movement. The lovers had acted as though they lived only on the human plane: they now discover that their love partook of the divine. 'Denn es waltet ein Gott in uns.' In the full vowel and the strong accentuation of the syllable 'Gott' that discovery flashes upon us, illuminating the ravages around, shedding light on the mysterious 'wie Mord' of the second line.

In deciding to separate, the lovers are murdering a god: they are acting, as the opening of stanza 2 tells us, the part of Judas the Traitor. The whole of this second stanza conveys revolt against such betrayal, moves passionately to the renunciation implicit in its final word. The god who informed their love first gave them a soul in a soulless world, protected them from the meaninglessness of life; the line-division

> ... *den beseelenden*
> *Schutzgott* ...

lingers over these benefits, lends them their proper weight. The last line of the stanza, with its determined stresses, seems therefore to reverse the decision of the opening, to refuse to murder and betray.

But on the agitated, nervously energetic second stanza follows the inexorable even third, which speaks of the world in which the lovers live. 'Der Weltsinn', 'der Gebrauch'—these are not simply abstractions, they are *seen*, become a monstrous actuality crushing the lovers with the iron tread suggested by the rhythm; the tread which comes down three times on the word 'andern', suggesting the remoteness of these monsters from the laws of true gods. Their law, their code, is 'ehern'. The word describes at once the nature and the object of the world's worship. It suggests on the one hand the juggernaut inexorability already noted; and on the other a worship of brute power, of heathen idols. Life in a world dedicated to such service as this gradually kills the soul bestowed on the lovers by their god. Custom steals it cunningly away:

> *Und es listet die Seele*
> *Tag für Tag der Gebrauch uns ab.*

Another image of unnatural, criminal activities—activities justified, almost sanctified, by an unnatural heathen worship.

'Wohl ich wusst es zuvor.' Now we realize that the previous stanzas have been agitated by a submerged memory, which insists at last on rising to the surface.

> *... seit die gewúrzelte*
> *Úngestálte die Fúrcht Götter und Ménschen trénnt.*

In these lines we can see *Fear* rearing itself up—as we pass from the first adjective over the line-division to the second and thence (over the repeated article) to the noun 'Furcht'; as we are jerked from one stress, one ominous *u* vowel, to the next. The modern world separates gods and men, therefore—and the realization of this is delayed as long as possible, until the very last word of the stanza, whose movement is agitated by the dread of which it speaks—the lovers must kill their own soul, their own love. They have no choice. That repeated heavily-stressed 'muss' seems to mock at the 'Trennen *wollten* wirs uns' of the opening, with its suggestion of free will; at the passionate resolution not to betray the true god, towards which the second stanza had moved. There is a cosmic reason for the lovers' pain, a cosmic necessity for murder and betrayal. The world in its worship of idols, the monster Fear, exact blood sacrifices, the sacrifice of the lovers' heart. 'Mit Blut ... sühnen.' The unnatural has become the sacred. The blood of the lovers, the murder and betrayal of their god, is a sacrifice of atonement. The lovers are at the same time Judas and Christ.

The poet's personal tragedy has now become cosmic: it has become the tragedy of his age. But this is a consciousness which Hölderlin cannot, as yet, bear; a vision to which he tries to close his eyes in the exclamatory sentences which make up stanzas 5 and 6. Even his own isolation holds no terrors compared with 'dieses Tödliche', the death-bringing recognition that his own fate is the fate, not of an individual, but of a generation. He asks first for silence (thus renouncing his vision as a poet) and then (renouncing it as a man) for blindness:

> *Lass mich schweigen! o lass nimmer von nun an mich*
> *Dieses Tödliche sehn . . . ;*

hoping to wander into his destined solitude in peace, in the belief that the parting is but his and Diotima's and not that of all who have the same aspirations, that it is a private and not a general fate. But just then the closeness with which the lovers are bound to their world becomes terrifyingly clear. The lovers too, at this supreme moment, are involved in the paradox of the world. For them too the unnatural becomes the sacred.

> *Reich die Schale mir selbst, dass ich des rettenden*
> *Heilgen Giftes genug, dass ich des Lethetranks*
> *Mit dir trinke . . .*

As the poet prays for total annihilation, oblivion, Lethe; as he gives way for the moment to that 'wunderbare Sehnen dem Abgrund zu' which he shared with the German Romantics, we see in his mind the sacred and the poisonous ('heiliges Gift') come together as inevitably and inextricably as in the rest of the benighted world.

On this almost hysterical outburst follows calm, and the vision of a possible future in which the pyres are out and valediction said. The calm, as the ambiguity of 'Hingehn' already suggests, is the calm of death. '*Verblutet* ist dann das Wünschen.' The blood-sacrifice has been accomplished. The lovers' hearts, their desires, have bled to death. The mysterious and beautiful lines which describe a strange disembodied walk through the landscape in some possible future (ll. 25–30), seem themselves to ebb away, as life ebbs out of the lovers. 'Verblutet' is the keyword; 'Sinnend, zögernd' characterizes the movement. Yet suddenly, in the middle of line 30, the movement is reversed. Instead of the expected cessation comes a new flood of life, echoed by the rhythms, a new flowering of life and hope. 'Es erwarmet...' 'Duftet... auf.' Instead of the dissonance which yoked together the unnatural and the sacred we have infinite harmony, as from a by-gone age (wie aus voriger Zeit): a vision of purity, love and hope concentrated in the inexhaustible

DER ABSCHIED

synaesthetic symbol of the lily wafting a golden fragrance over the brook. The poem ends, not with revolt, but with acceptance. It ends with the vision of a possible happier future, apprehended, not intellectually, but through contemplation of one of the beauties of this world: the beauty, purity and fragrance of the lily. There is no 'Trennung', no separation here. Through its fragrance the flower unites itself with the aether and aspires towards the lovers, who (themselves united) thus partake of it. Harmony has been and will be again.

Hölderlin, as we have seen, experienced more painfully than any German poet before him the isolation of the individual, and especially of the poet, in the modern world. The theme of *Der Abschied* is therefore separation, the separation of that which belongs together: the theme also of Goethe's *Trilogie der Leidenschaft*.

> *Denn Scheiden endlich — Scheiden ist der Tod.*

But for Goethe parting was a private grief. The world remained as great and good as it had ever been; others were not and should not be affected by the sorrows of the poet.

> *Verlasst mich hier, getreue Weggenossen!*
> *Lasst mich allein am Fels, in Moor und Moos.*
> *Nur immer zu! Euch ist die Welt erschlossen,*
> *Die Erde weit, der Himmel hehr und gross.*

Hölderlin—though he cannot as yet face the full implications of this—sees his own separation from Diotima as part of the separation of man from man and man from his gods in the world as he knew it.

'Had I grown up with Themistocles, had I lived in the time of Scipio, my soul would not have experienced what it experiences now.' (*Hyperion.*)

He sees everywhere the parting of that which ought to be one and the union of the incongruous; a union perfectly conveyed by those images which 'yoke the most heterogeneous ideas by violence together'. The violence of the juxtaposition reflects the violence done to nature. Such realization of a cosmic necessity for personally experienced pain and anguish lends Hölderlin's lyrics a tragic intensity new in German poetry; leads him to express, again and again, his longing for annihilation, for the peace of death.

> *Indessen dünket mich öfter*
> *Besser zu schlafen, wie so ohne Genossen zu sein,*
> *So zu harren, und was zu tun indes und zu sagen*
> *Weiss ich nicht, und wozu Dichter in dürftiger Zeit?*

Yet he never—and this distinguishes him sharply from the German Romantics—gave way to such yearning for more than a moment. Seeing the terror of life more clearly than ever Goethe did, Hölderlin, while he could not flee, with Klopstock, into happier regions of the mind, refused to look, like his contemporary Novalis, towards death and night and life beyond the skies. *Der Abschied*, which had begun with images of separation and disharmony, ends with the vision of the lily, one of the beauties of this world, which becomes, as the poet gazes, the symbol of a possible, happier, more harmonious existence *on earth*. 'Hier die Stelle des Abschieds' (l. 31)—that directs our attention to an actual landscape, makes it clear that we have not left the planet on which we live. Just as the asclepiad stanzas hold and contain the flow of grief, so yearning is checked by this final vision. Not by any means a certain vision—'vielleicht', 'einst', perhaps, in some possible future: but one which holds out at least the possibility of consolation, and makes it possible for the poet to go on living and seek for consolation in the world which has caused his suffering.

(b)
WIE WENN AM FEIERTAGE...

> *Wie wenn am Feiertage, das Feld zu sehn*
> *Ein Landmann geht, des Morgens, wenn*
> *Aus heisser Nacht die kühlenden Blitze fielen*
> *Die ganze Zeit und fern noch tönet der Donner,*
> *In sein Gestade wieder tritt der Strom,*
> *Und frisch der Boden grünt*
> *Und von des Himmels erfreuendem Regen*
> *Der Weinstock trauft und glänzend*
> *In stiller Sonne stehn die Bäume des Haines:*

WIE WENN AM FEIERTAGE...

So stehn sie unter günstiger Witterung
Sie die kein Meister allein, die wunderbar
Allgegenwärtig erzieht in leichtem Umfangen
Die mächtige, die göttlichschöne Natur.
Drum wenn zu schlafen sie scheint zu Zeiten des Jahrs
Am Himmel oder unter den Pflanzen oder den Völkern,
So trauert der Dichter Angesicht auch,
Sie scheinen allein zu sein, doch ahnen sie immer.
Denn ahnend ruhet sie selbst auch.

Jetzt aber tagts! Ich harrt und sah es kommen,
Und was ich sah, das Heilige sei mein Wort.
Denn sie, sie selbst, die älter denn die Zeiten
Und über die Götter des Abends und Orients ist,
Die Natur ist jetzt mit Waffenklang erwacht,
Und hoch vom Äther bis zum Abgrund nieder
Nach festem Gesetze, wie einst, aus heiligem Chaos gezeugt,
Fühlt neu die Begeisterung sich,
Die Allerschaffende wieder.

Und wie im Aug ein Feuer dem Manne glänzt,
Wenn Hohes er entwarf; so ist
Von neuem an den Zeichen, den Taten der Welt jetzt,
Ein Feuer angezündet in Seelen der Dichter.
Und was zuvor geschah, doch kaum gefühlt,
Ist offenbar erst jetzt,
Und die uns lächelnd den Acker gebauet,
In Knechtsgestalt, sie sind bekannt, die
Alllebendigen, die Kräfte der Götter.

Erfrägst du sie? im Liede wehet ihr Geist,
Wenn es der Sonne des Tags und warmer Erd
Entwacht, und Wettern, die in der Luft, und andern
Die vorbereiteter in Tiefen der Zeit
Und deutungsvoller, und vernehmlicher uns
Hinwandeln zwischen Himmel und Erd und unter den Völkern.
Des gemeinsamen Geistes Gedanken sind
Still endend in der Seele des Dichters.

Dass schnellbetroffen sie, Unendlichem
Bekannt seit langer Zeit, von Erinnerung

HÖLDERLIN

Erbebt, und ihr, von heilgem Strahl entzündet,
Die Frucht in Liebe geboren, der Götter und Menschen Werk
Der Gesang, damit er beiden zeuge, glückt.
So fiel, wie Dichter sagen, da sie sichtbar
Den Gott zu sehen begehrte, sein Blitz auf Semeles Haus
Und die göttlichgetroffne gebar,
Die Frucht des Gewitters, den heiligen Bacchus.

Und daher trinken himmlisches Feuer jetzt
Die Erdensöhne ohne Gefahr.
Doch uns gebührt es, unter Gottes Gewittern,
Ihr Dichter! mit entblösstem Haupte zu stehen,
Des Vaters Strahl, ihn selbst, mit eigner Hand
Zu fassen und dem Volk ins Lied
Gehüllt die himmlische Gabe zu reichen.
Denn sind nur reinen Herzens,
Wie Kinder, wir, sind schuldlos unsere Hände,

Des Vaters Strahl, der reine versengt es nicht
Und tieferschüttert, die Leiden des Stärkeren
Mitleidend, bleibt das ewige Herz doch fest.

This poem, one of the great free verse *Hymnen* of Hölderlin's last years of sanity, begins at the point towards which *Der Abschied* had moved: begins with contemplation of nature. Contemplation, indeed, seems the keynote of the opening lines, in which all main stresses fall on nouns: 'Feiertag', 'Felde' (the alliteration gives the stresses greater weight and force), 'Landmann', 'Morgen'. Correspondingly slow and deliberate is the movement of the verse, which echoes the unhurrying holiday walk (described in the first lines) of the farmer through his fields.

The peace, the beautiful calm of the landscape has only just been re-established after turmoil, after the thunderstorm which is recalled in lines that seem themselves to fall like the lightning they describe—

wenn
Aus heisser Nacht die kühlenden Blitze fielen
Die ganze Zeit ... —

and whose distant rumblings can still be heard in the onomatopoeic 'und fern noch tönet der Donner'. In these lines (2-4), conflict of speech-movement and technical norm, overflowing of line-endings, sufficiently suggest to the reader an experience of turmoil barely calmed. The thunderstorm, however, has brought not disaster but refreshment: itself uniting and balancing extremes ('*heisse* Nacht', '*kühlende* Blitze'), it has lent new beauty and freshness to a landscape now once again still, bathed in the light of the sun.

glänzend
In stiller Sonne stehn die Bäume des Haines.

Peace, stillness, content, the ineffable beauty and calm of the scene described, are mirrored in these magnificent balanced cadences. The more we scrutinize the scene—and the deliberate movement, the heavy stresses thrown on individual words, invite such scrutiny—the more evidences we find of unity and harmony: harmony between heaven, earth and mankind. The river in its bed of earth, the rooted grass, the vine and trees tended by man, are nourished from above, first by the tumultuous rain, then by the silent sun. But this is not the kind of unity in which everything is chaotically confounded. The river, which had overflowed its banks, has once again returned; the rains and lightnings have ceased; and the separate features of the landscape—so far from merging in a general flood or conflagration—keep their identity, their separateness, while tending towards one another, towards the earth, and towards heaven. Raindrops fall from the vines, and the leaves shine in the sun. Sharp, painful divisions, the result of sunlight without rain, have disappeared. Turmoil, the rain-storm, has played its part in, has been a necessary precondition of, the achievement of this perfect harmony and calm content.

The reader, however, cannot share entirely the calm of this landscape, cannot give himself up (like the 'Landmann' of line 2) to delighted contemplation. The very first word of the poem, the 'Wie' looking forward to a 'So', had warned him that this landscape in holiday mood was not to be described for its own sake. Throughout the opening description, there had been a straining forward, an expectancy, which line 10 seems, at last, to be about to satisfy.

So stehn sie unter günstiger Witterung ...

But who are these 'Sie'? The sentence does not supply the answer. Instead, it introduces a new element of expectancy, as it moves to its climax. Hölderlin so controls his stress that it falls successively on the attributes of an as yet unknown power; that we have first an impression of miraculous omnipresence, then one of tender embrace joining that which is divided, then one of might and one of divinity and beauty:

> die wúnderbár
> Àllgègenwä̀rtig erzíeht in léichtem Úmfángen
> Die mä́chtige, die gö́ttlichschö́ne ...

Expectation is satisfied only with the very last word of the sentence. 'Natur.' We come to the word, to the concept, with a sense of awe, of excited discovery, paralleled in a later passage rising towards the same word, the same central concept:

> *Denn sie, sie selbst, die älter denn die Zeiten*
> *Und über die Götter des Abends und Orients ist,*
> *Die Natur ...*

But the main subject of the long opening sentence, the *sie* of line 10, has not yet been elucidated. The reader must still strain forward to complete the meaning.

Lines 14–15 widen the focus from a particular moment in time to all time. The landscape, while remaining itself, becomes simultaneously the landscape of history. The season of the year becomes a season in the history of mankind:

> *zu Zeiten des Jahrs*
> *Am Himmel oder unter den Pflanzen oder den Völkern.*

At the same time, we become aware of a mode of existence radically different from that suggested by the landscape; a mode of existence adumbrated in the projected preface to Hölderlin's novel *Hyperion*:

'Happy unity, existence in the true sense of the word, is lost to us ... We tear ourselves away from the peaceful ἓν καὶ πᾶν of the world ... We are at variance with Nature, and what was once, as we believe, united, is now disparate and at enmity.'

Only now, when we have reached awareness of life in an era in

WIE WENN AM FEIERTAGE...

which Nature seems asleep, is the main subject of the first sentence, almost casually, revealed.

So trauert der Dichter *Angesicht auch.*

We realize at once why the subject had to be withheld, why the reader had not been allowed to rest and contemplate, why he had constantly to strain forward, away from 'Feiertag' and happy landscape. 'Günstige Witterung', actual in the landscape, was not yet actual in world-history. Poets were not, in Hölderlin's time, gently nurtured by a kind fate. The opening scene was an objective correlative, not of an actual, but of a prospective human situation; something towards which nature was striving (as the reader had also to strive, to strain forward), not something already attained.

Sie scheinen allein zu sein, doch ahnen sie immer.

The first half of this line conveys directly the situation of the poet, apparently so isolated, in the modern world. It mirrors the introspection of loneliness, seeming constantly—such is the effect of the *ei* assonance—to turn about its own axis. But the second half of the line breaks through this magic circle into 'Ahnung', intimations of a unity and harmony yet to come. Hölderlin is not satisfied, at rest within nature—he is writing, to use Schiller's terminology, not naïve but sentimental poetry.

The landscape and its storms have now without losing their concrete reality become symbols for world-historical processes: and the third section of the poem fixes the point at which Hölderlin believes himself to stand. It is a moment before that of the 'Landmann's' walk, the moment of dawn (Jetzt aber tagts!) while the storms are still raging. A clash of arms is heard: the turmoil of the French Revolution and Napoleonic wars, waking Nature from its stagnant sleep. It is a time of Bacchic enthusiasm—

Fühlt neu die Begeisterung sich,
Die Allerschaffende wieder —

of enthusiasm, the child of Chaos, the greatest imaginable unity in which all is confounded. Characteristically, however, Hölderlin does not evince a one-sided delight in chaos and aorgic merging.

'Nach festem Gesetze.' That brings us back to the characteristic Hölderlin balance. The storms of time herald a happiness akin to that of the opening landscape: the harmony, but not the confounding of all things. Liberty and law must balance and combine.

At a moment such as this, at a moment of storm, the poet has an important mission. He is Nature's most conscious organ, the point at which Nature first shows consciousness of her designs —in his own bold image, he is the flashing eye (again an image connected with storms! The 'Feuer' is another kind of lightning) announcing the great plan of Nature and the gods. It is the poet's mission to wait patiently until Nature wakes and grows, and then to announce this waking, this growth, to others:

> *Ich harrt und sah es kommen*
> *Und was ich sah, das Heilige sei mein Wort;*

to make explicit what others only dimly feel:

> *Und was zuvor geschah, doch kaum gefühlt,*
> *Ist offenbar erst jetzt.*

The end of the fourth section shows how this is accomplished. The poet looks at a landscape, a field seen a thousand times by others; and to him it suddenly reveals the existence of the gods, who had seemed departed from the earth.

> *Und die uns lächelnd den Acker gebauet,*
> *In Knechtsgestalt, sie sind bekannt, die*
> *Alllebendigen, die Kräfte der Götter.*

By withholding the subject of the sentence until the very end, and so controlling his stress that it falls heaviest on 'Alllebendigen', Hölderlin makes the reader share the very process of his discovery, startles him with the recognition that even when the world seems forsaken, the gods are alive and omnipresent.

This view of the poet's task is central to the whole poem. Hölderlin began with contemplation of a landscape after a storm which became naturally and unforcedly a symbol for world-historical processes. Throughout the poem, Hölderlin now meditates on this landscape, these storms, allows them to reveal more and more symbolical meaning. His is the thought, not of a philo-

WIE WENN AM FEIERTAGE...

sopher, but of a poet; a way of apprehending truth which has been well described by Louis MacNeice: 'The poet is often not completely sure what he is trying to say until he has said it. He works up to his meaning by a dialectic of purification.' *Wie wenn am Feiertage* ... is the disciplined exploration of a given reality.

In the fifth section of the poem, this exploration continues, and the landscape is seen to be a symbol also of the poet's song. Like the trees, like the vines, poetry too must have roots in the earth, must be agitated by storms. At one level this means—characteristically for Hölderlin—that the poet must not cut himself off from the world in which he lives, that he must contemplate and experience the sun, the earth, and 'Wetter... in der Luft'. But ll. 39–43 suggest another level at which the symbol operates.

> und ándern
> Die vórbereiteter in Tíefen der Zéit
> Und deútungsvóller, und vernéhmlicher úns
> Hínwandeln zwischen Hímmel und Érd und únter den Vólkern.

It is not actual thunderbolts, but the thunderbolts of history, which crash down in these lines, in the successive heavily stressed comparative adverbs, each of which startles us anew, until majesty and beauty oust terror in the stately line that ends the sentence. 'Sonne des Tags' and 'warme Erd' thereby also take on a new meaning, a meaning suggested by the well-known lines from *Patmos*:

> *Wir haben gedienet der Mutter Erd,*
> *Wir haben jüngst dem Sonnenlichte gedient ...*

They characterize different ages of mankind and different attitudes to life: an era of 'heiliges Chaos', of unconscious unity with nature; and an era of clear distinction, of *Aufklärung*. To all these forces, the poet's song must be open. All that the community experiences the poet must experience.

> *Des gemeinsamen Geistes Gedanken sind*
> *Still endend in der Seele des Dichters.*

What thunders and lightens in the outside world (we note the *g* alliteration and the flashes of the *ei* assonance) becomes suddenly still (how the stress is controlled to fall on this word!) as it enters, as enter it must, the soul of the poet.

The landscape has now become, by a further extension of meaning, a landscape of the poet's soul, struck by the lightning of experience. We have entered (on tiptoe almost) the soul of the poet, and are enabled to share—in ways no other German lyric has ever enabled us to do—the very process and labour of creation. In the sixth section, speech-rhythms and line-division come to be sharply at variance; we seem to be jerked forward from stress to stress, shaken as by a storm or earthquake:

> ... *von Erinnerung*
> *Erbebt* ...

The sentence-structure becomes more and more crabbed and intricate, the clauses are boxed up one within the other, so that the effort required of us as we read the lines reproduces the labour of the poet who, struck by the lightning of communal and divinely inspired experience, brings forth the fruit of song. We come to rest, appropriately, at the word 'glückt'. The difficult task has been achieved. The labour is over. The song, fruit of the union of god and man, has been brought forth. And when we come later (l. 65) to the term 'Tieferschüttert', we feel it to be more than an empty word: Hölderlin has here made us share, physically, the terrible agitation of which he speaks.

We have now seen the landscape and its storms opening up into symbols of ever-widening application, until at last—inevitably—it flowers into myth. The myth of Semele who, struck by the lightnings of Zeus, gave birth to Bacchus. Thunder and lightning seem to have entered the very lines in which this is accomplished.

> *So fiel, wie Dichter sagen, da sie sichtbar*
> *Den Gott zu sehen begehrte, sein Blitz auf Semeles Haus*
> *Und die göttlichgetroffene gebar*
> *Die Frucht des Gewitters, den heiligen Bacchus.*

The vines described at the opening, burgeoning after a storm;

the world labouring to bring forth a new era of harmony and unity; the poet's song enabled by divine influences to proclaim a coming truth; the poet's soul, agitated by experience of nature, god and man, and creating poetry—all these are taken up by, are copresent in, a myth which finally justifies suffering and danger. Semele is the exceptional individual who exposes herself to perils for the benefit of mankind:

> *Und daher trinken himmlisches Feuer jetzt*
> *Die Erdensöhne ohne Gefahr.*

Her dangerous union with the tempest brought Bacchus into the world—Bacchus, who submits men to heavenly influences, holding out to them a pledge that the gods are not dead:

> *Brot ist der Erde Frucht, doch ists vom Lichte gesegnet*
> *Und vom donnernden Gott kommet die Freude des Weins*
> *(Brot und Wein)*

and who represents a stage of happy unity in the progress of mankind.

> *Wie Fürsten ist Herkules. Gemeingeist Bacchus. Christus aber ist*
> *Das Ende.*
> *(Der Einzige)*

All men may, thanks to Semele, quaff heavenly fire without danger to themselves.

Hölderlin has now found, in the myth of Semele, an analogy to his own fate: but ll. 55–65 insist on contrast rather than resemblance.

> *Doch uns gebührt es, unter Gottes Gewittern,*
> *Ihr Dichter! Mit entblösstem Haupte zu stehen ...*

What here impresses itself, is not so much that the poet is like Semele—for Semele is only a figment of his own brain, 'wie Dichter sagen' (l. 51); it is rather that poets are unlike other men. Other men may quaff heavenly fire without danger: but the poet has to expose himself, humbly, receptively, to the very lightnings of the gods, to all perils, all experiences of life, a servant alike of gods and men. If he maintains his innocence and humility—

> *Denn sind nur reinen Herzens,*
> *Wie Kinder, wir, sind schuldlos unsere Hände —*

he too may be saved, may not be destroyed by the storm which buffets him.

The poem was not to have ended here. A fragment of its real ending has been preserved. If, so these final lines were to have told us, the poet allows his loneliness, his exposure to god's lightning, to overwhelm him with grief felt as private grief—

> *Doch weh mir! wenn von selbstgeschlagener Wunde*
> *Das Herz mir blutet, und tiefverloren*
> *Der Frieden ist, und freibescheidenes Genügen . . . —*

then a fearful destiny awaits him. He will incur the wrath of the gods.

> *Sie selbst, sie werfen mich tief unter die Lebenden alle,*
> *Den falschen Priester ins Dunkel, dass ich, aus Nächten herauf,*
> *Das warnend ängstige Lied*
> *Den Unerfahrenen singe.*

The poem thus ends, if not with the reconciliation, then with the simultaneous awareness of conflicting emotions—a sense of loneliness and untold peril, and at the same time the consciousness of a vital mission: to act as mediator between gods and men, between past, present and future.

The difficulty of Hölderlin's later poetry is not accidental. The poet remains open, receptive, to all experience: he shuts out nothing, he flees from nothing. He renders, sensitively, all the fluxes and refluxes of thought and emotion, and makes the reader share—as we have seen—his very mode of apprehending, thinking and feeling. Yet far from merely recording successive unconnected impressions, Hölderlin makes a tremendous intellectual and emotional effort to balance and combine, to penetrate meanings, the very meaning of life. That effort too the reader must make with him. He must become conscious of the terrors of the world: the terrors of a lonely life exposed to the storms of the gods (or to put it in social terms: the terrors of a life in which the ideals of the poet are hopelessly at variance with those of the society into which he has been born); and he must at the same time

attempt to maintain his faith in the world, o see in present pain only a preparation for greater good, greater joy to come. It is this concern to bring 'more than usual order' into 'more than usual emotion' which makes Hölderlin so pre-eminently the *poet in ideal perfection* as Coleridge has described him for all time:
'The poet, described in ideal perfection, brings the whole soul of man into activity, with the subordination of its faculties to each other, according to their relative worth and dignity. He diffuses a tone and spirit of unity, that blends and (as it were) fuses each into each, by that synthetic and magical power to which we have exclusively appropriated the name of imagination. This power, first put into action by the will and understanding, and retained under their irremissive, though gentle and unnoticed control (laxis effertur habenis) reveals itself in the balance or reconciliation of opposite or discordant qualities; of sameness with difference; of the general with the concrete; of the idea with the image; the individual, with the representative; the sense of novelty and freshness, with old and familiar objects; a more than usual state of emotion, with more than usual order; judgment ever awake and steady self-possession, with enthusiasm and feeling profound and vehement; and while it blends and harmonizes the natural and artificial, still subordinates art to nature; the manner to the matter; and our admiration of the poet to our sympathy with the poetry.'
Nowhere could we hope to find a more complete and exact definition of Hölderlin's greatness.

CHAPTER SEVEN

The Romantics

(a)
NOVALIS
SEHNSUCHT NACH DEM TODE

Hinunter in der Erde Schoss,
Weg aus des Lichtes Reichen,
Der Schmerzen Wut und wilder Stoss
Ist froher Abfahrt Zeichen.
Wir kommen in dem engen Kahn
Geschwind am Himmelsufer an.

Gelobt sei uns die ew'ge Nacht,
Gelobt der ew'ge Schlummer.
Wohl hat der Tag uns warm gemacht
Und welk der lange Kummer.
Die Lust der Fremde ging uns aus,
Zum Vater wollen wir nach Haus.

Was sollen wir auf dieser Welt
Mit unsrer Lieb' und Treue?
Das Alte wird hintangestellt:
Was soll uns dann das Neue?
O! einsam steht und tiefbetrübt,
Wer heiss und fromm die Vorzeit liebt.

Die Vorzeit, wo die Sinne licht
In hohen Flammen brannten,
Des Vaters Hand und Angesicht
Die Menschen noch erkannten.
Und hohen Sinns, einfältiglich
Noch mancher seinem Urbild glich.

Die Vorzeit, wo noch blütenreich
Uralte Stämme prangten

*Und Kinder für das Himmelreich
Nach Qual und Tod verlangten.
Und wenn auch Lust und Leben sprach,
Doch manches Herz für Liebe brach.*

*Die Vorzeit, wo in Jugendglut
Gott selbst sich kundgegeben
Und frühem Tod in Liebesmut
Geweiht sein süsses Leben.
Und Angst und Schmerz nicht von sich trieb,
Damit es uns nur teurer blieb.*

*Mit banger Sehnsucht sehn wir sie
In dunkle Nacht gehüllet;
In dieser Zeitlichkeit wird nie
Der heisse Durst gestillet.
Wir müssen nach der Heimat gehn,
Um diese heil'ge Zeit zu sehn.*

*Was hält noch unsre Rückkehr auf,
Die Liebsten ruhn schon lange.
Ihr Grab schliesst unsern Lebenslauf,
Nun wird uns weh und bange.
Zu suchen haben wir nichts mehr —
Das Herz ist satt — die Welt ist leer.*

*Unendlich und geheimnisvoll
Durchströmt uns süsser Schauer —
Mir deucht aus tiefen Fernen scholl
Ein Echo unsrer Trauer.
Die Lieben sehnen sich wohl auch,
Und sandten uns der Sehnsucht Hauch.*

*Hinunter zu der süssen Braut,
Zu Jesus, dem Geliebten —
Getrost, die Abenddämmrung graut
Den Liebenden, Betrübten.
Ein Traum bricht unsre Banden los,
Und senkt uns in des Vaters Schoss.*

In one of the most moving poems of his later years, *Reif sind, in Feuer getaucht...*, Hölderlin draws, as it were, the sum of his existence. It is a poem of maturity: maturity achieved, not through steady and harmonious growth, but in purgatorial fires. Hölderlin tells how the consciousness of many, of too many things winds itself snake-like into his mind, and speaks, in rhythms that jerk themselves forward as with strained exertion, of heavy burdens carried over difficult roads in times that seemed unpropitious:

> *Und vieles*
> *Wie auf den Schultern eine*
> *Last von Scheitern ist*
> *Zu behalten. Aber bös sind*
> *Die Pfade. Nämlich unrecht,*
> *Wie Rosse, gehn die gefangenen*
> *Element' und alten*
> *Gesetze der Erd.*

Bowed down by this terrible load the poet longs for annihilation and chaos:

> *Und immer*
> *Ins Ungebundene gehet eine Sehnsucht,*

but conquers his desires, resolving to bear all steadfastly and faithfully—

> *Vieles aber ist*
> *Zu behalten. Und not die Treue —*

and to accept whatever the present may bring without yearning for irrevocable past or unattainable future.

> *Vorwärts aber und rückwärts wollen wir*
> *Nicht sehn. Uns wiegen lassen, wie*
> *Auf schwankem Kahne der See.*

That is the characteristic Hölderlin movement, the Hölderlin complexity. Realizing the terrors of life, allowing them to enter his verse and mould its rhythms, he yet resolves to bear all without succumbing to the lure of chaos or the transcendental.

The older generation of poets generally labelled 'Romantic'— August Wilhelm and Friedrich Schlegel, Ludwig Tieck (1773-1853) and, greatest of all, Novalis (Friedrich von Hardenberg, 1772-1801)—found itself in the same world, the same situation, as Hölderlin. A world in turmoil of social change, a world beginning to be dominated by a class which cared little or nothing about literature. But the reaction of these poets, in easier circumstances, differed sharply from that of their greater contemporary. Not for them the full acceptance of terror as well as joy; not for them the resistance, the heroism of a sensitive soul, so characteristic of Hölderlin. With Tieck, they tended to despise their own time, 'its stock-jobbing, its veneration of low cunning, its deification of the modern age'; to regard it with abhorrence as an age of prose:

'Heaven and earth as they now are are prosaic; the world has entered an era in which 'usefulness' is the only recognized criterion.'

(NOVALIS)

Despising their own age of 'sophisters, economists and calculators' the Romantics dreamt of the recreation of the 'age of chivalry', longed for death, night, the transcendental. Unable to deal with the problems of their time, they tended to withdraw from firsthand experience and allow themselves to be inspired by literature rather than life. They hoped, by retiring into their own minds, to transform prose into poetry, the world into literature. An aim never to be attained—a blue flower always beyond their grasp. And so their poetry becomes one pre-eminently of longing:
'The poetry of the ancients was that of possession, ours is that of longing; the former stands on the firm ground of the present, the latter hovers between recollection and divination.

(A. W. SCHLEGEL)

of the abnegation of sense and first-hand experience in favour of the imagination, 'the wondrous faculty (as Novalis calls it) which can replace all our senses'. The mysterious path of the Romantic poet leads inwards.[1]

Sehnsucht nach dem Tode, the final, culminating poem of Novalis's 'Hymnen an die Nacht', communicates the experience of one who views the present, the real contemporary world, with existential *Angst*. 'Einsam' and 'tiefbetrübt', lonely and sorrowful, the poet stands in a hostile time; 'mit banger Sehnsucht', 'weh und bange', he contemplates the lot of those who have gone before.

[1] 'Nach innen geht der geheimnisvolle Weg; in uns oder nirgends ist die Ewigkeit mit ihren Welten' (Novalis).

This Anxiety is the lot of man on this earth—Christ too had to take it upon himself when he walked among men:

> *Und Angst und Schmerz nicht von sich trieb ...*

It is the condition of humanity in a godless age. Man is, as line 11 suggests, a stranger on earth. He is condemned, while among the living, to that eternal longing which determines the very title of the poem.

From this feeling of *Geworfenheit*, of being cast into a situation not of his own choosing or making, the poet seeks comfort and shelter. The first lines indicate where such comfort and shelter are to be found: they seem, almost consciously, to reverse the direction in which we have seen Goethe's lyrics to move. *Auf dem See* had moved from early youth (mother-imagery!) to maturity, from darkness to light: *Sehnsucht nach dem Tode* thrusts itself vigorously backwards, to the womb of the mother, to darkness. 'Hinunter in der Erde *Schoss*.' The mother-imagery, bespeaking immaturity and unchecked desire to regress, is central to the poem.

> *Mit banger Sehnsucht sehn wir sie*
> *In dunkle Nacht gehüllet.*

The dead are sheltered, wrapped, swaddled in darkness—the object of longing; their thirst is stilled (gestillet) as the babe is stilled by the mother. All this reminds us of the opening imagery of *Auf dem See*. And sure enough, Novalis at once, in the first stanza, introduces the very symbol of that poem, the boat on the lake. Not a boat being rowed into harbour, but one driven, by the sharp pang of pain, from its accustomed moorings—

> *Der Schmerzen Wut und wilder Stoss*
> *Ist froher Abfahrt Zeichen —*

until it reaches the shore of heaven. The boat, characteristically, is the coffin, the grave (der *enge* Kahn). It moves towards night (Abenddämmrung), not towards day; towards sheltered immaturity (the 'Schoss' of the first line and the last), not towards manhood.

Mother-images are supplemented by protective father-imagery ('Zum Vater wollen wir nach Haus'. 'Des Vaters Hand und

Angesicht...'); and that in its turn gives the poem its religious colouring and tone. Longing for regression into the womb of night, for death, becomes longing for God the Father and the heavenly home. Images of regression, of mother and father triumphantly amalgamate in the last line of the poem. We *sink down* into the *womb* of the *Father*.

The darkness into which the whole poem moves thus holds suggestions of the womb, of protection, of home, of sleep, of death, and of another world beyond the grave promised by religion; and also, we must now add, of the past. The theme of 'Die Vorzeit', first announced in the last line of stanza 3, is elaborated in the fourth, fifth and sixth stanzas. The poet recalls with regret times of prelapsarian godliness, in which men were still uncorrupted; a time of aristocratic families and Children's Crusades (stanza 5 suggests, not only the early Christian era, but the Middle Ages too); a time in which God still walked the earth, and laid down His life for mankind. All this past is now not only irrevocable, but neglected and forgotten.

> *Das Alte wird hintangestellt*
> *Was soll uns dann das Neue?*

That is the voice of a man who feels himself unable to cope effectively with the problems of his own age. Hölderlin too loved 'das Alte': he too might have sung of the loneliness of those who piously and ardently love the times that have gone. But Hölderlin ever strove for a synthesis of the old and the new, for the establishment of a regenerated Greece in regenerated Germany. Not even in *Hyperion* did he reject all hope of reform as uncompromisingly as Novalis. 'Was soll uns dann das Neue' strikes a note not heard in German literature since the seventeenth century.

The final couplet of stanza 5 brings in another, the central concept of Novalis's poem: the concept of love.

> *Und wenn auch Lust und Leben sprach,*
> *Doch manches Herz vor Liebe brach.*

Alliteration assimilates love to joy and life, which are yet rejected in favour of death. A death for love—a *Liebestod*. 'In death,' Novalis tells us in an aphorism, 'love is sweetest; for the lover Death is a bridal night, a sweet mystery of mysteries.' Earthly love mingles inextricably with heavenly. The same terms of endearment are applied to the earthly bride and to Christ. In Night the poet feels reunited with both.

> *¡Oh noche amable más que la alborada:*
> *Oh noche, que juntaste*
> *Amado con Amada*
> *Amada en el Amado transformada!*
> (ST. JOHN OF THE CROSS)

Since Christ's own death for love of mankind was (as the sixth stanza tells us) the supreme example of a *Liebestod*, man's longing for death becomes an *imitatio Christi*:

> *Hinunter zu der süssen Braut,*
> *Zu Jesus, dem Geliebten!*

Darkness, protected childhood, the past, the earthly bride, Christ, God the Father: all these objects of longing may be fully attained only in love and death. They appear together, confounded and fused, in the last stanza of the poem, which is thus in a real sense the climax of the *Hymns to Night*.

The only relations that matter—those of man to his god and man to death—are seen by Novalis as relations between bridegroom and bride. One might speak of Pan-Eroticism. The poet desires to merge with God, with the world, as the lover merges with his beloved.

'The world has but one temple, and that is the human body. There is nothing more sacred. You touch heaven when you touch the human body.' (*Fragmente*.)

> *Einst ist alles Leib*
> *Ein Leib,*
> *In himmlischem Blute*
> *Schwimmt das selige Paar. —*
> *O! dass das Weltmeer*
> *Schon errötete*
> *Und in duftiges Fleisch*
> *Aufquölle der Fels!*
> *Nie endet das süsse Mahl,*
> *Nie sättigt die Liebe sich;*

NOVALIS: SEHNSUCHT NACH DEM TODE

> *Nicht innig, nicht eigen genug*
> *Kann sie haben den Geliebten.*
> (Hymne)

The essentially corrupt nature of this love-death cult is not as clear in *Sehnsucht nach dem Tode* as it is in the *Hymne* just quoted. One might point, however, to the close association in which pain and joy ever appear (the very first stanza brings together 'Der Schmerzen Wut' and 'frohe Abfahrt'), the perverse relishing of pain[1]; and to the cult of erotic *süsse Schauer*, of exquisite sensations of yearning for their own sake, bringing with it the usual penalties: a parched throat (heisser Durst),[2] cloyed heart and sense of emptiness. 'Das Herz ist satt, die Welt ist leer.' A relish for death as the last most exquisite sensation is the obvious, the only logical consequence.

It is difficult to escape the spell of this self-indulgent, supremely escapist poem. Nothing in it is precisely seen: Novalis *will* not look closely at the world, his adjectives have only the vaguest visual connotations. We are thus made conscious of the emptiness of a world with which the voluptuary is sated. We do not find, however, mere weary resignation. No reader can fail to be affected by the energy of the opening stanza, with its key word *Stoss*, and of all the lines with their predominantly masculine endings: all is impulsion, effort, perverted effort away from this world. Paradoxically, this poem of death and sleep has nothing tired about it. The note of fear and insecurity may indeed be heard, in lines whose echoing *e* vowels suggest languors and longings:

> *Mit banger Sehnsucht sehn wir sie*
> *In tief Nacht gehüllet;*

but the rhythm of every stanza is informed by an ardent energy born of the certain knowledge that it is good to merge with Night as with the beloved. In the most magic lines of the poem, Novalis evokes an answer from beyond, uncertain but compelling:

> *Unendlich und geheimnisvoll*
> *Durchströmt uns süsser Schauer;*

---

[1] Cf. *Fragmente*: 'It is possible to conceive of an infinitely alluring pain.'
[2] Cf. *Die Lehrlinge zu Lais*: 'In thirst the soul of the world reveals itself, in a powerful yearning towards deliquescence.'

> *Mir deucht, aus tiefen Fernen scholl*
> *Ein Echo unsrer Trauer.*

Just so, from afar, from the depths ('aus tiefen Fernen') these languorous lines with their long vowels and liquid consonants, seem to reach the reader. The answer comes at once, redressing the balance:

> *Hinunter zu der süssen Braut,*
> *Zu Jesus, dem Geliebten!*

The languors have gone: energy—the positive thrust towards the negative—is triumphant.

Never before Wagner has the death-cult found a more attractive, and therefore more dangerous exponent than Novalis, 'perhaps' (as Friedrich Schlegel said) 'the first man of our present time who has an artist's appreciation of Death'. What Hölderlin had feared, the yearning away from life, away from this world—

> *Das heimatlos die Seele mir nicht*
> *Ueber das Leben hinweg sich sehne —*

becomes relished reality in the *Hymns to Night*. Novalis tasted to the full that 'pure Despair' of which another poet has spoken in our own day, in lines which seem to distil the essence of this most dangerous, most fascinating and most elusive of the Romantic poets of Germany.

> *He did not die with loathing of the worms,*
> *Or fear of pain, or tunnel's gloom ahead,*
> *But with a pure despair refusing terms*
> *That suns of summer for his kindness made,*
> *Turned his desire from green and flowered growth*
> *To rocky dark and long before he died*
> *A lonely miner, worked new ores of death.*[1]

---

[1] Quoted, without author's name, in *New Writing and Daylight* (Hogarth Press), Summer 1943, p. 104.

(b)
BRENTANO
DER SPINNERIN LIED

Es sang vor langen Jahren
Wohl auch die Nachtigall,
Das war wohl süsser Schall,
Da wir zusammen waren.

Ich sing' und kann nicht weinen
Und spinne so allein
Den Faden, klar und rein,
So lang der Mond wird scheinen.

Da wir zusammen waren,
Da sang die Nachtigall,
Nun mahnet mich ihr Schall,
Dass du von mir gefahren.

So oft der Mond mag scheinen,
Gedenk' ich dein allein,
Mein Herz ist klar und rein,
Gott wolle uns vereinen!

Seit du von mir gefahren,
Singt stets die Nachtigall,
Ich denk' bei ihrem Schall,
Wie wir zusammen waren.

Gott wolle uns vereinen,
Hier spinn' ich so allein,
Der Mond scheint klar und rein,
Ich sing' und möchte weinen!

No one could accuse Goethe of having been deaf to the music of language: but Goethe ever insisted that speech has a rational as well as a musical content, and that the former must be given precedence.

'I honour rhythm and rhyme, which first makes poetry what it is: but its real depth and most profound effect, that which fashions truth and furthers mankind, is what remains of poetry after it has been translated into prose.'

The Romantics tended to shift the emphasis: to use their feeling for syllable and rhythm to penetrate far below the conscious levels of thought and feeling. 'One may think', writes Novalis in *Heinrich von Ofterdingen*
'of stories without logical connecting links, associative, like dreams; of poems composed of beautiful sounds and lovely words, but without meaning, without connections, understandable only in isolated stanzas... This *true* poetry can have but an allegorical meaning and affect men indirectly, like music.'
The music of language thus becomes divorced from its meaning, independent (almost) of thought:

> *Liebe denkt in süssen Tönen*
> *Denn Gedanken stehn zu fern,*
> *Nur in Tönen mag sie gern*
> *Alles, was sie will, verschönen.*

Ludwig Tieck (whose *Liebe* has just been quoted) attempts to use language purely to convey *Stimmung*. In famous lines, Tieck conveys through sound the mood of a moon-lit night:

> *Mondbeglänzte Zaubernacht*
> *Die den Sinn gefangen hält,*
> *Wundervolle Märchenwelt*
> *Steig auf in der alten Pracht*

or the mysterious forest-murmurs heard by Bertha in *Der blonde Eckbert*:

> *Waldeinsamkeit*
> *Die mich erfreut*
> *So morgen wie heut;*
> *In ewger Zeit,*
> *O wie mich freut*
> *Waldeinsamkeit.*

In the work of his more interesting contemporary Clemens Brentano (1778–1842), one of a group of poets known to literary history as the *Jüngere Romantik*, *Stimmung* condenses itself into haunting refrains:

> *Nach Sevilla, nach Sevilla...*
>
> *Hüte dich, schöns Blümelein!*[1]

[1] Brentano took this over from a Volkslied.

> *O lieb's Mädel, wie schlecht bist du!*
>
> > *Lore Lay!*
> > *Lore Lay!*
> > *Lore Lay!*

or into mysterious individual lines whose music and rhythm, once heard, are never forgotten:

> *O Stern und Blume, Geist und Kleid*
> *Lieb', Leid und Zeit und Ewigkeit!*

We must now look in greater detail at *Der Spinnerin Lied*, one of Brentano's most characteristic productions; and though the contrast is by no means new, we may best appreciate its originality if we hold it against another well-known spinning song, the Song of Gretchen in *Faust*.

> *Meine Ruh' ist hin,*
> *Mein Herz ist schwer;*
> *Ich finde sie nimmer*
> *Und nimmermehr.*
>
> *Wo ich ihn nicht hab',*
> *Ist mir das Grab,*
> *Die ganze Welt*
> *Ist mir vergällt.*
>
> *Mein armer Kopf*
> *Ist mir verrückt,*
> *Mein armer Sinn*
> *Ist mir zerstückt.*
>
> *Meine Ruh' ist hin,*
> *Mein Herz ist schwer;*
> *Ich finde sie nimmer*
> *Und nimmermehr.*
>
> *Nach ihm nur schau' ich*
> *Zum Fenster hinaus,*
> *Nach ihm nur geh' ich*
> *Aus dem Haus*

> *Sein hoher Gang,*
> *Sein' edle Gestalt,*
> *Seines Mundes Lächeln,*
> *Seiner Augen Gewalt,*
>
> *Und seiner Rede*
> *Zauberfluss,*
> *Sein Händedruck,*
> *Und ach sein Kuss!*
>
> *Meine Ruh' ist hin,*
> *Mein Herz ist schwer;*
> *Ich finde sie nimmer*
> *Und nimmermehr.*
>
> *Mein Busen drängt*
> *Sich nach ihm hin.*
> *Ach dürft' ich fassen*
> *Und halten ihn,*
>
> *Und küssen ihn,*
> *So wie ich wollt',*
> *An seinen Küssen*
> *Vergehen sollt'!*

The most obvious feature of Goethe's poem is its steady progression, its mounting intensity. The poem begins with a stanza which conveys directly both Gretchen's state of mind and her occupation. We can hear the whirring of the spinning-wheel. Then follow two stanzas of dull misery, recording Gretchen's thoughts of her absent lover, her fearful confusion; until—with calming effect—the spinning-wheel breaks in again, as the first stanza is repeated. After that, with mounting intensity, Gretchen re-evokes her lover's physical presence—until the first stanza is repeated, the wheel whirs again, in a moment of precarious calm. And then, at last, the final outburst, overflowing line-endings and stanza-endings: the physical passion of Gretchen for her lover. No calming movement, no return to the spinning-wheel, is possible after that. The climax has been reached.[1]

[1] Schubert has quite destroyed this effect in his setting of the poem: he repeats *Meine Ruh' ist hin* ... after the final stanza. But then, Schubert was pre-eminently a Romantic.

This progression, this steady ascent towards a climax, is matched by the plastic particularity with which Goethe makes us apprehend the very detail of Gretchen's experience. '*Ich bin ein Plastiker*', he said to Boisserée. The most notable instance occurs in stanzas 6 and 7, in which we share Gretchen's habitual experience of her lover's approach. At first, only his gait is discerned in the distance; then his contour; then his mouth and his eyes; and then, with his handclasp and his kiss, touch supplements and supplants sight.

To all this, Brentano's *Spinnerin Lied* (from *Aus der Chronika eines fahrenden Schülers*) presents the most complete contrast imaginable. There is clearly no progression, no mounting towards a climax. Phrase is joined to phrase, line to line, in listlessly wistful succession of end-stopped lines. A single mood is presented: the mood of a lonely spinner sitting in the moonlight and dreaming of a happiness that is gone. In alternate stanzas, she remembers past happiness and laments present sorrow. We cease, after the first two stanzas, to be aware of any intellectual content: nightingale, moonshine, loneliness, longing—the same note is struck over and over again. One might read the poem backwards as well as forwards, continue it to infinity. It has no beginning, it has no middle, it has no end.

The mood conveyed is that of a whole *fin-de-siècle* generation, tired, listless, unable to deal with life; a generation of late-comers, who felt that there had been greatness and zest, but that it all lay in the past. And that mood is conveyed almost entirely through appeal to the *ear*. Where Goethe's poem had been plastic, Brentano's is musical.

> *Es sang vor langen Jahren*
> *Wohl auch die Nachtigall —*

the long *a* associates itself with 'Nachtigall', and the alternate stanzas in which the nightingale appears—1, 3, 5—all rhyme on stressed syllables containing this vowel. The other stanzas, which speak of the moon and of present misery, all rhyme on *ei*—a vowel obviously recalling *Mondschein*.[1] No effort of response is

---

[1] Miss Margaret Atkinson, in an article on *Musical Form in some Romantic Writings* (MLR, XLIV, 221), observes: 'Each theme is musically characterized by the continued recurrence of the same two rhymes, and each variation brings

required of the reader: he is asked merely to submit himself, to allow himself to be swept on by waves of beautiful sound. The reader is to be as passive as the spinner, as Brentano himself, as the Romantic generation. Above all, he is never asked to visualize anything clearly. The adjectives 'klar und rein' are used successively to describe the thread, the moonlight, the spinner's heart. They mean nothing at all: they are used only because of their sound, *a* for nightingale and remembrance, *ei* for moonshine and grief.

In characterizing this kind of poetry as *musical*, we are of course using the adjective only in a special, limited sense. In an essay on *The Music of Poetry*, T. S. Eliot tells us
'I believe that the properties in which music concerns the poet most nearly, are the sense of rhythm and the sense of structure ... There are possibilities for verse which bear some analogy to the development of a theme by different groups of instruments; there are possibilities of transitions in a poem comparable to the different movements of a symphony or a quartet; there are possibilities of contrapuntal arrangement of subject-matter.'
None of these possibilities were realized by the lyric poetry of the German Romantics. Brentano's poem—and it is representative—has no structure, no organization. It is amorphous. There is no place for intellect or will. Such poems as these enable us therefore to understand A. W. Schlegel's definition: 'Romanticism expresses the secret impulsion towards chaos which hides itself beneath the most ordered creations, in their very womb', as well as the later strictures of Stefan George, who saw so clearly that the Romantic tradition prevented the most important contemporary interests from getting into poetry, that it debilitated authors and readers alike.

(c)
EICHENDORFF
MARIAS SEHNSUCHT

Es ging Maria in den Morgen hinein,
Tat die Erd' einen lichten Liebesschein,

a musical echo from the previous statement. The very form of the poem thus turns our attention backwards through reminiscence of the past, and so reflects the content.'

Und über die fröhlichen grünen Höhn
Sah sie den bläulichen Himmel stehn.
'Ach, hätt ich ein Brautkleid von Himmelsschein,
Zwei goldene Flüglein — wie flög' ich hinein!'

Es ging Maria in stiller Nacht,
Die Erde schlief, der Himmel wacht',
Und durchs Herze, wie sie ging und sann und dacht',
Zogen die Sterne mit goldener Pracht.
'Ach, hätt ich das Brautkleid von Himmelsschein
Und goldene Sterne gewoben drein!'

Es ging Maria im Garten allein,
Da sangen so lockend bunt Vögelein,
Und Rosen sah sie im Grünen stehn,
Viel' rote und weisse so wunderschön.
'Ach, hätt ich ein Knäblein, so weiss und rot,
Wie wollt ichs liebhaben bis in den Tod!'

Nun ist wohl das Brautkleid gewoben gar,
Und goldene Sterne im dunkelen Haar,
Und im Arme die Jungfrau das Knäblein hält,
Hoch über der dunkelerbrausenden Welt,
Und vom Kindlein gehet ein Glänzen aus,
Das ruft uns nur ewig: 'Nach Haus, nach Haus!'

Der Spinnerin Lied already showed clearly, in theme and treatment, the influence of German folk-song, for which Brentano had done so much: for it is to Brentano and his friend Achim von Arnim that Germany owes its best-loved collection of Volkslieder, *Des Knaben Wunderhorn* (1805-8). Many factors combined to endear folksong to the poets of German Romanticism. They saw their own age as an overcultivated 'era of books' (the phrase is Friedrich Schlegel's) and longed for the child-like simplicity of earlier times, reflected in folk-song; loved its mysterious ellipses and associative formulae; saw in it, like Herder, a truly national German poetry (for they could not well escape the national enthusiasm of the Wars of Liberation); and found in it a link with the German past and with a *Volk* conceived as feudally opposed to the 'unhistorical' principles of the French Revolution. It is not surprising, therefore, that the editors of the best-known collections of German folk-songs and folk-tales should all have been associated with the Romantic movement: Arnim and Brentano; the brothers Grimm (*Kinder- und Hausmärchen*, 1812-15, and *Deutsche Sagen*, 1816-18); and Josef Görres (*Die teutschen Volksbücher*, 1807).

Josef von Eichendorff (1788-1857) is generally recognized as the greatest of the second generation of Romantic poets; and his *Marias Sehnsucht* shows unmistakably, like many others of his lyrics, the influence of the *Volkslied*. Its very theme—scenes from the life of the Virgin—is a popular one, and as always in such popular songs, the Virgin appears in what is unmistakably a *German* landscape.

> *Dort droben auf der Aue*
> *Geht der Morgenstern auf,*
> *Und da sitzt unsre liebe Fraue*
> *Mit dem Jesulein drauf.*

or again:

> *Maria die ging über d'Heid',*
> *Da weinte Gras und Blum vor Leid*
> *Sie fand nicht ihren Sohn.*

The third stanza especially draws on folk-song traditions: for here as there virgins and flower-gardens (the carefully sheltered and cultivated) appear together:

> *Regina wollt' in Garten gehn*
> *In Garten wollt sie gehn;*
> *Rote Röslein wollt' sie brechen ab,*
> *Die in dem Garten stehn;*

here as there the mother of God appears in her garden:

> *Maria in den Garten trat,*
> *Begegnen ihr drei Jüngling zart ...*

and:

> *Maria's Morgens früh aufsteht,*
> *Maria, Maria, o Maria, Königin!*
> *Sie kleidet sich gar schöne an,*
> *Maria, Maria, o Maria Königin!*

> *Sie geht hinaus in'n Rosengarten,*
> *Maria, Maria, o Maria Königin!*

In *Volkslied* style, Maria makes three wishes (three, the magic number of popular tradition, here united with suggestions of the Trinity); well-known formulae from folk-song and fairy-tale are employed throughout the poem[1]; and its whole structure—four scenes juxtaposed without connecting links—as well as its simple vocabulary clearly indicate the tradition from which the poem derives.

The world of *Marias Sehnsucht* seems, at a first glance, as far as possible removed from that of Novalis, who also loved to make the Virgin Mary the theme of his song. It is a beautiful world, full of light and colour. 'Light', indeed, may be said to be the keyword of the opening stanza. Without any close description of detail—even colours are vague and imprecise, '*bläulich*' instead of '*blau*'—Eichendorff conveys an impression of light and joy, the rapture of a clear spring-morning.

> *Tăt dĭe Erd einen lichten Liebesschein ...*

The opening anapaest makes this line leap up, as in joy at seeing the Virgin. And when in line 3 an unexpected accusative

> *Und über die fröhlichen grünen Höhn*
> *Sah sie den bläulichen Himmel stehn*

directs our gaze dynamically over the heights instead of at them, we too like everything in nature are made to share this joyous movement. The rhyme which predominates in this stanza obviously associates itself (through the repeated 'Schein') with light, the light of a beautiful spring morning on God's earth.

Yet Maria, as the last two lines of the stanza show, yearns away from all this beauty to the greater beauty of another kind, another order of existence.

If the keynote of the first stanza had been 'light', that of the second is 'nocturnal peace'; not the rapture of night as we know it from Novalis, but rather a clear starlit night of peace and calm. The dominant vowel of the rhyme-words is now, not

---

[1] e.g. 'ein Knäblein so weiss und rot', 'goldne Flüglein', 'goldne Sterne', 'Es ging Maria ...'

THE ROMANTICS

ei, but the *a* associated with 'Nacht' and 'dacht' and 'Pracht', darkness and reflection and majesty. The world at night has a stately beauty different from but not inferior to the beauty of day. This reflective beauty moulds the very rhythms of lines which, with their slow stately movement

> *Und durchs Hérze, wie sie gíng und sánn und dácht*
> *Zógen die Stérne in góldener Prácht*

indicate a calm fully justified:

> *Die Erde schlief, der Himmel wacht.*

The last word of this line unites two levels of meaning: at one level it suggests that heaven is 'awake', i.e. that stars are glittering in the sky when all is dark below; at another, that heaven 'watches', i.e. that God guards the sleep of the world. Yet the theme of the stanza, as its last lines make clear, is again that of the first: in face of all this beauty and peace, Maria yearns for something beyond.

Where the first stanza had insisted on the light and the second on the calm of this world, the third is filled with its sweet sounds and sights, its birds and flowers.

> *Da sangen so lockend bunt Vögelein ...*

Colour and sound all allure ('locken') mankind. The world seems here to be exerting itself as never before to make the lonely wanderer in the garden feel its tempting beauty. Yet Maria still yearns beyond the actual, this time, in folk-song fashion, for a child. The child, we know, is to be a *heavenly* child; and it is obviously significant that the stanza ends with thoughts of the supreme transcendence, which will remove man from all the beauty of this earth.

> *Bis in den Tod.*

That is the answer to the 'allure', the 'Lockung', of birds and flowers.

The sonorous last stanza shows Maria's yearning rewarded, all her wishes fulfilled at last. The bridal gown is woven, the stars are in her hair, and she holds the infant Jesus in her arms.

Hoch über der dunkelerbrausenden Welt.

The adjective startles: for it is quite foreign to folksong, though characteristic of Eichendorff, who loved to hear sound coming from an unseen source.[1] With a shock we realize that the world of the previous stanzas—light, calm, full of sweet sights and sounds—has been completely transformed. From the vantage-point of one who has achieved transcendence, it appears dark and tumultuous, with a sound as of rushing waters. Light and sweetness are now all concentrated in the Virgin and her heavenly child. Light is her bridal-veil, the stars (and the calm they bring) adorn her person—

Und vom Kindlein gehet ein Glänzen aus
Das ruft uns nur ewig: 'Nach Haus, nach Haus!'

Here, in the last stanza, the yearning of the previous stanzas reasserts itself, more strongly than ever. But it is not now the yearning of Maria: it has become the supreme nostalgia of all humanity for a better life, a home in another world.

(d)

EICHENDORFF

ZWIELICHT

Dämmrung will die Flügel spreiten,
Schaurig rühren sich die Bäume,
Wolken ziehn wie schwere Träume — ,
Was will dieses Graun bedeuten?

Hast ein Reh du lieb vor andern,
Lass' es nicht alleine grasen,
Jäger ziehn im Wald und blasen,
Stimmen hin und wieder wandern.

Hast du einen Freund hienieden,
Trau' ihm nicht zu dieser Stunde,
Freundlich wohl mit Aug' und Munde,
Sinnt er Krieg im tück'schen Frieden.

---

[1] Eichendorff's favourite rhyme is 'rauschen'–'lauschen'.

Was heut' müde gehet unter,
Hebt sich morgen neu geboren.
Manches bleibt in Nacht verloren —
Hüte dich, bleib' wach und munter!

What distinguished *Marias Sehnsucht* from Novalis's hymns to the Virgin Mary was its delight—despite its transcendent orientation—in the beauty of this world. And it is of course as a nature poet that Eichendorff is known above all: as one who loved the woods and hills and streams of his native landscape and saw in them, like his 'froher Wandersmann', a reflection of the goodness of God.

Die Bächlein von den Bergen springen,
Die Lerchen schwirren hoch vor Lust,
Was soll ich nicht mit ihnen singen
Aus voller Kehl und frischer Brust?

Den lieben Gott lass ich nur walten,
Der Bächlein, Lerchen, Wald und Feld
Und Erd' und Himmel will erhalten,
Hat auch mein Sach' aufs best bestellt.

But it has often been noticed how consistently Eichendorff refused to look closely at nature. The landscape of his poems lies in the past (*Jugendsehnen*) or in darkness or twilight (*Nachts, Im Walde*); it is dimly seen in the distance or glimpsed in passing (*Wanderschaft, Wandernder Dichter*). Eichendorff never affords his readers that close view of the natural scene or that sense of the unity of Nature and man, to which Goethe has accustomed us. He is pre-eminently the poet of twilight, the gloaming in which the noise and bustle of the world abates so that isolated sounds (ein Posthorn im stillen Land) may be heard all the more clearly.

Zwielicht opens with the image, characteristically vague and undefined, of Dusk as a being (birdlike? batlike? Icarean?) about to spread its wings, and at once proceeds to suggest an attitude to the natural phenomenon described, to establish a mood.

Schaurig rühren sich die Bäume.

'Schaurig.' Nature at dusk, the rustling of the leaves, inspires vague but none the less potent fears.

> *Nur von den Bergen noch rauschet der Wald*
> *Und mich schauert im Herzensgrunde.*
>
> (Im Walde)

Twilight transforms Eichendorff's beloved woodland landscape into a nightmare in which clouds pass overhead—as the slow, dragging, heavily stressed third line so ominously tells us—like oppressive dreams. With characteristic subtlety, the poet fuses the image of a darkening world with one of apprehension in the poet's mind:

> *Was will dieses Graun bedeuten?*

'Graun'—outside all grows grey, dark: inside the human mind there is dismay and dread. Both meanings come together in one ambiguous word.

The falling cadences of this opening stanza, its exclusively feminine endings, and its slow progress from one end-stopped line to the next (a movement characteristic of *Zwielicht* as a whole) establish the tone of the poem. This is at once tired and wary. The poem conveys the experience of a man who would gladly rest (the idea of sleep is implicit in the falling cadences and feminine endings, and explicit in the image: 'schwere Träume') but who is beset by fears and must search, as the final questioning line of the stanza tells us, for their cause and explanation.

Instead of an explanation, however, the poem brings only a deepening sense of the sinister and dangerous. We are told nothing exact about the peril that awaits the doe—the dearest thing we have: only of vague sounds of horns, of voices dimly heard, now here, now there. 'Lass es nicht alleine grasen.' That is the *Angst* we know so well from Novalis. The lonely individual wanders, terrified, in a hostile and dangerous world, surrounded by echoing sounds he cannot understand. The contiguous rhymes 'grasen': 'blasen' perfectly render the echoing horn-calls while assonance and alliteration combine at the end of the stanza—

> *Stimmen hin und wieder wandern —*

to convey the shifting mysterious voices calling one to the other. Who is the hunter and who the hunted? We know as little as Eichendorff's mad minstrel:

> *Durchs Leben jag ich manch trügerisch Bild,*
> *Wer ist der Jäger da, und wer das Wild?*
> (*Der irre Spielmann*)

Whom do the sounds of horns and hunting, the calling voices pursue? We know as little as the knight in *Waldgespräch*

> *Wohl irrt das Waldhorn her und hin ...*

or the peasants in *Der Kehraus:*

> *Wer weiss, wem sie geigen —*
> *Hüt' dich, Gesell!*

We only know that such sounds as these portend danger and death.

The third stanza lifts the danger more definitely to the human plane, brings it nearer to the reader. He is warned now, not that the thing he loves is threatened by pursuers, the doe by hunters, but he himself is threatened by false friends. 'Hast du einen Freund *hienieden*'—that again suggests the transcendental orientation familiar from *Marias Sehnsucht*. It is here on earth that appearances deceive, that all is not what it looks. As dusk hides outlines and shapes, so the eye looking and mouth speaking friendship hide the heart devising war. In one final oxymoron—*tückscher Frieden*—peaceful appearance and dangerous reality join in unholy alliance.

While Danger—all the more terrifying for being undefined—seems to be coming closer and closer, the movement of the poem has continued to indicate, through falling cadences and slow progress from one end-stopped line to the next, a tiredness appropriate to the *evening*-scene described. This tiredness is now, in the last stanza of the poem, made explicit.

> *Was heut' müde gehet unter ...*

At the same time, a new optimism seems to assert itself. Give way to your tiredness, the poet seems to tell himself and us, for tomorrow the sun will rise again and danger will have passed.

> *Was heut' müde gehet unter*
> *Hebt sich morgen neu geboren.*

But this last line (which has its own ominous ambiguity[1]) is at once echoed by another that reverses its tenor and denies its optimism. Danger is *not* passed. One must not sleep but watch.

> *Manches bleibt in Nacht verloren —*
> *Hüte dich, bleib' wach und munter!*

The urgency of the last line is unmistakable. Harking back warningly to the 'gehet unter' of line 13, it disrupts the tired flow of the rest of *Zwielicht*. The two warnings it embodies are separated by a strong caesura, the first in the poem. Beware of sleep! Nature at this hour is dangerous, demonic, ready to swallow up those who give way to the weariness it induces.

Eichendorff's poem strikingly contrasts with one written on the same theme by Goethe in his old age.

> *Dämmrung senkte sich von oben,*
> *Schon ist alle Nähe fern;*
> *Doch zuerst emporgehoben*
> *Holden Lichts der Abendstern!*
> *Alles schwankt ins Ungewisse,*
> *Nebel schleichen in die Höh';*
> *Schwarzvertiefte Finsternisse*
> *Widerspiegelnd ruht der See.*
>
> *Nun am östlichen Bereiche*
> *Ahn' ich Mondenglanz und -glut,*
> *Schlanker Weiden Haargezweige*
> *Scherzen auf der nächsten Flut.*
> *Durch bewegter Schatten Spiele*
> *Zittert Lunas Zauberschein,*
> *Und durchs Auge schleicht die Kühle*
> *Sänftigend ins Herz hinein.*

Goethe, characteristically, depicts a process—the coming of dusk, apprehended through the eye; and this process of sheer *Schauen*, of gazing on the wonder of the world, is seen to have, in the very last lines of the poem, an effect on the mind of the beholder.[2]

---

[1] Perhaps it is *danger* which tires to-day to menace us afresh to-morrow.

[2] Dr. E. M. Wilkinson comments on the significance of these last two lines of Goethe's poem in her perceptive and valuable essay on *Goethe the Poet*. Thees lines, she maintains, 'would serve as a poetic illustration to (Goethe's)

The poet is of course implicitly present throughout, but only in the last line does he point to his own psyche calmed by the coolness attending the dusk. Eichendorff's poem is seen, by contrast, to be essentially static. It evokes a single mood: weariness coupled with apprehension: and it concentrates on the depiction of that mood almost to the exclusion of the natural scene. Where Goethe's organ was the eye, Eichendorff's is the ear. We are back again at the contrast between plastic poetry, appealing through the eye to the intellect and emotions

> *und durchs Auge schleicht die Kühle*
> *sänftigend ins Herz hinein*

and musical poetry, appealing through the ear to the emotions, to the virtual exclusion of intellect. And where the 'Augenmensch' Goethe sees dusk as the coming of a different kind of light.

> *Doch zuerst emporgehoben*
> *holden Lichts der Abendstern*
>
> *Durch bewegter Schatten Spiele*
> *Zittert Lunas Zauberschein*

Eichendorff conceives it as the coming of darkness and terror, as the coming (to use his own poetically ambiguous term) of 'Graun'. Nature to Goethe is divine, partakes with man of the essence of God: there is therefore an indissoluble unity between man and the world he perceives. For Eichendorff, the Fall of Man had transformed a Nature originally beautiful and good into something no less demonic than those undercurrents of the human mind which E. T. A. Hoffmann so terrifyingly presented. Unity is lost. Man must *beware* of a Nature grown mysterious and dangerous. Man can no longer feel at home in his twilight world.

'Our own time', writes Eichendorff in his novel *Ahnung und*

statement that the objects of his perception entered his thoughts and were permeated by it, so that his perceiving was itself thinking and his thinking perceiving. He does not begin with his own feeling, or idea, and projects it into nature. He just looks; he contemplates the evening, his eyes wide open, until at the end its essence enters through the eye and permeates the mind. His heart and mind submit themselves to the objects of the outer world, to know them as they are and to be transmuted by them.' (*German Life and Letters*, October 1949.)

Gegenwart, 'seems to me to resemble a vast uncertain twilight. Strangely massed, light and the encroaching shadows are grappling, dark clouds dragging ominously among them, while below the world waits expectantly in vast darkling silence. Comets and portents again illumine the sky, spectres stalk again through the night, out of the sea the fabulous Sirens rise once more to sing before the storm; everything points with warning, bloody finger to a great, an unavoidable catastrophe. *Our* youth does not know the carefree play or the glad repose of our fathers; too soon life's seriousness has overcome us. In the midst of struggle we were born, and struggling we will fall, whether defeated or exulting. For the magic smoke-wreath of our knowledge will condense into an armed phantom of War, with pale dead features and blood-boultered hair; our eyes practised in solitude may discern already the outlines of this spectre softly suggested in convolutions of smoke. He is lost whom the time finds unprepared and unarmed; and many a man, made for joy and the soft delights of poetry, desiring nothing but peace with the world, will have to say to himself like Prince Hamlet:

> *The world is out of joint: o cursed spite*
> *That ever I was born to set it right.*

For once again the world will be "out of joint"; the old and the new will join in dreadful battle; the passions, which now slink about in masks, will doff their disguises; and with flaming torches burning Madness will fling herself into the confusion as though all hell had been let loose. Right and Wrong will be on both sides blindly confounded.—At last, for the sake of the just, there will once again be miracles. The sun, new and yet eternally the same, will break through the horror, the thunder will roll but afar in the mountains, the white dove will cleave the air, and in new glory the earth will rise again through its tears, like Beauty unchained.'

CHAPTER EIGHT

Heine and Platen

(a)
HEINE
SEEGESPENST

*Ich aber lag am Rande des Schiffes,
Und schaute, träumenden Auges,
Hinab in das spiegelklare Wasser,
Und schaute tiefer und tiefer —
Bis tief, im Meeresgrunde,
Anfangs wie dämmernde Nebel,
Jedoch allmählich farbenbestimmter,
Kirchenkuppel und Türme sich zeigten,
Und endlich, sonnenklar, eine ganze Stadt,
Altertümlich niederländisch,
Und menschenbelebt.
Bedächtige Männer, schwarzbemäntelt,
Mit weissen Halskrausen und Ehrenketten
Und langen Degen und langen Gesichtern,
Schreiten, über den wimmelnden Marktplatz,
Nach dem treppenhohen Rathhaus,
Wo steinerne Kaiserbilder
Wacht halten mit Scepter und Schwert.
Unferne, vor langen Häuserreihn,
Wo spiegelblanke Fenster
Und pyramidisch beschnittene Linden,
Wandeln seidenrauschende Jungfern,
Schlanke Leibchen, die Blumengesichter
Sittsam umschlossen von schwarzen Mützchen
Und hervorquellendem Goldhaar.
Bunte Gesellen, in spanischer Tracht,
Stolzieren vorüber und nicken.
Bejahrte Frauen,*

In braunen, verschollnen Gewändern,
Gesangbuch und Rosenkranz in der Hand,
Eilen, trippelnden Schritts,
Nach dem grossen Dome,
Getrieben von Glockengeläute
Und rauschendem Orgelton.

Mich selbst ergreift des fernen Klangs
Geheimnisvoller Schauer!
Unendliches Sehnen, tiefe Wehmut
Beschleicht mein Herz,
Mein kaum geheiltes Herz; —
Mir ist, als würden seine Wunden
Von lieben Lippen aufgeküsst,
Und täten wieder bluten, —
Heisse, rote Tropfen,
Die lang und langsam niederfall'n
Auf ein altes Haus, dort unten
In der tiefen Meerstadt,
Auf ein altes hochgegiebeltes Haus,
Das melancholisch menschenleer ist,
Nur dass am untern Fenster
Ein Mädchen sitzt,
Den Kopf auf den Arm gestützt,
Wie ein armes, vergessenes Kind —
Und ich kenne dich, armes, vergessenes Kind!

So tief, meertief also
Verstecktest du dich vor mir
Aus kindischer Laune,
Und konntest nicht mehr herauf,
Und sassest fremd unter fremden Leuten,
Jahrhundertelang,
Derweilen ich, die Seele voll Gram,
Auf der ganzen Erde dich suchte,
Und immer dich suchte,
Du Immergeliebte,
Du Längstverlorene,
Du Endlichgefundene —
Ich hab' dich gefunden und schaue wieder

> *Dein süsses Gesicht*
> *Die klugen, treuen Augen,*
> *Das liebe Lächeln —*
> *Und nimmer will ich dich wieder verlassen,*
> *Und ich komme hinab zu dir,*
> *Und mit ausgebreiteten Armen*
> *Stürz' ich hinab an dein Herz —*
>
> *Aber zur rechten Zeit noch*
> *Ergriff mich beim Fuss der Kapitän,*
> *Und zog mich vom Schiffsrand,*
> *Und rief, ärgerlich lachend:*
> *'Doktor, sind Sie des Teufels?'*

Heinrich Heine (1797–1856) in many ways carries on the tradition of German Romanticism. *Seegespenst* thus begins with the Romantic picture of the lonely poet, apart from his fellows. The word 'aber' in the first line suggests this: it implies a contrast between the poet at the edge of the ship and the other passengers, gregariously enjoying themselves. A dreamy-eyed poet, yearning away from life into the imagined Atlantidean city under the ocean. All the Romantic paraphernalia make their appearance: the evocation of a more stately past; otherworldly religious suggestions (in the irresistible call of church-bell and church-organ); lovers irrevocably parted; the bleeding heart; exile in strange lands, 'fremd unter fremden Leuten'; loneliness, in a house 'melancholisch menschenleer'—everything seen in a haze, the haze of water.

But this is not the Romanticism of Novalis, Tieck, Brentano or Eichendorff: a mode of composition which betrayed, beneath all apparent artlessness and simplicity, the presence of taste and tact, of a highly cultured personality. The self-dramatization of *Seegespenst* is crude, the Romanticism extreme.

> *...mein Herz,*
> *Mein kaum geheiltes Herz;*
> *Mir ist, als würden seine Wunden*
> *Von lieben Lippen aufgeküsst,*
> *Und täten wieder bluten...*

This is Romanticism raised to the *n*th power: Romanticism, one is tempted to say, reduced to absurdity.

The poem opens, *in mediae rebus*, with the poet's telling a tale of his own past. And throughout, from the opening lines, we are made conscious of the setting of the tale: the sea, through which the ship cuts its even path.

> *Ich aber lag am Rande des Schiffes*
> *Und schaute, träumenden Auges,*
> *Hinab in das spiegelklare Wasser* ...

Sounds and rhythms echo the smooth passage of the ship, and continue to do so even when the poet ostensibly departs from the real world of which he is telling, the world of the ship, for one of the imagination, the world of Atlantis.

> ... *vor langen Häuserreihn*
> *Wo spiegelblanke Fenster*
> *Und pyramidisch beschnittene Linden,*
> *Wandeln seidenrauschende Jungfern,*
> *Schlanke Leibchen, die Blumengesichter*
> *Sittsam umschlossen von schwarzen Mützchen* ...

Yet within this constant pattern, the rhythms never become monotonously inexpressive. To take but one example out of many: we respond to the languorously falling cadences of

> *Und schaute, träumenden Auges,*
> *Hinab in das spiegelklare Wasser,*
> *Und schaute tiefer und tiefer* ...

until we reach the lowest depths with the heavily, evenly accentuated line

> *Bis tief, im Meeresgrunde,*

after which the rhythms fluctuate and rise as the city gradually appears:

> *Anfangs wie dämmernde Nebel,*
> *Jedoch allmählich farbenbestimmter,*
> *Kirchenkuppel und Türme sich zeigten,*

until, as the word 'sonnenklar' is isolated grammatically and rhythmically, the contour becomes perfectly clear:

Und éndlich, / sonnenklár, / eine gánze Stádt.

We have already seen that in the course of *Seegespenst* Heine departs, in true Romantic fashion, from the real world of his poem (the world of the ship) into an imaginary one (that of the Atlantidean city). As he does this, the mark of the narrator and of distance, the past tense, gradually and imperceptibly disappears: 'Bis ... Kirchenkuppel und Türme sich *zeigten*' gives way to 'Bedächtige Männer | *Schreiten* über den wimmelnden Marktplatz'. No longer is Heine telling us of an experience that is past: he himself, and we, are reliving the experience.

'Poetry ... takes its origin from emotion recollected in tranquillity: the emotion is contemplated till by a species of reaction the tranquillity gradually disappears, and an emotion, kindred to that which was before the subject of contemplation, is gradually produced and does itself actually exist in the mind.'
All distance between poet and reader, poet and subject, gradually disappears. At first there is still a puckish, mischievous touch, bespeaking distance, in the description of those thoughtful men

Mit langen Degen und langen Gesichtern:

but the Romantic emotion, a sense of grief and loss, of unspeakable yearning, of longing for the ἓν καὶ πᾶν of death, rises perceptibly until it reaches its hysterical climax.

Und mit ausgebreiteten Armen
Stürz ich hinab an dein Herz.

After the languorous passion and slow yearning the swift fall, in sense and rhythm alike.

But suddenly, at the climax, we are jerked back across two dimensions: from timeless lyric present to the real present in which we are reading the poem ('Ergriff', the verb, is in the past tense!); from Atlantidean city to the company on board ship; from Heine the romantic wanderer in search of phantom worlds to bourgeois Dr. Heine with his university degree; in short—from dream to reality. This is by no means, as so many have thought, a mere anticlimax, entirely unexpected and unprepared. Rhythms and consonants had kept us, throughout the poem, subconsciously aware of the ship moving through the waters, of the voyage of which we are told, in the past tense, at the opening of the poem. These rhythms seem in retrospect like an eye unobtrusively and ironically watching the growing excitement of the poet, and of his readers, in their lyric present. The 'Herr Doktor', the prosaic Heine living in a real world and its social relations, has throughout the poem been watching with amused detachment the doings of the Romantic, the self-dramatizing *Weltschmerzler*. And of these two Heines, it is the former who conquers. As the captain pulls the poet away from the edge of the ship, so Heine pulls us away from the fatal attractions of a crude Romanticism.

Romanticism has been transcended by one who feels its attractions, by the singer of 'Das letzte | Freie Waldlied der Romantik'. It has been beaten with one of its own most powerful weapons: the weapon of *Ironie*. Yet for Heine, and his generation, this victory is only temporary. The struggle between escapist and realist self went on in this generation of *Zerrissene* characterized by Platen:

Ein Geschlecht das stets zerrissen, stets vom Halben halb erfasst,

a weary struggle, without defeat or victory. In his *Geständnisse* of 1853, Heine confessed:
'Despite my exterminatory warfare against Romanticism, I always remained a Romanticist in a higher degree than I could myself divine.'
Romanticism here implies a turning away from social reality, from the demands of the time, from truth even, to a realm of pure beauty, to the past; to imagination. In *Seegespenst* this tendency has been, for a time at least, reversed.

(*b*)

DIE WEBER

Im düstern Auge keine Träne,
Sie sitzen am Webstuhl und fletschen die Zähne:
'Deutschland, wir weben dein Leichentuch,

> *Wir weben hinein den dreifachen Fluch —*
> *Wir weben, wir weben!*
>
> '*Ein Fluch dem Götzen, zu dem wir gebeten*
> *In Winterskälte und Hungersnöten;*
> *Wir haben vergebens gehofft und geharrt,*
> *Er hat uns geäfft und gefoppt und genarrt —*
> *Wir weben, wir weben!*
>
> '*Ein Fluch dem König, dem König der Reichen*
> *Den unser Elend nicht konnte erweichen,*
> *Der den letzten Groschen von uns erpresst,*
> *Und uns wie Hunde erschiessen lässt —*
> *Wir weben, wir weben!*
>
> '*Ein Fluch dem falschen Vaterlande,*
> *Wo nur gedeihen Schmach und Schande,*
> *Wo jede Blume früh geknickt,*
> *Wo Fäulnis und Moder den Wurm erquickt —*
> *Wir weben, wir weben!*
>
> '*Das Schiffchen fliegt, der Webstuhl kracht,*
> *Wir weben emsig Tag und Nacht —*
> *Altdeutschland, wir weben dein Leichentuch,*
> *Wir weben hinein den dreifachen Fluch.*
> *Wir weben, wir weben!*'

Goethe had felt at one with nature and the world; Schiller had been able to hope that by striving towards an ideal recognized as unattainable he would be able to remould an actuality he could not admire; the Romantics had found solace by retiring into the world of books and of imagination, and there building up an intellectual dream-world to which they sought to approximate the real. Heine, in *Seegespenst* and elsewhere, tried to take the Romantic path ('Nach innen geht der geheimnisvolle Weg') but found himself constantly pulled up by a world very different from that he imagined. Faery beckonings—

> *Aus alten Märchen winkt es*
> *Hervor mit weisser Hand —*

were inevitably followed by harsh awakening.

> *Ach, dieses Land der Wonne*
> *Das seh' ich oft im Traum;*
> *Doch kommt die Morgensonne*
> *Verfliesst's wie eitel Schaum.*

And so Heine becomes, as *Seegespenst* already demonstrated, the poet of *Katzenjammer*, of disillusion and disenchantment. He presents himself as one who has tried, and tries again and again, to delude himself, but finds the world so much harsher, uglier and more unbearable than his dreams.

Reality, for the young poets of the 30's and 40's, increasingly meant political or socio-political reality. The political lyric had flowered briefly during the Wars of Liberation (Körner, Schenkendorff), and again during the Polish and Greek revolts against their Russian and Turkish overlords ('Anastasius Grün', Platen). But it was not until the death of Frederick William III and the accession of Frederick William IV of Prussia (1840) that the political lyric began to come into its own in Germany. The new king had awakened hopes that the stagnation and backwardness of Prussia at least was to be remedied by liberal reform: hopes which inspired Georg Herwegh's *Lieder eines Lebendigen* (1841) and whose disappointment was to drive Ferdinand Freiligrath, hitherto a fanatically unpolitical[1] singer of exotic 'lion and desert songs', into the arms of the most extreme section of German reformers. In 1842, Freiligrath said farewell to his desert poetry:

> *Zum Teufel die Kamele,*
> *Zum Teufel auch die Leun!*
> *Es rauscht durch meine Seele*
> *Der alte deutsche Rhein!*
> *Er rauscht mir um die Stirne*
> *Mit Wein und Eichenlaub;*
> *Er wäscht mir aus dem Hirne*
> *Verjährten Wüstenstaub*
>   (*Auch eine Rheinsage*)

while Herwegh maintained, with pardonable exaggeration: 'In the last analysis our times have no interests which are *not* political.'

---

[1] *Der Dichter steht auf einer höhern Warte*
Als auf den Zinnen der Partei.

The problems of national unity, of constitutional liberty and of incipient industrial revolution entered more and more deeply into the everyday experience of German poets. They thus became fit and inevitable subjects for lyric poetry.

Die Weber, a poem written soon after a Luddite revolt by Silesian weavers (1844), owes not a little of its power and impressiveness to the mould in which Heine chose to cast it. It recalls in effect, two of the most primitive forms of poetry. The first of these is the song of labour—a song in which the task at which a group of workmen is engaged (rowing, beating the anvil, grinding corn, weaving) suggests a refrain, while the reflections of the workmen on their actual situation, their aspirations and antipathies fill the intervening stanzas.[1] The other primitive form recalled by *Die Weber* is the charm or incantation. The famous Merseburg charm, for instance, begins like Heine's poem, by setting the scene and introducing the speakers at their work:

> *Eiris sazun idisi   sazun hera duoder.*
> *suma hapt heptidun   suma heri lezidun*
> *suma clubodun   umbi cuoniouuidi*

and only then goes on to give the actual incantatory formula:

> *insprinc haptbandun   invar vigandun!*

The occupations of weaving and spinning in any case recall the Norns, who magically control the fate of the world: and the conjuring repetition of words and sounds —

> *Deutschland, wir weben dein Leichentuch,*
> *Wir weben hinein den dreifachen Fluch,*
> *Wir weben, wir weben —*

still further suggest magical formulae and incantations. All this, together with the suggestions of direst destitution and fierce hatred give the poem a primitive savage intensity that is hardly equalled in modern poetry.

[1] Schopp (*Das deutsche Arbeitslied*, pp. 325 ff.) notes that the rhythm of weaving at a hand-loom consists of three noises, a strong, half-strong and weak one. Most weaving-songs are therefore in a sort of dactylic rhythm. It is possible that Heine knew this and allowed it to mould the rhythms of *Die Weber*.

The opening line seems explicitly concerned to distinguish these 'weavers' and all they stand for from the Heine of the *Buch der Lieder* (1817–24); to lift them out of the copious flood of tears in which this poet above all others so loved to immerse himself. We are to hear, instead of the loud laments of yesterday, 'curses not loud but deep', a silent and therefore all the more ominous gnashing of teeth. Throughout the poem we *hear* this hissing subdued menace.

> *Sie sitzen am Webstuhl und fletschen die Zähne:*
> *Deutschland ...*

(the assonantic juxtaposition of *fletschen* and *Deutschland* turns the very name of Germany into a curse, a gnashing of teeth!):

> *Ein Fluch dem Götzen,*[1] *zu dem wir gebeten,*
> *In Winterskälte und Hungersnöten ...*
>
> *Ein Fluch dem falschen Vaterlande ...*

The first four stanzas all follow the same pattern. They begin with a couplet with feminine rhymes, whose fall might indicate weariness and consequent inaction (Träne, Zähne — gebeten, Nöten — Reichen, Weichen, etc.); but this is followed by the energetic, rising menace of masculine rhymes ending on progressively harsher (or hissing) sound-groups: Fluch, Tuch — geharrt, genarrt — erpresst, lässt — geknickt, erquickt. After this open threat comes the return to the task in hand, and also to the curse which will surely work itself out. 'Wir weben, wir weben' —a quiet, almost purring menace more terrible than any open revolt. The last stanza, the climax of the whole, in one way modifies the pattern: both couplets here end with harsh masculine rhymes, thus indicating that the end is nearing, that revolt and the downfall of the old order are imminent; but in the closing line the familiar purring menace of the refrain once more, ominously, supervenes.

The cold fury of this poem is again, as so often with Heine, the fruit of disillusion. *With God for King and Country*—the weavers too had once believed in the common adage, had venerated what they saw venerated by others; but they are now driven to curse God, king and country alike. The force of the poem

[1] Or, as another version has it: 'Ein Fluch dem Gotte, zu dem wir gebeten ...'

depends on our simultaneous consciousness, induced by the poet, of a love and faith that are gone and a hatred that has taken their place. All the three 'curse'-stanzas contain, negatively, suggestions of hope, pity, beauty—hope blighted, pity suppressed, beauty destroyed.

Wir haben vergebens gehofft und geharrt.

Hope and expectation has been in vain: instead there comes a mocking echo:

Er hat uns geäfft und gefoppt und genarrt.

Gehofft, geäfft—geharrt, genarrt. The folly of hope and of expecting good could not be more strikingly, more horribly, underlined. A similar function is fulfilled by '*erweichen*', in stanza 3, with its suggestions of a pity that is not there, and (in stanza 4) by 'gedeihen', 'Blume', 'erquickt', with their disenchanted evocation of prosperity, beauty, refreshment. These terms give body to disappointment by showing what has been disappointed; make disillusion real by embodying, concretely, the illusion which preceded it.

The last three lines of the poem repeat, with one significant variation, those of the opening stanza. The shroud is not now to be woven for *all* Germany:

Altdeutschland, wir weben dein Leichentuch.

Heine seems here specifically to align himself with the *Jungdeutschland* movement: with those young German liberals whom Wienbarg had greeted in his *Ästhetische Feldzüge* (1834): 'To you, *Young* Germany, I dedicate these pages, not to the old!'[1] The lines seem to suggest Heine's positives, to look forward to a new Germany which will rise out of the ruins of the old. But here Heine's essential weakness reveals itself. It is obvious that he really

[1] The term *Jungdeutschland* describes a group of liberal revolutionary writers active after 1830: they never formed a 'school' (indeed they were rivals rather than confederates) but were united by their political tendencies and their desire to make literature a vehicle for social, political and ethical reforms. Chief among them, besides Heine, were Ludwig Börne (1786–1837), Ludwig Wienbarg (1802–72), Theodor Mundt (1808–61), Karl Gutzkow (1811–78) and Heinrich Laube (1806–84). They were in the main prose-writers and dramatists rather than lyric poets.

has no positives, that he cannot visualize, cannot make concrete, what is to be new-created. A master of attack, satirical or earnest, a master of destruction, he cannot build up. He never found, throughout his life, a political or social or religious creed to satisfy himself—or his modern readers; least of all the jejune Saint-Simonian 'Hellenism' to which he paid lip-service at this period of his life.

Yet Heine has so chosen the subject of the poem that this very defect, this lack of positives and standards, becomes almost a merit. The triple curse is placed in the mouth of weavers toiling day and night, conscious of nothing but their miseries: men who would not be articulate enough to formulate or foresighted enough to visualize the standards of the future. How much more convincing, and how much more truly menacing, are Heine's figures than Freiligrath's famous stoker, exulting in the strength and power of the proletariat:

Du bist viel weniger als ich, o König, ein Titan!
Beherrsch' ich nicht, auf dem du gehst, den allzeit kochenden
  Vulkan?
Es liegt an mir; — ein Ruck von mir, ein Schlag von mir zu
  dieser Frist,
Und siehe, das Gebäude stürzt, von welchem du die Spitze bist!
                                        (*Von unten auf!*)

How much more effective is Heine's threat of revolution than Herwegh's crude versification of Lassalle:

> *Mann der Arbeit, aufgewacht!*
> *Und erkenne deine Macht!*
> *Alle Räder stehen still,*
> *Wenn dein starker Arm es will.*

Yet for all that Heine leaves us in no doubt that *Die Weber* embodies his own experience, his own disillusion; that the weavers' curse is in a measure his own. The opening lines of the poem are not, like the rest, spoken by the weavers, but by the poet himself, introducing his subject. The hissing menace of the second line, the gnashing of teeth both spoken of and reproduced in sound, are the poet's own.

Despite its dramatic guise, therefore, *Die Weber* may be called a true lyric, embodying a personal experience of life: an experience of disenchantment characteristic not only of Heine but of a whole post-romantic generation.

(c)
HEINE
ZWEI RITTER

Krapülinski und Waschlapski,
Polen aus der Polackei,
Fochten für die Freiheit, gegen
Moskowiter-Tyrannei.

Fochten tapfer und entkamen
Endlich glücklich nach Paris —
Leben bleiben, wie das Sterben
Für das Vaterland, ist süss.

Wie Achilles und Patroklus,
David und sein Jonathan,
Liebten sich die beiden Polen,
Küssten sich: 'Kochan! Kochan!'

Keiner je verriet den Andern,
Blieben Freunde, ehrlich, treu,
Ob sie gleich zwei edle Polen,
Polen aus der Polackei.

Wohnten in derselben Stube,
Schliefen in demselben Bette;
Eine Laus und eine Seele,
Kratzten sie sich um die Wette.

Speisten in derselben Kneipe,
Und da Keiner wollte leiden,
Dass der Andre für ihn zahle,
Zahlte keiner von den Beiden.

Auch dieselbe Henriette
Wäscht für beide edle Polen;
Trällernd kommt sie jeden Monat, —
Um die Wäsche abzuholen.

HEINE: ZWEI RITTER

Ja, sie haben wirklich Wäsche,
Jeder hat der Hemden zwei,
Ob sie gleich zwei edle Polen,
Polen aus der Polackei.

Sitzen heute am Kamine,
Wo die Flammen traulich flackern;
Draussen Nacht und Schneegestöber
Und das Rollen von Fiakern.

Eine grosse Bowle Punsch
(Es versteht sich, unverzückert,
Unversäuert, unverwässert)
Haben sie bereits geschlückert.

Und von Wehmut wird beschlichen
Ihr Gemüte; ihr Gesicht
Wird befeuchtet schon von Zähren,
Und der Krapülinski spricht:

'Hätt' ich doch hier in Paris
Meinen Bärenpelz, den lieben
Schlafrock und die Katzfell-Nachtmütz',
Die im Vaterland geblieben!'

Ihm erwiderte Waschlapski:
'O du bist ein treuer Schlachzitz,
Denkest immer an der Heimat
Bärenpelz und Katzfell-Nachtmütz.

'Polen ist noch nicht verloren,
Unsre Weiber, sie gebären,
Unsre Jungfraun tun dasselbe,
Werden Helden uns bescheren,

'Helden, wie der Held Sobieski,
Wie Schelmufski und Uminski,
Eskrokewitsch, Schubiakski,
Und der grosse Eselinski.'

Heine has suffered a good deal from his admirers no less than his detractors: from readers who demanded of poetry above all solemnity and 'high seriousness',[1] and thought they found the admired qualities in those poems of the *Buch der Lieder* in which Heine fooled himself into enchantment (cf. *Auf Flügeln des Gesanges*). But an experience of life such as that communicated by *Seegespenst* and *Die Weber* must inevitably seek to express itself in wit and more especially in satire. Satire, ridiculing the vices and follies of mankind, pricks the soap-bubbles of illusion that float around this world. It is unthinkable without a background of seriousness: and we do indeed find Heine writing to Moses Moser that wit in its isolation is worth nothing at all, that he can brook it only if its basis is serious. The satirical poems of Heine's later years—of which *Zwei Ritter* is one of the best-known examples —embody and communicate an experience no less individual no less bitter than such nightmare ballads as *Nächtliche Fahrt* and *Pfalzgräfin Jutta*, or the heartrending laments of the *Lazarus* cycle. They are therefore, although they frequently wear a cloak of impersonality, true lyric poetry.

Superficially, the humour of *Zwei Ritter* seems facile enough. It seems to be little more than a skit on Slav sounds, especially Slav names (so barbarous to Western ears!), in the manner of Southey's *March to Moscow*

> *Oncharoffsky and Rostoffsky*
> *And all the others that end in -offsky*

or, more especially, in the manner of Byron's *Don Juan*:

> *Achilles' self was not more grim and gory*
> *Than thousands of this new and polished nation,*
> *Whose names want nothing but—pronunciation.*
> *Still, I'll record a few, if but to increase*
> *Our euphony: there was Strongenoff and Strokonoff,*
> *Meknop, Serge Lvow, Arséniew of modern Greece,*
> *And Tschitschakoff, and Roguenoff, and Chokenoff,*
> *And others of twelve consonants apiece . . .*

On the model of Byron's 'Roguenoff' and 'Chokenoff', Heine admixes with uncouth Polish words (kochany, szlachcic) and actual Polish names (Sobiesky) pseudo-names, embodying Ger-

---

[1] It will be remembered that the critic who gave currency to this term denigrated Chaucer.

man and French terms of opprobrium: dissoluteness ('Krapüle'), cowardice and weakness ('Waschlappen'), roguery ('Schelm', 'Escroc', 'Schubiak') and stupidity ('Esel').

For the effect of the poem it is, however, essential to realize that *Poles*, not Russians, are here being satirized: those heroic Poles whose rebellion against 'Muscovite tyranny' had endeared them to liberals all over Europe in the 30's and 40's of the nineteenth century. Herwegh had called on all peoples to avenge 'the death-rattle of poor murdered Polonia'; Platen had likened the Polish rebels to the heroes of Leonidas:

> *Einst kommen wird ein freies Volk und pflanzen eine Siegestrophä'*
> *Für euch, und ein Simonides besingen dies Thermopilae;*

while Maltitz, in his now-forgotten *Polonia*, had expressed what was in the hearts of all—that in singing of Polish he was dreaming of German liberty:

> *Kann mein Lied nicht deutsche Freiheit bringen,*
> *Muss es einem fremden Volke singen;*
> *Denn der Deutsche hat kein Vaterland.*

Now, in the '50's, Heine takes another look at these 'heroes' of mankind's war of liberation.

> *Polen aus der Polackei,*
> *Fochten für die Freiheit.*

The plosive and fricative alliteration communicates the deepest contempt. Here are your heroic Poles, your fighters for freedom: rogues, cowards and fools, like the rest of mankind. This is indeed the depth of disillusion and despair. There is no longer any hope of that true wholehearted revolt against tyranny whose mutterings had informed *Die Weber*.

But it is Heine's greatness, the distinguishing mark of his poetry, that he can make disillusion concrete by conjuring up the co-presence (in the reader's consciousness) of the preceding illusion. He portrays reality together with the ideal it disappoints. The opening stanza depicts, through pause and enjambement, the effort of resistance against Muscovite tyranny, the ideal of Herwegh, Platen and Maltitz:

> *Fochten für die Freiheit, gegen*
> *Moskowiter-Tyrannei.*

The uncouth compound of that second line seems to be the very obstacle which is to be dislodged by the effort so concretely embodied in the verse. But the element of contempt and parody already apparent in these lines is strengthened, made conscious, by the presentment (through similar rhythmic devices) of another kind of effort in the lines that follow:

> *Fochten tapfer und entkamen*
> *Endlich glücklich nach Paris.*

The 'fochten' of line 5 mocks that of line 3. The effort is now an effort of escape from danger: it is rendered by the passage from 'entkamen' to 'endlich' (the glottal stop enhances the effect), while glottal stops and the unaccented echoing '-lich' convey the panting of these heroic Poles in their headlong flight.

> *... entkamen*
> *Endlich glücklich ...*

Heine is indeed a master of conveying, through the very texture of his poetry, a fully apprehended situation.

The mocking echo—reality mocking the ideal—returns in the lines that follow those just analysed, where Heine uses, to great effect, one of his favourite devices: the inverted commonplace.

> *Leben bleiben, wie das Sterben*
> *Für das Vaterland ist süss.*

At once the Horatian tag springs to mind, the accepted commonplace, the ideal of conduct. 'Dulce et decorum est pro patria mori.' But reality is otherwise. Echo answers—where?[1] In the past perhaps there was true greatness, true friendship, true heroism—so at least the introduction, in a mock-comparison, of Achilles and Patroclus, David and Jonathan, seems to tell us; but the present belongs to rogues and cowards, to Krapülinski and Waschlapski.

[1] The lines

> *Eine Laus und eine Seele*
> *Kratzten sie sich um die Wette*

bring a similar echo of a commonplace: 'ein Herz und eine Seele'. This, Heine says in effect, is what friendship is really like.

> *Speisten in derselben Kneipe*
> *Und da Keiner wollte leiden*
> *Dass der Andre für ihn zahle,*
> *Zahlte Keiner von den Beiden.*

How perfectly the lilting tune of this, helped by the *ei* assonance, conveys the spirit of mockery! The first two lines introduce the tune; the third seems to interrupt it, to introduce (with its deeper *a* sounds) a serious note of friendship and self-sacrifice, carried on by the first word of the fourth line; but with the unexpected, witty ending of this fourth line the earlier tune, the *ei* tune, triumphantly reasserts itself. Again and again we find this realization of all the possibilities of poetry in the service of parody:

> *Und von Wehmut wird beschlichen*
> *Ihr Gemüte; / ihr Gesicht*
> *Wird befeuchtet schon von Zähren* ...

A serious note seems once again about to be introduced. The lines are broken, as if stifled by sobs. And then at once, in the same verse-movement, comes the parody:

> *Hätt' ich doch hier in Paris*
> *Meinen Bärenpelz, / den lieben*
> *Schlafrock / und die Katzfell – Nachtmütz* ...[1]

With mock-pathos achieved by superb rhythmic control, Heine here throws the main stresses on the objects of desire: on furcoat, dressing-gown, catskin nightcap. The emblems of German Philistinism and inertia, no less potent instruments of reaction than the censorship itself, desired by the Polish heroes of liberty. O the difference of man and man.

And so the poem goes on. Courage, friendship, patriotism, cleanliness (the juxtaposition is characteristic), chastity, fidelity—all are mockingly denied. As a last turn of the screw comes the refrain—

> *Ob sie gleich zwei edle Polen* ... —

suggesting that there are none better, but many worse. We are prepared therefore for the horrifying dissonance of the ending. There is hope yet, suggests Waschlapski, in

[1] Such rhymes as *Schlachzitz — Nachtmütz* add to the effect.

> *Helden, wie der Held Sobieski,*
> *Wie Schelmufski und Uminski,*
> *Eskrokewitsch, Schubiakski,*
> *Und der grosse Esselinski.*

Hope itself (which Schiller had called the greatest boon of mankind) is derided. There can be no hope, for all men are rogues —and if not rogues they are fools. 'Der grosse Eselinski' fittingly ends the poem, as he was to end one of the most moving personal poems of Heine's last years.

> *Da war zumal der Esel Bileams,*
> *Der überschrie die Götter und die Heil'gen!*
> *Mit I-a, I-a, dem Gewieh'r*
> *Dem schluchzend ekelhaften Misslaut, brachte*
> *Mich zur Verzweiflung schier das dumme Tier,*
> *Ich selbst zuletzt schrie auf — und ich erwachte.*
> (Für die Mouche)

Here as there the aspirations of mankind are at last defeated by a nightmare of stupidity.

Disillusion is complete. And even if we find this later poetry too negative, too little concerned with the attainment of true standards and values, we cannot but admire the force and originality with which Heine communicates a vision of life familiar not only to his contemporaries but to so many of his readers of the present day.

(d)
PLATEN
VENEDIG (Sonnet 5)

> *Venedig liegt nur noch im Land der Träume,*
>   *Und wirft nur Schatten her aus alten Tagen,*
>   *Es liegt der Leu der Republik erschlagen,*
>   *Und öde feiern seines Kerkers Räume.*
>
> *Die ehrnen Hengste, die durch salz'ge Schäume*
>   *Dahergeschleppt, auf jener Kirche ragen,*
>   *Nicht mehr dieselben sind sie, ach! sie tragen*
>   *Des korsikan'schen Ueberwinders Zäume.*

PLATEN: VENEDIG (SONNET 5)

> *Wo ist das Volk von Königen geblieben,*
> *Das diese Marmorhäuser durfte bauen,*
> *Die nun verfallen und gemach zerstieben?*
>
> *Nur selten finden auf der Enkel Brauen*
> *Der Ahnen grosse Züge sich geschrieben,*
> *An Dogengräbern in den Stein gehauen.*

Zwei Ritter, in the lines about Achilles and Patroclus, David and Jonathan, skirted a theme often treated by Heine: the theme of degeneration, of the decay of what had once been great and noble, explicit in the very title of the earlier poem *Entartung*. In *Entartung*, Heine shows demoralization spreading from humanity to the plant and animal world. The lily has lost its chastity, the violet its modesty, the nightingale its sincerity. What remains only serves to emphasize what has been lost:

> *Die Wahrheit schwindet von der Erde,*
> *Auch mit der Treu' ist es vorbei.*
> *Die Hunde wedeln noch und stinken*
> *Wie sonst, doch sind sie nicht mehr treu.*

This theme, inevitably in the air at a time when Germany was having the worst of both worlds—when commercial values began to invade all spheres of life, while at the same time a feudal reaction muzzled press and people—commended itself with special force to Heine's old enemy, August Graf von Platen-Hallermünde (1796–1835). Not only did he see German life and literature in decay (witness his satires on both in *Die verhängnisvolle Gabel* and *Der romantische Oedipus*), poisoned by a degenerate Romanticism:

> *(der) Pesthauch jener dämonischen Schar*
> *Welche des Geists unklaren Begriff und des Herzens Verderbtheit*
> *Als tiefsinnig sogar, Kindern und Knaben verkauft;*

but he looked on himself too, physically puny and sexually abnormal as he was, as the degenerate scion of a noble race, changed even from what he had been:

> *Wer aber gäbe mir die vollen Wangen*
> *Der ersten Jugend und den Glanz zurücke,*
> *Woran allein der Menschen Blicke hangen?*

It is this consciousness of personal and general decay which unmistakably pervades Platen's *Venedig* sonnet-cycle of 1824, and crystallizes in the fifth sonnet which is now to be examined.

Platen's sonnet is more than an exercise in gentle nostalgia. All the well-known nostalgic sign-posts do indeed appear: a 'land of dream', 'shadows from days of yore', decay ('verfallen', 'zerstieben'), graves, the 'ach' of impotent lament; but the movement of the poem warns us at once that Platen, unlike Lenau, refuses to revel in his grief. The very opening of the poem pulls the reader up. 'Venédig liégt núr noch ...' These heavy stresses following one on the other suggest that the poet is finding it difficult to speak out, that he tries to keep back what nevertheless insists on utterance. We experience resistance, resistance which is gradually overcome by the urgency within. At first the poem moves slowly, jerkily, with great effort from heavy stress to heavy stress, from end-stopped line to end-stopped line; but it gathers momentum as it moves towards the 'ach' of the seventh line[1] and the lament which follows it. In the broken rhythms of lines 5 to 8 nostalgic emotion seems at last to have free rein, to mould speech at will:

> Die ehrnen Hengste, / die durch salz'ge Schäume
> Dahergeschleppt, / auf jener Kirche ragen,
> Nicht mehr dieselben sind sie, / ach! / sie tragen
> Des korsikan'schen Ueberwinders Zäume.

In the sestet, however, the rhythms grow progressively quieter: at first in a comparatively agitated question, then in a measured statement. The keyword 'gemach' (l. 11) makes this slowing-down explicit. Emotion is once more reined in, resistance re-introduced, surface calm re-established. Platen forces his poem to move in calm, impersonal, super-personal measure. It comes to rest, appropriately, on an image of sculptured death.

Conflict between nostalgic emotion and controlling will, reproduced by the verse-movement, is at the heart of Platen's poem. It has dictated its very form: for what could seem more inappro-

---

[1] Cf. the seventh sonnet of this cycle:

> Es scheint ein langes, ew'ges **Ach** zu wohnen
> In diesen Lüften, die sich leise regen ...

priate to the theme of decay, of degeneration, than the strict form of the sonnet? Yet this very 'inappropriateness' is essential. Just as Platen tries to distance his emotions, to contemplate them (as it were) from the outside by not speaking directly of his personal problems but using an Italian city as a symbol for them—so he counteracts nostalgia and chaos by the strictest emphasis on *form*.

> *Ein Trost nur bleibt mir, dass ich jeder Bürde*
> *Vielleicht ein Gleichgewicht vermag zu halten*
> *Durch meiner Seele ganze Kraft und Würde.*

His is the endeavour so well described in *The Poetic Image*, by C. Day Lewis, who declares it reasonable to argue 'that, when a social pattern is changing, when the beliefs or structure of a society are in process of disintegration', poets should compensate for the incoherence of the outside world by 'a more insistent emphasis on order in the world of their imagination'.

As has already been shown, Platen's concern for form in an era of disintegration is connected with his attempt to distance strong and personal emotions. This attempt—the attempt to distance, to contemplate from the outside—assures his poem of a mature complexity of attitude very different from the nostalgia of his Romantic predecessors. One striking example will suffice. At the opening of his sonnet the poet enumerates the signs of degeneracy and decay he sees in Venice. One of these signs is the emptiness of the dungeons once guarded by that lion of the Republic whose death is now lamented. Republican greatness, it seems, was inevitably associated with a measure of cruelty and oppression, with which the poet, in Nietzschean fashion, has a deal of sympathy. Yet the line which introduces the dungeons introduces at the same time a more ambivalent attitude towards them:

> *Und öde feiern seines Kerkers Räume.*

'Öde feiern.' The adverb laments the degenerate emptiness of the present: but the verb holds suggestions of rejoicing, of celebration. Even in the nostalgic appraisal of a regretted past the weighing intellect, the critical spirit, have their part.

But there is about the *Venedig* cycle another, a tragic complexity, one which most endears Platen to the reader of to-day.

It is quite obvious that Platen loves Venice *as it is*: that he loves the very decay and degeneration he laments.

> *Welch eine Fülle wohnt von Kraft und Milde*
> *Sogar im Marmor hier, im spröden, kalten,*
> *Und in so manchem tiefgefühlten Bilde!*
>
> *Doch um noch mehr zu fesseln mich, zu halten,*
> *So mischt sich unter jene Kunstgebilde*
> *Die schönste Blüte lebender Gestalten.*

Decay, chaos and death have a beauty, an attraction, of their own. Beauty and death, as the Romantics knew, are near allied. That is the theme of Platen's *Tristan*, so admired (for obvious reasons) by Thomas Mann:

> *Wer die Schönheit angeschaut mit Augen*
> *Ist dem Tode schon anheimgegeben . . .*

That is ultimately the theme also of the *Venedig* sonnets: all the more moving because of the poet's heroic resistance to the lure of chaos and the lure of death; his refusal to give way without a struggle to 'the recurring human desire to escape the burden of life and thought'.

CHAPTER NINE

Poetic Realism

(a)
ANNETTE VON DROSTE-HÜLSHOFF
MONDESAUFGANG

*An des Balkones Gitter lehnte ich
Und wartete, du mildes Licht, auf dich.
Hoch über mir, gleich trübem Eiskristalle,
Zerschmolzen schwamm des Firmamentes Halle;
Der See verschimmerte mit leisem Dehnen,
Zerflossne Perlen oder Wolkentränen? —
Es rieselte, es dämmerte um mich,
Ich wartete, du mildes Licht, auf dich.*

*Hoch stand ich, neben mir der Linden Kamm,
Tief unter mir Gezweige, Ast und Stamm;
Im Laube summte der Phalänen Reigen,
Die Feuerfliege sah ich glimmend steigen,
Und Blüten taumelten wie halb entschlafen;
Mir war, als treibe hier ein Herz zum Hafen,
Ein Herz, das übervoll von Glück und Leid
Und Bildern seliger Vergangenheit.*

*Das Dunkel stieg, die Schatten drangen ein —
Wo weilst du, weilst du denn, mein milder Schein? —
Sie drangen ein, wie sündige Gedanken,
Des Firmamentes Woge schien zu schwanken,
Verzittert war der Feuerfliege Funken,
Längst die Phaläne an den Grund gesunken,
Nur Bergeshäupter standen hart und nah,
Ein finstrer Richterkreis, im Düster da.*

*Und Zweige zischelten an meinem Fuss
Wie Warnungsflüstern oder Todesgruss;*

POETIC REALISM

Ein Summen stieg im weiten Wassertale
Wie Volksgemurmel vor dem Tribunale;
Mir war, als müsse etwas Rechnung geben,
Als stehe zagend ein verlornes Leben,
Als stehe ein verkümmert Herz allein,
Einsam mit seiner Schuld und seiner Pein.

Da auf die Wellen sank ein Silberflor,
Und langsam stiegst du, frommes Licht, empor;
Der Alpen finstre Stirnen strichst du leise,
Und aus den Richtern wurden sanfte Greise,
Der Wellen Zucken ward ein lächelnd Winken,
An jedem Zweige sah ich Tropfen blinken,
Und jeder Tropfen schien ein Kämmerlein,
Drin flimmerte der Heimatlampe Schein.

O, Mond, du bist mir wie ein später Freund,
Der seine Jugend dem Verarmten eint,
Um seine sterbenden Erinnerungen
Des Lebens zarten Widerschein geschlungen,
Bist keine Sonne, die entzückt und blendet,
In Feuerströmen lebt, im Blute endet —
Bist, was dem kranken Sänger sein Gedicht,
Ein fremdes, aber o! ein mildes Licht.

The historian of literature who takes up a convenient term coined by Otto Ludwig and designates a number of nineteenth-century authors as 'poetic realists', must make it clear that he refers neither to a 'school' of writers (like, for example the older Romantics) nor even to as homogeneous a group as *Jungdeutschland*. The term conveniently describes a number of very different writers, living in different provinces of Germany and Switzerland around the middle of the nineteenth century. These were poets who had learnt a great deal from Romantic poetry, but rejected its outré subjectivism, its exotic avenues of escape, and the paucity of its themes:

O Mondscheinglanz und Lindenglanz, um aus der Haut zu fahren
Wie seid ihr, Dichter und Gesell'n, verblichen mit den Jahren!
(TH. MOMMSEN)

while at the same time they could not agree with their *Jungdeutschland* contemporaries that literature ought to conduce directly to social and political change. They were content to present their own life, the life and ethics of the German Bürgertum in provinces usually remote from world-shaking events

> (*Kein Klang der aufgeregten Zeit*
> *Drang noch in diese Einsamkeit*)

without searching for the Blue Flower of romantic or liberal Utopias.

Annette von Droste-Hülshoff (1797–1848) was, as a Westfalian 'Landedelfräulein', the only one of the Poetic Realists who did not belong to the Bürgertum; yet her poems (of which *Mondesaufgang*, written about 1843 in Castle Meersburg near Konstanz, is one of the most universally admired) show her to have had sufficient in common with Mörike, Storm and to a lesser extent Keller, to warrant her inclusion in this particular chapter of German literature.

Mondesaufgang records, as did Goethe's *Auf dem See*, the experience of several consecutive moments: twilight, complete darkness, moonrise; and like Goethe's poem merges with this objective a subjective movement. The poem passes from passive expectation, through hopes of drifting to peace and rest, through increasing terror, to a feeling of shelter and calm. The verse-movement, however, of Annette von Droste's poem is by no means as flexible, as adapted to every twist and turn of emotion, as that of Goethe's. It is harsh, unmelodious, almost jerky. The reader's voice is forced to pause at the end of every line, and often in the middle of the lines as well:

> *Es rieselte, / es dämmerte um mich, /*
> *Ich wartete, / du mildes Licht, / auf dich. /*
> *Hoch stand ich, / neben mir der Linden Kamm, /*
> *Tief unter mir Gezweige, / Ast / und Stamm ...*

Nor is the language of the poem musical in itself. Annette von Droste speaks, she does not sing—even when addressing that moon which had traditionally called forth, in the poetry of Klopstock, Hölty, Goethe, Brentano, Eichendorff and Heine, all the resources of word-music and melody.

POETIC REALISM

Passive expectation, 'warten', begins the poem: expectation not unmixed with apprehension. The appearances of the natural world, so the opening description of the evening sky seems to warn us, are deceptive, are not always what they seem. The sky appears to the observer alternately firm and dissolved: an image of impenetrable solidity (turbid ice-crystals) is succeeded by one of liquefaction (melting, swimming—'zerschmolzen schwamm') and by another of solidity (the *hall* of the firmament). As a result, the observer's attitude to this shifting world becomes uncertain and problematical.

Zerflossne Perlen oder Wolkentränen?

Is the lake, stretched to infinity in the mist, something infinitely precious or something ineffably sad? When, therefore, the second line of the poem is repeated at the end of the first stanza, the line takes on a deeper meaning, a new colouring. 'Ich wartete, du mildes Licht, auf dich.' Waiting for the mild light of the moon: that means, waiting for something which is both steady in itself, and towards which man can take up a definite attitude. It implies a conquest of uncertainty.

The second stanza seeks (as do so many of Annette von Droste's poems) to counterpoise uncertainty of sensation and attitude by the most exact notation possible of the physical *données* of the outside world. Chaos can be avoided by a clutching of the actual. The reader is given first the exact position of the observer on her balcony (poised, symbolically, between heaven and earth), then the sights to be seen, down to the tiniest (branches and tree-trunk, fire-flies), and familiar sounds to be heard (night-moths rustling in the foliage). But however firmly seized and held, physical sensation melts in the mind of the poetess into something more uncertain, more problematical: into moral apprehension. The sights and sounds of the evening suggest the evening of a life which has known too much both of bliss and of sorrow, and now yearns for oblivion. This sense of the dangers and discomforts of excessive experience, whether happy or unhappy, Annette von Droste shares with many another of the Poetic Realists: notably with Eduard Mörike, whose *Gebet*:

Wollest mit Freuden
Und wollest mit Leiden

> *Mich nicht überschütten —*
> *Doch in der Mitten*
> *Liegt holdes Bescheiden*

voices perfectly the feelings of a whole generation.

The sense of apprehension and uncertainty now steadily increases. It is reinforced by the jerky and hesitant movement of the stanzas: we have an impression of groping our way in an unknown terrifying region. The outside world grows darker and more menacing, as firefly and moth disappear, the shadows close in, and the mild moon fails to rise. 'Schwanken', uncertain wavering, now becomes the keyword; the darkening physical world merges into a strange, unexplored, dreaded inner world. Shadows closing in become thoughts of Sin; the mountains the tribunal of conscience.

> *O the mind, mind has mountains, cliffs of fall*
> *Frightful, sheer, no-man-fathomed; hold them cheap*
> *May, who ne'er hung there.*

As the trees hiss out their warning or annunciation of death, the whole world seems to turn into a tribunal arrayed against man, pitifully alone and thwarted, conscious of nothing but guilt and pain. 'Zagend', 'verloren', 'verkümmert', 'einsam' (the stress, we must note, falls heaviest on this last word!), 'Schuld', 'Pein'—we are suddenly conscious of an abyss of terror for which the opening of the poem had failed to prepare us.

But just then the moon begins, slowly and steadily, to rise, illuminating the world, transforming terror—a little mawkishly even—into benevolence:

> *Und aus den Richtern wurden sanfte Greise.*

Expectation has not been disappointed. The mild light has come, magically transforming each drop of dew into an image of home, symbol of shelter and peace. 'Der Heimatlampe Schein'—that is the answer to a plethora of experience, to visions of guilt and terror. Annette von Droste, in the face of an abyss of which she is only too conscious, clutches at that which is nearest to her: at her home, her native region, at all the sights and sounds which are familiar and harmless. To these sights the moon pre-eminently belongs. The moon is apostrophized, in the final stanza, as something which does not overwhelm with love and affection, but brings friendship. Not a stormy, dangerous friendship, but such friendship as a young man might feel for an ageing one, bringing —not life itself, but a mild reflection of it among the other's dying memories. The moon does not delight or dazzle, cannot—unlike the sun—be made to symbolize great elation and great disaster:

> *Bist keine Sonne, die entzückt und blendet,*
> *In Feuerströmen lebt, im Blute endet.*

It is a mild solace, that does not overwhelm. Mankind can find in the moon what the sick poet—how startling, and yet how right, is his introduction here!—finds in his poem.

> *Bist was dem kranken Sänger sein Gedicht,*
> *Ein fremdes, aber o! ein mildes Licht.*

The sick poet contemplating lonely man faced with a world terrifying and uncertain: we have met all this before, in the work of the German Romantics. Unlike her *Jungdeutschland* contemporaries, Annette von Droste conceives life, not as something infinitely perfectible, something intrinsically good that can be made ever better, but rather as the brink of a nameless abyss into which it is only too easy to fall. One can never be sure just how near one is, at any moment, to that abyss, which opens so terrifyingly in the third and fourth stanzas of *Mondesaufgang*. Yet unlike the Romantics, Annette von Droste has come to see a way out of this existential situation: through wariness, the careful step conveyed by the very movement of her poetry; through avoidance of what men generally call 'great', of the kind of life symbolized by the sun which begins in fire and ends in blood; through deliberate confinement to the 'mild' existence for which the moon is here seen to stand, the narrow round of home.

> *Und jeder Tropfen schien ein Kämmerlein,*
> *Drin flimmerte der Heimatlampe Schein.*

That is the answer. Keep to what you know, stay within the sphere into which you are born, do not seek too much 'experience' for its own sake. The moon becomes a symbol, in Annette von Droste's poem, of that 'gentle law' so many of her contemporaries sought in nature and history—a law decreeing not revolution but evolution, not heroic adventure but sweet contentment (Mörike's 'holdes Bescheiden') in traditional provincial life. The best-known formulation of this principle, of the *Biedermeier* world-picture, comes from the preface to Adalbert Stifter's collection of short stories, *Bunte Steine* (1852):

'As in the world of nature, so it is in the inner, human world. A whole life full of justice, simplicity, self-control, reasonableness, activity within one's proper sphere, admiration of beauty, culminating in a calm, serene death—that I call great. Powerful emotional upheavals, fearful wrath, the lust for revenge, the excited spirit which must have activity, which tears down, alters, destroys, and often in its excitement flings away life itself—these I call smaller, not greater, for such things as these are as much the product of isolated, of one-sided forces, as are tempests, volcanoes, and earthquakes. We shall endeavour to recognize the gentle law which guides humanity.'

It would be hard to find a better commentary on *Mondesaufgang*. The poetess shows herself aware of the terrors of life; but she seeks to conquer them by not looking for contentment beyond her actual situation, however impoverished, sick and even alien (verarmt, krank, fremd) she may feel in it. A strangely unstable contentment it may be; but the effort to reach it—or rather, more characteristically, the patient waiting for it—recorded in *Mondesaufgang*, make the poem one of the most moving in the German language.

(b)
EDUARD MÖRIKE
MEIN FLUSS

O Fluss, mein Fluss im Morgenstrahl!
Empfange nun, empfange
Den sehnsuchtsvollen Leib einmal,
Und küsse Brust und Wange!
— Er fühlt mir schon herauf die Brust,
Er kühlt mit Liebesschauerlust
Und jauchzendem Gesange.

*Es schlüpft der goldne Sonnenschein
In Tropfen an mir nieder,
Die Woge wieget aus und ein
Die hingegebnen Glieder;
Die Arme hab' ich ausgespannt,
Sie kommt auf mich herzugerannt,
Sie fasst und lässt mich wieder.*

*Du murmelst so, mein Fluss, warum?
Du trägst seit alten Tagen
Ein seltsam Märchen mit dir um
Und mühst dich, es zu sagen;
Du eilst so sehr und läufst so sehr,
Als müsstest du im Land umher,
Man weiss nicht wen, drum fragen.*

*Der Himmel, blau und kinderrein,
Worin die Wellen singen,
Der Himmel ist die Seele dein:
O lass mich ihn durchdringen!
Ich tauche mich mit Geist und Sinn
Durch die vertiefte Bläue hin
Und kann sie nicht erschwingen!*

*Was ist so tief, so tief wie sie?
Die Liebe nur alleine.
Sie wird nicht satt und sättigt nie
Mit ihrem Wechselscheine.
— Schwill an, mein Fluss, und hebe dich!
Mit Grausen übergiesse mich!
Mein Leben um das deine!*

*Du weisest schmeichelnd mich zurück
Zu deiner Blumenschwelle.
So trage denn allein dein Glück,
Und wieg auf deiner Welle
Der Sonne Pracht, des Mondes Ruh:
Nach tausend Irren kehrest du
Zur ew'gen Mutterquelle!*

When Eduard Mörike died in 1875, his friend Friedrich Theodor

Vischer delivered an *oraison funèbre* that sought to forecast what would be the fate of Mörike's works among the generations to come. Never, Vischer declared, would these poems be 'popular'; nor would they ever stir men's hearts and minds like those of a Dante or a Goethe.

'But there is a community—and it can be called "small" only in comparison with the mass of the vulgar—a still community, which will find in your clear and blessed dreams refreshment and delight, and will recognize truth in them ... And this community will grow, will conquer circle after circle of readers, and one link after another will be forged between initiates who understand your work.'

This prophecy was to be fulfilled. The 'stille Gemeinde' that had, from the first, gathered around the poetry of Mörike has grown from year to year and from generation to generation; a 'still' community indeed, for no poetry has ever proved less suited for appeal to the crowd, less apt even for loud recitation, than his. It is pre-eminently a poetry of twilight, of the time that is neither completely night nor completely day:

> *Da noch der freche Tag verstummt ...*
>
> *O flaumenleichte Zeit der dunkeln Frühe! ...;*

and of subtly balanced emotions between sadness and joy, partaking of both without being either:

> *Halb ist es Lust, halb ist es Klage ...*
>
> *Zwischen süssem Schmerz, zwischen dunklem Wohlbehagen ...*

To maintain this poise, Mörike ever strove to avoid overpowering experiences, demonic forces of which he was only too well aware (for those 'clear and blessed dreams' of which Vischer speaks are nothing but deceptively idyllic surface); to avoid the insistent claims of the world, avoid elation as well as misery:

> *Lass, o Welt, o lass mich sein!*
> *Locket nicht mit Liebesgaben ...*
>
> *Wollest mit Freuden*
> *Und wollest mit Leiden*
> *Mich nicht überschütten ...*

POETIC REALISM

Some of his most successful lyrics depend for their greatest effects on this effort to balance and restrain: *Um Mitternacht* (that most perfectly poised of poems), the *Peregrina* cycle, *Denk es, o Seele, Mein Fluss*. And so Mörike became the poet, not of overpowering emotions, but of subtle half-tones and feelings; cultivating a natural sensitivity to the finest sensations (a crystal purity of soul described in the lyric which fitly ushers in his slender volume of Gedichte, *An einem Wintermorgen vor Sonnenaufgang*:

> *Einem Kristall gleicht meine Seele nun*
> *Den noch kein falscher Strahl des Lichts getroffen;*
> *Zu fluten scheint mein Geist, er scheint zu ruhn,*
> *Dem Eindruck naher Wunderkräfte offen . . .*

Mein Fluss is well adapted to show at once Mörike's greatness as a lyric poet and his peculiar vision of the 'Wunderkräfte', the wondrous powers, he felt at work in the world and in man's mind.

At its most obvious level, the poem records a particular physical experience at a particular time—that of a swimmer in a river on a sunny summer's day. In the first stanza we see the swimmer, after hesitating on the bank, wade slowly into the water; the second and third show him actually swimming; in the fourth he submerges his head, to experience, in the fifth, that not unpleasant drowning sensation which usually accompanies this feat; and in the sixth, he is carried back, by the waves, to the river bank.

But the tone of the opening invocation of the river at once suggests another level of meaning. First comes a tell-tale possessive:

> *O Fluss, mein Fluss . . . ;*

then a delicately modulated appeal:

> *Empfange nun, empfange*
> *Den sehnsuchtsvollen Leib einmal . . . ,*

with its effective pause, repetition, and enjambement so controlling the stress that it falls heavily on 'sèhnsuchtsvollen Leíb'; then echoing, tactile imagery:

> *Er* fühlt *mir schon herauf die Brust,*
> *Er* kühlt . . . ;

and then, at last, what may now be recognized as the keyword:

> *Mit Liebesschauerlust.*

For Mörike (as later in the poem we are told explicitly) another experience merges with that of the swimmer: an experience of love, more especially of physical love, with its shudder and delight.

It is hardly necessary, once this has been pointed out, to analyse in detail how the rhythm of the swimmer's progress assumes a new significance in terms of the love-relationship. The force of the verb 'hingegeben', in stanza 2, where the wave is seen as skittish girl and mothering woman at the same time, should be sufficiently plain:

> *Die Woge wieget aus und ein*
> *Die hingegebnen Glieder;*
> *Die Arme hab ich ausgespannt,*
> *Sie kommt auf mich herzugerannt,*
> *Sie fasst und lässt mich wieder.*

In stanza 3, the climax approaches, as we hear of the desire to enter, as it were, the very soul of the river beloved (once again, the verb should be noted):

> *Der Himmel ist die Seele dein,*
> *O lass mich ihn durchdringen;*

while the orgiastic fifth stanza unmistakably reminds us of the analogy:

> *Was ist so tief, so tief wie sie?*
> *Die Liebe nur alleine.*

Then follows the climax, for lover as for swimmer—again it is the verbs which amalgamate the experience of both:

> *Schwill an, mein Fluss, und hebe dich,*
> *Mit Grausen übergiesse mich ...*

After that comes inevitably the relaxation, the separation, the calm of the final stanza, as the swimmer leaves the river.

Mörike has here fused, then, two disparate experiences, and has thereby fulfilled what Wordsworth regarded as one of the prime functions of poetry:

> *The song would speak*
> *Of that interminable building, reared*
> *By observation of affinities*
> *In objects where no brotherhood exists*
> *To passive minds.*

By linking up the experience of the swimmer with one of the basic human experiences, Mörike has given the former an archetypal significance, and the latter a new sanction. There is no logical connection between swimmer and lover; but the fusion of their separate experiences into one rhythmic and emotional unit gives both a new meaning. A new pattern has been formed, new relationships have been discovered.

The last stanza of the poem suggests, however, yet a third level at which *Mein Fluss* must be read. Like *Auf dem See*, to which we have so often had to return, *Mein Fluss* assimilates in the compass of one single experience (that of the swimmer) the whole course of an individual human life. The poem begins with 'Sehnsucht', a yearning for experience:

> *Empfange nun, empfange*
> *Den sehnsuchtsvollen Leib einmal . . . ;*

this is followed by a delighted plunging into life (the last line of stanza 1, we feel, is really a cry of joy, 'Jauchzen', as it harks back through its rhyme to what has gone before); and then comes an abandonment to all life has to offer, in the passively swaying rhythms of

> *Die Woge wieget aus und ein*
> *Die hingegebnen Glieder.*

After this, we are confronted with the first *questionings*. There has been a significant progress: the poem began with an exclamation, passed to statements, and thence, at the opening of stanza 3, to a question. Life holds something unexplained, mysterious, to which an answer must be found—but where? The movement, after the abandonment of the opening, becomes hesitant:

> *Du murmelst so, / mein Fluss, / warum? . . .*

The river too is seen as anxiously seeking answers which cannot be given. And after that, in an attempt to drown all questionings, comes confusion, turmoil mental chaos. As high and low, up and down, are confounded—'Ich tauche (downwards) mich mit Geist und Sinn | Durch die vertiefte (downwards) Bläue hin | Und kann sie nicht erschwingen (upwards)'—we reach a romantic desire to be submerged in infinite variety (Wechselschein), to find death in love, love in death.

Mein Leben um das deine!

But this is overcome, in the last stanza, by the resignation so characteristic of Mörike. 'Du weisest schmeichelnd mich zurück ... So trage denn allein dein Glück.' By a subtle shift, we see the river become a symbol of human life, of the kind of life the swimmer has just lived through in his brief moment. Varied impressions, splendid and restful, but all of equal beauty and significance:

Und wieg auf deiner Welle
Der Sonne Pracht, des Mondes Ruh;

many human errors (tausend Irren); and at last greater peace, a greater calm, in a return to the origin of all. We pass from the yearning of the opening, through the delighted abandon of all life has to offer, through 'Todeslust', to the resigned acceptance of the close.

And it might well be said that Mörike has here evoked for us, through his intensely personal experience, the experience of the whole epoch to which he belonged.[1] We might call it, abstractly, the conquest of Romanticism and the attainment of the *Biedermeier* outlook. Mörike lives through, and makes his readers live through, romantic yearning for experience at any price, for love as for death, for the unattainable, in a romantic confusion of high and low; but he ends, not like Novalis with a *unio mystica*, but with contemplation of the beauty and significance of this world. Not for him the quest of the impossible—'So trage denn allein dein Glück': for him only the steady gaze on the river, on the beauty of day and night mirrored in it, and on the prospect of peace which awaits it at the end of its wanderings.

[1] This is the paradox of great art—the secluded poet, not at all, so it would seem, in touch with the great issues of his time, distils the essence of his time and expresses what future ages may recognize as its true nature and most powerful aspirations.

This is not yet, however, a joyous, delighted affirmation of the workaday world: Mörike still experiences a sense of exile, of having been banished—however gently—from significant love and life

Du weisest schmeichelnd mich zurück...

The final gaze of the poet is therefore directed towards the peace of death: the present, despite its beauty, is part of those 'tausend Irren' of which the penultimate line speaks. Mörike, like Annette von Droste-Hülshoff, is the poet of an era of transition.

(c)
GOTTFRIED KELLER
ABENDLIED

Augen, meine lieben Fensterlein,
Gebt mir schon so lange holden Schein,
Lasset freundlich Bild um Bild herein:
Einmal werdet ihr verdunkelt sein!

Fallen einst die müden Lider zu,
Löscht ihr aus, dann hat die Seele Ruh';
Tastend streift sie ab die Wanderschuh',
Legt sich auch in ihre finstre Truh'.

Noch zwei Fünklein sieht sie glimmend stehn
Wie zwei Sternlein, innerlich zu sehn,
Bis sie schwanken und dann auch vergehn,
Wie von eines Falters Flügelwehn.

Doch noch wandl' ich auf dem Abendfeld,
Nur dem sinkenden Gestirn gesellt;
Trinkt, o Augen, was die Wimper hält,
Von dem goldnen Ueberfluss der Welt!

In the work of the Swiss poet Gottfried Keller (1819–90) we reach the goal towards which both Annette von Droste-Hülshoff and Eduard Mörike had seemed to strive: that complete affirmation of the beauty and goodness of the everyday familiar world which no German poet after Goethe had found possible. In the materialist optimism of Gottfried Keller (a disciple, it must be remembered, of Ludwig Feuerbach), Poetic Realism finds at last its philosophical justification.

Abendlied opens with the delighted recognition of a familiar, friendly, beloved world, and with gratitude to the eyes which admit images of this world into man. The rhythms of the first line indicate an eagerness of affection like that of a child seeing —and calling to—someone it loves (Aúgen!) and then running towards him (meine lieben Fensterlein). 'Lieb', 'hold', 'freundlich' are keywords, reinforced by endearing diminutive (Fensterlein), many liquid consonants, and the rhyme on *ei*, associated with 'Schein', with light. The opening of the poem expresses satisfaction with a present in which the past is contained (Gebt mir *schon so lange* holden Schein). The last line of the stanza, however, leaves this delightful present to look forward to the future.

Einmal werdet ihr verdunkelt sein.

The *u* sound of 'verdunkelt', between the *ei* of 'einmal' and 'sein', seems to bring in darkness itself, as thoughts of the future impinge on present joy.

The second stanza takes this *u*, now associated with darkness, into its rhymes. We are thus given the feeling of a darkening world as the future (still implicit in 'fallen *einst*') becomes in the imagination the present. We enter a dark cottage[1] in which the soul, tired of its wanderings, takes off its travel-stained shoes and retires to rest. With the image of the eyes as *windows* admitting the sights of the world now merges another image: that of the eyes as candle-flames about to extinguish (löscht ihr aus ...). The opening word of

Tastend *streift sie ab die Wanderschuh'*

makes the darkness wonderfully concrete: it characterizes at once the uncertain groping of the tired wanderer, and the failing faculties of old age. The second stanza ends on an image which brings out unmistakably the emotional ambivalence of the situation. 'Finstre Truh.' This suggests on the one hand the bed

---

[1] Cf. *The soul's dark cottage, battered and decayed,*
Lets in new light through chinks that time has made.
(EDMUND WALLER)

(a Swiss wall-bed), which must seem delightful to the weary wanderer; on the other fear of the narrowness and darkness of the grave, fear of a death which slays the man of flesh and soul.

The process of extinction (as which the materialist must see death), Keller magnificently records in the third stanza. The world is still the beloved and familiar world of the opening—the diminutives 'Fünklein' and 'Sternlein' hark back to the 'Fensterlein' of the first stanza; but it is gradually vanishing away. The eyes, which had before admitted image after image, now appear to the dying soul as no more than two tiny sparks: as stars twinkling, not in the sky, but within the soul itself; as two candle-flames glimmering in the darkness and slowly fading, until at last (as though a night-moth had brushed against them) they too are extinguished. This gradual, gentle, painless dying away is reflected in the rhythms of lines 12 and 13. The stresses, hitherto so heavy, become less marked (as though a heart were ceasing to beat!), and the stanza comes to a gentle close with the f, w, s and l sounds of

> W*ie* von *eines* Fa*lters* Fl*ü*gelwehn.

'Vergehn', 'wehn'. The pyres are out and valediction said.

But from this contemplation of an imagined (though inevitable) future the last stanza energetically recalls us to the present. Three stresses pull the reader back:

> Dóch nóch wándl' ich auf dem Abendfeld.

From the world of the mind ('innerlich zu sehn') we look out once more, through the windows of the eyes, on the actual world. And only now do we realize what prompted the poet's meditation on death. He is walking, alone, through the fields at sunset: and the evening scene apprehended by the eyes—'Abendfeld', 'sinkendes Gestirn'—inevitably suggests thoughts of the evening of life. But, as Goethe knew, the setting sun can awaken other thoughts too:

> *Dankst du dann, am Blick dich weidend,*
> *Freien Blicks der Grossen, Holden,*
> *Wird die Sonne, rötlich scheidend,*
> *Rings den Horizont vergolden.*

Flooding the horizon with light, the setting sun can become a symbol of God's foison, of the 'golden superabundance' of this earth. 'Der goldne Überfluss der Welt'—here the physically apprehended fact (the sun 'overflowing' the horizon) merges with the consciousness of God's plenty in the whole world.

Keller's poem thus ends, as it began, with an invocation of the human eye, which is to drink its fill of the beauty of the earth, until death finally closes it. Death, thinks the materialist, is the end of all: but that obliges us all the more to savour while we can what the world has to give us. Hence the finality, the assurance, of the lines which end the poem.

Gone are the *Angst* of Annette von Droste-Hülshoff, the sense of banishment, the insecurity, of Mörike: there is resignation still, but not the shrinking, timid retiring from great issues which characterized so many of the earlier Poetic Realists. Keller knew well enough that he lived in times unpropitious for poets. He spoke more than once of his 'painful resignation':
'the painful resignation of a poet who hears every day that only in the future will poetry once again be given a beautiful reality on which to work, that only the future will once again bring forth great poets. He himself realizes this: and he feels within himself a power and energy which would enable him to create something worth while in that prophesied time, if only he could live in it. There is within him a burning desire to base his poetry on a life fully lived—but he cannot do this, because he knows that everything merely anticipated is *false idealism*, and because he is too proud to ally himself with the poetry of an irrevocable past.'
Yet Keller accepted these limitations without demur, and without undue sadness and introspection. 'There is something healthy', he wrote, 'in every age, and on that the poet must seize: for here he will find the material for beautiful, even if episodic, poetry.'

(d)
THEODOR STORM
HYAZINTHEN

Fern hallt Musik; doch hier ist stille Nacht,
Mit Schlummerduft anhauchen mich die Pflanzen;

Ich habe immer, immer dein gedacht,
Ich möchte schlafen; aber du musst tanzen.

Es hört nicht auf, es rast ohn' Unterlass;
Die Kerzen brennen und die Geigen schreien,
Es teilen und es schliessen sich die Reihen,
Und Alle glühen; aber du bist blass.

Und du musst tanzen; fremde Arme schmiegen
Sich an dein Herz; o leide nicht Gewalt!
Ich seh' dein weisses Kleid vorüberfliegen
Und deine leichte, zärtliche Gestalt. — —

Und süsser strömend quillt der Duft der Nacht
Und träumerischer aus dem Kelch der Pflanzen.
Ich habe immer, immer dein gedacht;
Ich möchte schlafen; aber du musst tanzen.

With the Schleswig poet Theodor Storm (1817–88) we return from the sunlit world of Keller to one more akin to that of Mörike and Annette von Droste-Hülshoff. His most characteristic productions are in a minor key, even when their ostensible subject is praise—praise of homeland, or of family life. Constantly, Storm gives expression to nostalgia for a simple life and loyalty that the poet knows to be passing, and for a love lost or never attained. Of love-poetry, Storm has said:
'In such poetry, all must be full of *latent passion*, everything only suggested and yet powerfully evocative; all must be in darkness, lit up, of a sudden, by a blinding flash of lightning which may—in different circumstances—terrify or delight us.'
Nowhere in Storm's work is this 'latent passion' more strikingly revealed or nostalgic emotion more magically evoked, than in *Hyazinthen*, a poem Thomas Mann has put to striking new uses in *Tonio Kröger*.

The slow, reflective movement of the poem is suggested at once by its first line, with its three stresses, one closely after the other, followed by a pause.

Férn hállt Musik; ...

Soft consonants (*l* and *n* predominate) and dark vowels (*a*, *u*) combine with this slow movement to convey languor; a languor which distils itself most purely in the unbroken second line, with its unmistakable keyword, bearing the main stress: 'Schlummerduft'. All sounds of the outside world—the music of which the first line speaks—are far away ('fern'); the poet is conscious of nothing but the stillness of night, and the heavy, drowsy odour of the hyacinths. The pang of remembrance, recorded in the third line with its insistent repetition ('immer, immer'), sinks into vague, inactive regret in the last line of the stanza.

> *Ich möchte schlafen ...*

Dark vowels ('schlafen', 'tanzen'—the vowel of all the rhyme-words of stanza 1), soft consonants, grammatical pause, frequent stresses, reintroduce and reinforce the slow movement of the opening, as though the odour of hyacinths had sapped the poet's strength.

But even at the end of this first stanza, thought of a 'Du', another being with different desires and more active longings, had obtruded themselves: and now in the second stanza the sounds of the outside world—so far away in the first!—thrust themselves assertively and painfully into the poet's consciousness. *Ei* rhymes, associated with 'schreien', replace the *a* of the first stanza, which had conveyed so much of the stillness and darkness of the night. The altered rhyme-scheme (abba instead of abab) allows these *ei* sounds to follow more closely, more obtrusively one upon the other. Light and noise, the sights and sounds of a bustling ballroom, break in on the darkness and silence of solitude.

> *Die Kerzen brennen und die Geigen schreien,*
> *Es teilen und es schliessen sich die Reihen,*
> *Und alle glühen ...*

The movement too is swifter, we seem to be whirled from line to line as the dancers are whirled in the dance. But this movement, this bright and noisy world, is disturbed by the evocation of one who is pale in the midst of a glowing crowd.

> *... aber du bist blass.*

The dark vowels and soft consonants are, by now, familiar. They link the dancer immediately to the poet and his languorous solitude. The poet sees her as *in* the ballroom but not *of* it; as belonging, like himself, to the hyacinths and their sweet, heavy, intoxicating scent.

Between the second stanza and the third there is hardly any pause. The pale dancer may not belong to the ballroom, may differ from the other dancers, may be akin to the solitary poet outside—but she is swept on resistlessly.

> *... aber du bist blass.*
> *Und du musst tanzen ...*

At this point, in the broken enjambed lines that follow, the poem achieves an emotional intensity hitherto unsuspected. This is the 'lightning-flash' of which Storm had spoken, the flash which lights up 'with a blinding glare' the darkness of 'latent passion'. Seeing his beloved caught in the arms of strangers, the poet calls out to her to renounce this world which violates her loneliness. But she dances on ...

> *Ich seh' dein weisses Kleid vorüberfliegen*
> *Und deine leichte, zärtliche Gestalt.*

The *ei* vowel, so consistently associated with the ballroom and all it stands for; the white light dress; the swift and easy movement—all separate the dancer from the poet. However closely linked in his solitude, she belongs even more to the ballroom, to the world of light and turmoil and movement.

And so, after a long pause of exhausted contemplation, the poet allows the odour of the hyacinths to reassert, with added potency, their languorous charm.

> *Und süsser strömend quillt der Duft der Nacht*
> *Und träumerischer aus dem Kelch der Pflanzen.*

Successive adverbs and adjectives associate with the hyacinths suggestions of sweetness, an oozing flow, the odour of night itself, dreaminess; suggestions reinforced by long vowels and liquid consonants. The verse-movement seems to bring two waves of this sweet, enervating narcotic odour, each more potent than the rest. The first of these comes with the first line of the stanza; the second with the significantly isolated, heavily stressed 'und träumerischer'. The *a* rhyme too predominates once again.

There is no revolt; there is only vague, dreamy recognition and regret, in the stammering repetition of slow, broken lines which ended the first stanza and now end the poem:

> *Ich habe immer, immer dein gedacht;*
> *Ich möchte schlafen; aber du musst tanzen.*

The experience recorded in *Hyazinthen* might be described as that of a man who feels himself far removed from the noise and bustle of the outside world (*Fern hallt Musik*), and suddenly becomes conscious of its claims. At first these claims seem only painful and disturbing—they are embodied in the glare of candles, in the wail of fiddles, in hot purposelessness. Gradually, however, the poet realizes that he is himself bound to that world through what he loves most, something, someone, belonging both to his own solitude and to the world. The pale dancer forges a link between the lonely watcher among the hyacinths and the gregarious, bustling ballroom. But this realization brings neither joy nor relief. After a momentary, passionate protest the poet relapses into a deeper solitude, disturbed only by constant thoughts of a gulf now recognized as unbridgeable. With consummate delicacy and tact, Storm conveys this experience through rhythms and sounds, and through a selection of isolated, of very few, sense-impressions: the odour of hyacinths, the glare of candles, the sound of violins, the sight of a pale dancer in a white dress whirling past the lighted window of a ballroom. It is both a basic human experience which is thus conveyed, and one forced upon German poets at a specific time: a time in which the gulf yawned more widely than ever between the ideals of poets and those of the community for which they wrote.

No wonder then that Thomas Mann, who felt more strongly than any of his contemporaries the inescapable conflict between poet and citizen, 'Künstler' and 'Bürger', art and life, confessed himself so powerfully drawn to Theodor Storm and his lyric poetry.

CHAPTER TEN

Munich Interlude and Naturalist Reaction

PAUL HEYSE
TREUESTE LIEBE

Ein Bruder und eine Schwester,
Nichts Treuers kennt die Welt,
Kein Goldkettlein hält fester,
Als eins am andern hält.

Zwei Liebsten so oft sich scheiden,
Denn Minne verglüht geschwind.
Geschwister in Lust und Leiden
Die bleiben sich hold gesinnt,

So treulich als wie zusammen
Der Mond und die Erde gehn,
Der ewigen Sterne Flammen
Alle Nacht beieinander stehn.

Die Engel im himmlischen Reigen
Frohlocken dem holden Bund,
Wenn Bruder und Schwester sich neigen
Und küssen sich auf den Mund.

In the first essay of his *Unzeitgemässe Betrachtungen*—an essay entitled *David Friedrich Strauss als Bekenner und Schriftseller*—Friedrich Nietzsche analysed the state of German cultural life in the early years of the Second Empire. He found prevalent the belief that German civilization had conquered French civilization in the Franco-Prussian war. The majority of his countrymen were satisfied with the cultural *status quo*, convinced 'that the best seeds of culture had either been sown or were already luxuriantly in bloom'. This, declared Nietzsche, accounted for the self-confidence of certain German poets and writers, 'journalists and fabricators of novels, tragedies, songs and histories', who felt themselves sacrosanct, spoke in magisterial tones, issued their 'Collected Works' and had themselves proclaimed as writers of classic status.

Such men, said Nietzsche, were mistaken. German arms, not German culture, conquered in the war. If culture consists in 'unity of style in all the manifestations of a people's cultural life', then the French could lay far greater claim to it than the Germans: for with all their learning and (unco-ordinated) knowledge, the Germans lived 'in barbarism, that is: absence of style, or the chaotic confusion of all styles'. Such barbarism Nietzsche saw everywhere—in German dress-styles, in furniture, architecture, painting and poetry. If this state of affairs were allowed to continue, then the long-desired unification of Germany could only result in 'the defeat, even extirpation of the German Spirit in favour of the German Empire'. ('Die Niederlage, ja Exstirpation des deutschen Geistes zugunsten des deutschen Reiches.')

The justice of Nietzsche's charge may be demonstrated by an examination of the poetry of the 'Munich School' (a number of poets attracted to his capital by King Maximilian II of Bavaria), and that of a number of fashionable writers whose elegantly bound volumes of lyric poetry adorned ladies' drawing-rooms in the 70's of the last century. Many such 'Goldschnittlyriker' have somehow found their way into the *Oxford Book of German Verse* (first published 1911, second edition 1927, now badly in need of revision); and it is some of these that will now be briefly examined.

The first characteristic of all the poets touched by Nietzsche's strictures is a conscious divorce from reality. From beginning industrialization they tried to take flight into a realm of absolute beauty. As Emanuel Geibel (1815–84) explicitly acknowledged, these poets often modelled themselves on Platen:

> *Das wollen wir Platen nicht vergessen*
> *Dass wir in seiner Schule gesessen;*
> *Die strenge Pflicht, die römische Zucht*
> *Sie trug uns alle gute Frucht;*

but they would not concern themselves, as Platen so often did, with contemporary problems. Apart from genuflections to King and Church—

> *Fern von dem Schwarm, der unbesonnen*
> *Altar und Herz in Trümmer schlägt,*
> *Quillt mir der Dichtung heil'ger Bronnen*
> *Am Felsen, der die Kirche trägt,*
> (GEIBEL, *An den König von Preussen*)

such poets shunned contact with political and social questions of the day.

> *Es trägt die Kunst ihr eisern Los mit Qualen,*
> *Lass, Herr, die Göttliche in ihrer Hoheit*
> *Nicht untergehn, ein Opfer der Vandalen*
> *In dieses Meinungsstreits ergrimmter Rohheit.*

This set the Munich poets apart from the political poets of the earlier part of the century; but they were equally remote from the Poetic Realists, who dealt so lovingly and carefully with their immediate surroundings. From their own world, the Munich poets fled in imagination to other countries (Paul Heyse's Italian Song-book is, thanks to Hugo Wolf, a well-known example) and into the historic past. But most of all, they were concerned to create a dream-world into which they might escape. Wilhelm Herz's *Unter blühenden Bäumen* is a case in point:

> *Unter blühenden Bäumen*
> *Lieg' ich in Einsamkeit,*
> *Von alter Zeit,*
> *Von alter Liebe zu träumen.*
>
> *Sehnsüchtige Stille ringsherum,*
> *Nur Bienengesumm*
> *Und fern im Tal ein Glockenklang:*
> *Ob Hochzeitläuten,*
> *Ob Grabgesang,*
> *Ich will's nicht deuten.*
>
> *Lenzwolken ziehn mit sanftem Flug.*
> *O Jugendleben,*
> *Das lang verblich,*
> *O Frühlingsweben,*
> *Was lockst du mich?*
> *Goldsonnige Fernen lachen.*

> *Neues Hoffen, neuer Trug!*
> *Lenz, des Zaubers ist genug!*
> *Nein, wieg mich ein*
> *Zur süssen Ruh*
> *Und decke du*
> *Mein träumend Haupt mit Blüten zu!*
> *Rosige Dämmrung hüllt mich ein:*
> *O seliges Verschollensein,*
> *Schlafen und nimmer erwachen!*

'To dream of a time and a love that are past.' We have met such a flight before—in German Romanticism; but there it had been achieved in the startlingly original ways already discussed. Herz's poem is nothing but a tissue of vague generalities

> *(O Jugendleben*
> *Das lang verblich,*
> *O Frühlingsweben,*
> *Was lockst du mich?)*

and conscious archaisms ('mein träumend Haupt'); it demands no attention on the part of the reader. 'Ich will's nicht deuten' might be called its key-line. It is a piece of escapist self-indulgence by writer and reader alike.

The Munich poets and their like wrote on outworn themes in outworn forms. Nothing, for instance, could be more purely derivative than Hermann Lingg's *Immer leiser wird mein Schlummer*:

> *Immer leiser wird mein Schlummer,*
> *Nur wie Schleier liegt mein Kummer*
> *Zitternd über mir.*
> *Oft im Traume hör' ich dich*
> *Rufen drauss vor meiner Tür,*
> *Niemand wacht und öffnet dir;*
> *Ich erwach' und weine bitterlich.*
>
> *Ja, ich werde sterben müssen,*
> *Eine andre wirst du küssen,*
> *Wenn ich bleich und kalt;*
> *Eh' die Maienlüfte wehen,*
> *Eh' die Drossel singt im Wald:*

MUNICH INTERLUDE AND NATURALIST REACTION

> *Willst du mich noch einmal sehen,*
> *Komm, o komme bald!*

Lingg, like Herz, is wallowing[1] in vague emotions, working on stock-responses evoked by stock-situations. The dreamer thinks he hears his beloved call outside—a theme often treated by the Romantics (Eichendorff has a lovely variation of it in *Auf meines Kindes Tod*); the dreamer, on awaking, 'weeps bitterly' (Heine); the dying man knows that his beloved will kiss another after his death (Volkslied, Romantics, Heine). There is neither originality nor appropriateness in rhythm or phrasing. The poem moves along in skipping measures which contrast absurdly with the 'sadness' of the subject. This indeed is 'the currency of poetry, not poetry itself'.

For the work of all these poets is, in the worst sense, 'literary', without relation to life or to experience. This applies as much to the 'gay' as to the 'serious' lyric—to such poems, for instance, as the much-loved *Alt-Heidelberg*[2] of Joseph Victor von Scheffel (1826–86); a poem in which Herr von Scheffel visualizes himself as a happy, carefree scholar, riding through the countryside genteelly kissing innkeepers' daughters.

> *Und stechen mich die Dornen,*
> *Und wird mir's drauss zu kahl,*
> *Geb' ich dem Ross die Spornen* (! !)
> *Und reit' ins Neckartal.*

No wonder that Scheffel was the first of those poets attacked by the brothers Hart in *Kritische Waffengänge*: poets 'who ceaselessly chew the end of our ancestors' love and drinking songs'.

Often, too, poetry was used as a means of instruction. Professors of history and archaeology versified history and archaeology, travellers described foreign countries. Felix Dahn's *Gotentreue* is a fair example:

---

[1] The word is not too strong:

> *Ja, ich werde sterben müssen,*
> *Eine andre wirst du küssen,*
> *Wenn ich bleich und kalt ...*

[2] From *Der Trompeter von Säckingen* (1854).

Erschlagen lag mit seinem Heer
Der König der Goten, Theodemer.

Die Hunnen jauchzten auf blut'ger Wal;
Die Geier stiessen herab zutal.

Der Mond schien hell; der Wind pfiff kalt;
Die Wölfe heulten im Föhrenwald.

Drei Männer ritten durchs Heidegefild,
Den Helm zerschroten, zerhackt den Schild.

Der erste über dem Sattel quer
Trug seines Königs zerbrochenen Speer.

Der zweite des Königs Kronhelm trug,
Den mittendurch ein Schlachtbeil schlug.

Der dritte barg mit treuem Arm
Ein verhüllt Geheimnis im Mantel warm.

So kamen sie an die Donau tief,
Und der erste hielt mit dem Ross und rief:

'Ein zerhauener Helm, ein zerspellter Speer —
Vom Reiche der Goten blieb nicht mehr!'

Und der zweite sprach: 'In die Wellen dort
Versenkt den traurigen Gotenhort!

Dann springen wir nach dem Uferrand —
Was säumest du, Vater Hildebrand?'

'Und tragt ihr des Königs Kron' und Speer,
Ihr treuen Gesellen, ich habe mehr!'

Auf schlug er seinen Mantel weich:
'Hier trag' ich der Goten Hort und Reich.

Und habt ihr gerettet Speer und Kron',
Ich habe gerettet des Königs Sohn.

Erwache, mein Knabe, ich grüsse dich,
Du König der Goten, Jungdieterich!'

We note at once the significant archaisms ('Wal', 'zerschroten', 'zerspellt') and the self-conscious introduction of historical figures; the clumsy versification ('herab zutal') and monotonous rhythm; the elaborate assumption of a *Volkslied* robe which slips off again and again. Dahn's ballad is of a piece with his monstrously long historical novels,[1] and with the equally still-born 'heroic' epics of Heyse, Geibel and Scheffel.

For an epitome of Munich poetry at its worst, we must go to the poem by Paul Heyse reprinted at the head of this chapter: *Treueste Liebe*. Its rhythm, its movement, tells us at once what we are to expect. There is no precise emotion *in* the poem at all[2] —it is, if anywhere, all *behind* it. Rhythmically, the work is dead. Nor must the images be followed out.

> *Kein Goldkettlein hält fester*
> *Als eins am andern hält.*

But a little golden chain ('Goldkettlein') is not at all firm, unbreakable. It holds suggestions of preciousness (which Heyse obviously wishes to convey), but hardly of firmness. Or again:

> *Geschwister in Lust und Leiden*
> *Die bleiben sich hold gesinnt,*
> *So treulich als wie zusammen*
> *Der Mond und die Erde gehn.*

How obviously untrue to experience; how inappropriate the image to the main statement! We can all think of plenty of brothers and sisters who do not 'go together as faithfully as earth and moon'. Characteristic of Munich poetry are once again the archaisms (denn Minne verglüht geschwind); the stock-phrase (der ewigen Sterne Flammen; die Engel im himmlischen Reigen); and above all, the strained pretty-pretty calendar picture of the final stanza.

The spectacle presented by the Munich School must be a familiar one to English readers: the later pages of the *Oxford Book of English Verse* will suggest many analogies. It is the familiar wilderness in which the voice of G. M. Hopkins cried in vain:

---

[1] It is indeed introduced into the best-known of these, *Ein Kampf um Rom*.
[2] Cf. D. H. Lawrence's letter to E. Collings, 14 November 1912: 'I can see all the poetry at the *back* of your verse—but there isn't much inside the lines.'

'I cut myself off from the use of "ere", "wellnigh", "what time", "say not" (for "do not say") because, though dignified, they neither belong to nor could ever arise from, or be the elevation of, ordinary modern speech. For it seems that the poetical language of the age should be the current language heightened, to any degree heightened and unlike it, but not (I mean normally: passing freaks and graces are another thing) an obsolete one.'
In seeking to escape a world grown too ugly, these poets severed themselves from that language of common speech which alone can give life to poetry.

An organized revolt against the authority of Munich began, in Germany, in the 1880's. The *Kritische Waffengänge* edited by the brothers Hart (1882-4) bitterly attacked Scheffel, Heyse, and many others. 'What we lack', declared Julius Hart, 'is truth and manliness; what we lack is writers who take life seriously.' According to a programme laid down (with characteristic exaggeration) by Arno Holz in *Die Kunst, ihr Wesen und ihre Gesetze* (1891), literature was to copy life as slavishly as possible; to deal with the triviality, the beauty and the ugliness of the modern city.

> *O wie so anders, als die Herren singen,*
> *Stellt sich der Lenz hier in der Grossstadt ein,*
> *Er weiss sich auch noch anders zu verdingen,*
> *Als nur als Vogelsang und Vollmondschein.*
> *Er heult als Südwind um die morschen Dächer*
> *Und wimmert wie ein kranker Komödiant,*
> *Bis licht die Sonne ihren goldnen Fächer*
> *Durch Wolken lächelnd auseinander spannt.*
>
> . . . .
>
> *Schon legt der Bäcker sich auf Osterkringel,*
> *Und seine Fenster putzt der Photograph,*
> *Der blaue Milchmann mit der gelben Klingel*
> *Stört uns tagtäglich nun den Morgenschlaf.*
> *Mit Kupfern illustriert die Frauenzeitung*
> *Die neusten Frühjahrsmoden aus Paris,*
> *Ihr Feuilleton bringt zur Geschmacksverbreitung*
> *Den neusten Schundroman von Dumas fils.*
>
> (HOLZ: *Lieder eines Modernen*)

But Naturalism, however influential, need not long detain us—for it produced no lyric poet of any importance.[1] Poetry was given new subject-matter, but its forms remained the old familiar ones in the work of Karl Henckell, Julius Hart and Gerhart Hauptmann. Such experiments with form as were made—notably Arno Holz's 'Mittelachsenverse'[2]—proved ultimately barren. It was not given to Arno Holz to infuse new life into the German lyric, and the rhythms of his *Phantasus* are as dead as the rhymed lilting verses they were intended to supplant.

[1] The only exception is a peripheral figure: Richard Dehmel (1863–1920). Dehmel had, however, little contact with the actual leaders of the Naturalist revolt.

[2] An excellent account of these will be found in A. Closs: *The Genius of the German Lyric*, pp. 387–8.

CHAPTER ELEVEN

Chaos and Control

(a)
C. F. MEYER
SCHWARZSCHATTENDE KASTANIE

> Schwarzschattende Kastanie,
> Mein windgeregtes Sommerzelt,
> Du senkst zur Flut dein weit Geäst,
> Dein Laub, es durstet und es trinkt,
> Schwarzschattende Kastanie!
> Im Porte badet junge Brut
> Mit Hader oder Lustgeschrei.
> Und Kinder schwimmen leuchtend weiss
> Im Gitter deines Blätterwerks,
> Schwarzschattende Kastanie!
> Und dämmern See und Ufer ein
> Und rauscht vorbei das Abendboot,
> So zuckt aus roter Schiffslatern'
> Ein Blitz und wandert auf dem Schwung
> Der Flut, gebrochnen Lettern gleich,
> Bis unter deinem Laub erlischt
> Die rätselhafte Flammenschrift,
> Schwarzschattende Kastanie!

The Munich poets had tended to see themselves as heirs of Platen, as preservers of form in a formless age: and they made it easy to suspect, as so many subsequent critics have done, any strict cult of form of hiding emptiness. Platen himself fell into disrepute, as though the sins of the children were to be visited on the fathers. It is therefore fortunate that a legitimate heir now appears on the scene, who—though he did not rout these bastard Platenides at the time—at least justifies Platen and his endeavours to posterity. That heir was Conrad Ferdinand Meyer

(1825–98). Meyer, like his great predecessor, stemmed from an old aristocratic family (a family, in this case, of Swiss patricians); he too felt, with some justice, physically abnormal and degenerate; he too sought to distance emotion and to conquer the chaos of grief by the severest emphasis on form.

But for the possessive pronoun in the second line, the poem we have selected to represent Meyer seems entirely *objective*. It seems to attempt purely to describe a chestnut-tree in summer. The very sound, however, of the opening invocation to the tree, so frequently echoed throughout the poem, suggests other levels of meaning. Meyer is a *symboliste* before Verlaine, whose word-music ('de la musique avant toute chose') haunts the mind in similar fashion.

Schwárzschättende Kastánie.

The two opening stresses make the line unusually weighty and impressive; the dominant *sch* and *w* sounds seem to muffle it, to convey a mystery or a threat; while the dominant vowel (associated with 'schwarz', 'Schatten') makes concrete the very darkness of which the line speaks.

The second line passes beyond mere invocation to suggest an attitude towards this shadowing darkness. The shade is felt as cool and refreshing—as a tent in summer, agitated by the breeze. The unmistakably ominous note of the opening line is all but forgotten. The verse moves lightly, almost trippingly, along—and (in strong contrast to the opening) *ei*, *i* and *e* predominate among the vowels. The suggestions of the tent-image appear to be strengthened by the following lines, which speak of 'slaking thirst': we are shown parched leaves refreshingly immersed in the waters of the stream. But heavier, more dragging rhythms here replace the tripping measures of the second line. The keyword is 'senkst':

Du senkst zur Flut dein weit Geäst.

After the fourth line, with its reflective pause, we then return—sink down, are dragged back—to the sonorous, ominous opening.

The poem now leaves the tree itself and passes to another, a more cheerful sight: that of children bathing in the river, quarrelling or shouting gleefully. That the children are designated as 'junge Brut'—a playful humorous term—seems to introduce a light-hearted note. But at once a startling contrast is introduced. The gleaming white bodies of the bathing children are offset by the black-shadowing foliage which overhangs them. Our attitude to the chestnut-tree changes. It is now, not a refreshing tent in the summer's heat, but part of that prison-house whose shades enclose the growing boy.

> *Im* Gitter *deines Blätterwerks.*

A prison or cage, something alien and inimical enclosing innocence, is at once suggested. The now familiar invocation ('schwarzschattende Kastanie') assumes therefore a doubly ominous ring. More and more meaning accumulates around it, and the careful exploratory movement of the first (end-stopped) lines gives way, as if under pressure, to a more flowing movement. The poet is being impelled towards full knowledge.

The last section speaks, significantly, of the coming of darkness. Dusk is falling: and the red lantern of a passing ship seems to figure strange broken characters on the black waves. The rhythm too is broken as it had not been before:

> *So zuckt aus roter Schiffslatern*
> *Ein Blitz / Und wandert auf dem Schwung*
> *Der Flut, / gebrochnen Lettern gleich . . .*

Where there had been light relieved only by a small tent of refreshing darkness, darkness now reigns supreme, relieved only by occasional flashes of lurid light. From a sunlit comprehensible world we have passed to one of shadow and mystery. 'Gebrochne Lettern'. 'Rätselhafte Flammenschrift'. And even such glimpses of light as are vouchsafed give way before the tree.

> *Bis unter deinem Laub erlischt*
> *Die rätselhafte Flammenschrift,*
> *Schwarzschattende Kastanie!*

In the penultimate line the familiar *a* vowel, the hushing *sch* consonants begin to assert themselves, to dominate the last as they had the first. And universal darkness buries all.

The chestnut-tree, which had first been seen as a patch of shadow in a sun-lit landscape, had then turned into a black cage imprisoning the white shapes of children at play: it now appears part of an all-enveloping darkness, swallowing up even such little, mysterious light as the ship's lantern and its trailing reflection could yield. An exploration of reality, even of so lovely a fragment of it as this chestnut-tree in summer, leads to mystery, foreboding, darkness, death. The sunlit world of the Poetic Realists is gone for ever. Yet Meyer, in his greatest lyrics, does not refuse to see the dark which surrounds us. An Oedipus, not a Jocasta, he seeks truth, however hard to bear:

> *Der Dichter nur kann euch die Fäden zeigen*
> *Des wundersam verworrenen Gewebes,*
> *Ursprung und Wachstum dieser dunklen Dinge ...*

And when he finds truth terrible and chaotic, he does not break down, but opposes his own light to the darkness, his will to chaos. The three lines about the poet's function just quoted are capped by a fourth, characteristic of Meyer and all *true* heirs of Platen:

> *Und Herrschaft lehren über euer Herz!*[1]

(b)
STEFAN GEORGE
MÜHLE LASS DIE ARME STILL...

> *Mühle lass die arme still*
> *Da die haide ruhen will.*
> *Teiche auf den tauwind harren·*
> *Ihrer pflegen lichte lanzen*
> *Und die kleinen bäume starren*
> *Wie getünchte ginsterpflanzen.*
>
> *Weisse kinder schleifen leis*
> *Ueberm see auf blindem eis*
> *Nach dem segentag· sie kehren*
> *Heim zum dorf in stillgebeten·*
> *DIE beim fernen gott der lehren·*
> *DIE schon bei dem naherflehten.*
>
> *Kam ein pfiff am grund entlang?*
> *Alle lampen flackern bang.*
>
> Zur Einweihung des neuen Züricher Stadttheaters.

> *War es nicht als ob es riefe?*
> *Es empfingen ihre bräute*
> *Schwarze knaben aus der tiefe ...*
> *Glocke läute glocke läute!*

Stefan George (1868–1933), strongly influenced in his beginnings by the French symbolistes, reacted alike against the emptiness of Munich poetry and the excesses of Naturalism. He tried to avoid the appeal to stock-responses, the loose and vague collocation of words and images, the trite phrases of poets who, in Livingston Lowes' phrase, 'ensconce themselves like hermit crabs in the cast-off shells of their predecessors'; and he condemned at the same time the naturalist attempt to confound Art and Nature. In the privately-printed *Blätter für die Kunst*, a journal he edited, George wrote:

'We do not want to invent histories, but to convey moods (Stimmungen); not to reflect, but to present; not to entertain but to impress. Poets of former times wrote their works—or wished these works to be considered—as illustrations of an opinion or a conception of the world. We see in every event, in every age, only a means of artistic excitation (ein mittel künstlerischer erregung).'

The nineties are upon us.

Superficially, *Mühle lass die arme still ...*[1] does 'invent a history'. The poem tells of a still wintry landscape just before the thaw; of white-clad children sliding on the ice after coming from confirmation 'with God in their hearts' (a God to whom they are nearer than they think, for they will soon die); of the flickering of the lamps carried by the children; how the girls sink into the thawing lake and are dragged down among the black tentacular waterplants; and of the ringing of the alarm bell announcing the disaster.

The poem's significance lies less, however, in the events described than in the feelings evoked in and through that description. 'We do not want to invent histories, but to convey moods.' It

---

[1] The poem has been taken from the first (earliest) volume of the George *Gesamtausgabe*, a volume entitled: *Hymen·Pilgerfahrten·Algabal·* (1890–92). The arrangement of this and the following volumes is so exquisite,·the poems so enhance one another in the position which George has assigned to them, that no *selection* can do full justice to George.

begins with an invocation to the mill, traditionally a symbol of divine justice and retribution ('The mills of God grind slowly ...'). The mill has, we learn, been motionless for some time (hence 'Lass die arme *still*' instead of 'lass die arme *stehen*'), and the poet asks it to remain like that. The landscape does not need, does not want, the wind to blow. The second line makes implicit a desire for rest, for inertia. Line 3, however, introduces 'harren': an air of expectation, apprehension, of a wind which will bring the thaw to ponds and lakes. The alliteration (Teiche, tauwind) makes this third line ring with the sound of footsteps on ice, and contrasts with the *l* alliteration of the following line, in whose softer sounds the thaw is already suggested.

Ihrer pflegen lichte lanzen.

Simultaneously, the line just quoted brings a sense of security, and apprehension: 'pflegen', as a mother would, or a nurse; 'lanzen', borne by soldiers to ward off danger. This ambiguity of attitude is further reinforced by the last two lines of the first stanza. The 'white washed' plants ('getüncht') give the snow-landscape on the one hand the appearance of a toy, something that can be handled without danger: at the same time, though, they seem to transform it into an unreal, a nightmare scene of which man would do well to beware.

Into this undecided, uneasily apprehensive landscape the poet now introduces, at the opening of the second stanza, white-clad children sliding on the ice.

Weísse kínder schleífen leís
Ueberm seé auf blíndem eís.

Whiteness and silence, the smooth gliding of the children (becoming bolder in 'überm see') are all made concrete in stresses, vowels and consonants. Ominously, the sentence comes to rest on—seems to glide towards—the last words of the second line: 'auf blindem eis'. 'Blindem', harking back to 'kinder', conveys the indifference of this winter-world to the children innocently at play in it; an indifference which makes the last three lines, with

GEORGE: MÜHLE LASS DIE ARME STILL...

their invocation of a 'gott der lehren' who is nearer to the children than they think, assume a terrible irony.

So far the poem, for all its apprehensive atmosphere and variety of metrical stress, has moved slowly and evenly, statement following on statement, line on line, in unbroken succession. The last stanza, however, begins with a *question*, and the even keel of the rhythm is disturbed at last.

> *Kám ein pfíff am gründ entláng?*
> *Álle lámpen fláckern báng.*

'Flackern' is obviously the keyword here. How well different grades of stress falling on the same (*a*) vowel render this flickering! The wind has come at last: the disturbance so feared at the opening has not been avoided after all. Then, at once, follows another question, more ominous than the first:

> *War es nicht als ob es riefe?*;

and that, in its turn, is followed by the eerie picture of dark wooers dragging the white-clad girls into the depths of the pond. The rising cadences, falling again at the end, render at once the weird uprising from the depths, and the dragging down of the children:

> *Es empfíngen íhre bräute*
> *Schwárze knáben aus der tíefe.*

The girls, we remember, have just been confirmed, consecrated to their God, with Whom their prayers still are. Instead of 'brides of God', however, they become brides of dark forces rising from the deep. Is that God's will, God's law? Is it an instance of the grinding of the mills of God that the innocents should perish?

At this point occurs a distinct break in the pattern of the poem. Hitherto, the rhyme-scheme had been: aa (masculine) bcbc (feminine); and the feminine rhymes had been interlinked by assonance (e.g. h*a*rren l*a*nzen st*a*rren pfl*a*nzen). Now, in the third stanza, that pattern is broken. 'Bräute' (the fearful irony of 'brides of the dark' as well as 'brides of God') and 'läute' (the ringing of the bell announcing calamity) disrupt the pattern, for they have no assonantic link with the other feminine rhymes of the stanza. Our sense of disaster, of destruction, crystallizes here.

It is no accident that the 'story' content of the poem, the story of the little girls and their death, should be so veiled, so difficult to follow at a first reading. Mystery, apprehension, are essential elements of the mood, the feeling about life, George conveys to his readers. This is how George felt the winter-landscape: and this is also how he apprehended life, the life of his times. The poem begins calmly, with a prayer for the continuance of calm and inertia; then follows rising fear, clutching at faith, destruction of faith as the (half-expected) disaster comes; and at last the outcry: 'Ring the alarm-bell!', a complete reversal of the opening demand for calm and peace. One is reminded of another poetic invocation of the thaw: of Nietzsche's chapter in *Also sprach Zarathustra*:

'When the water has planks, when bridges and railings span the stream, then he is not believed who says: "All things are a'flowing".

'But even the simple contradict him: "What", say the simple, "all things are a'flowing? But there are planks and railings over the stream!"

'Over the stream all is stable, all the values of things, the bridges and bearings, all 'good' and 'evil': all these stand firm!"—

'And when the hard winter comes, the stream-tamer, then even the wisest learn distrust; and it is not only the simple who then say: "Is not everything—standing still?"

' "At bottom all is standing still"—that is true winter-doctrine, good for an unproductive time, a great comfort for hibernators and fire-side loungers.

' "At bottom all is standing still"—the thaw-wind preaches against that!

'The thaw-wind, a bull who does not draw the plough—a raging bull, a destroyer, who breaks the ice with his angry horns! But ice—breaks bridges!

'O my brothers, is not everything a'flowing now? Have not all the railings and bridges fallen into the water? Who would now hold fast to "good" and "evil"?

' "Woe to us! Hail to us! The thaw-wind has come!"

'So should you preach, o my brothers, in every street.'

GEORGE: DER HERR DER INSEL

But in George's poem, the thaw brings no relief. George felt only, at this period, the demonic forces at work beneath the outward calm and prosperity of the early Wilhelmine Empire; he saw all mankind, at all times, at the mercy of dark irrational powers. He communicated his apprehensions in this masterly symboliste poem in much the same way as C. F. Meyer communicated *his* apprehensions in *Schwarzschattende Kastanie*.

(c)

GEORGE

DER HERR DER INSEL

Die fischer überliefern dass im süden
Auf einer insel reich an zimt und öl
Und edlen steinen die im sande glitzern
Ein vogel war der wenn am boden fussend
Mit seinem schnabel honer stämme krone
Zerpflücken konnte· wenn er seine flügel
Gefärbt wie mit dem saft der Tyrer-schnecke
Zu schwerem niedrem flug erhoben: habe
Er einer dunklen wolke gleichgesehn.
Des tages sei er im gehölz verschwunden·
Des abends aber an den strand gekommen·
Im kühlen windeshauch von salz und tang
Die süsse stimme hebend dass delfine
Die freunde des gesanges näher schwammen
Im meer voll goldner federn goldner funken.
So habe er seit urbeginn gelebt·
Gescheiterte nur hätten ihn erblickt.
Denn als zum erstenmal die weissen segel
Der menschen sich mit günstigem geleit
Dem eiland zugedreht sei er zum hügel
Die ganze teure stätte zu beschaun gestiegen·
Verbreitet habe er die grossen schwingen
Verscheidend in gedämpften schmerzeslauten.

George, as has been seen, was apprehensive of the trends of his time, and particularly disturbed by the state of German culture: the state of affairs described in Nietzsche's *Unzeitgemässe Betrachtungen*. But what was the place of the poet in a world such as

George lived in? A world of mass-production, whose values were increasingly material? *Der Herr der Insel* suggests the answer of the George of the 1890's.

The fabulous bird, the 'lord of the isle' of which the title of the poem speaks, is very obviously the poet in the modern world—the sort of poet, at least, George himself aspires to be. Such a poet lives 'auf einer Insel', away from the mainland, cut off from the life of the profane vulgar. One remembers that a famous journal, founded in 1899, also bore the name *Die Insel*. In the first number, the editors wrote:

'In calling our publication *The Island* we wished to show how little we feel inclined to join in the now customary rejoicing at the glorious results of modern artistic endeavours, and how conscious we are of the enormous inner and outer difficulties impeding the desirable development of our art ... We endeavour to collect together the few seeds, the few beautiful remnants, which are still left to us and to adorn with these a garden, an oasis ... To do this, artists withdraw into a beautiful island-life away from the world.'

There is, about the poet and his isle in George's poem, something unmistakably sacerdotal. His is a world of spices, oils, rich jewels, Tyrian purple. All is precious, rich and glittering:

> *und edlen steinen die im sande glitzern ...*
>
> *im meer voll goldner federn goldner funken ...*

Unlike Shelley's skylark, this 'lord of the isle' does not soar. His very size, his *greatness*, forces him to heavy low flight, keeps him to the earth and his little island of experience. For those who see him, he is like a dark cloud—an ominous rather than a cheerful sight, alluding perhaps to the poet's function as *warner* of his times. He shuns the garish light of day, and comes to the shore only in the gloaming to sing

> *im kühlen windeshauch von salz und tang.*

The image is opportune—for it serves to relieve the somewhat oppressive atmosphere suggested by the images of spice and oil and jewels, reminiscent of the world of Dorian Gray and Des Esseintes and George's own Algabal. The air in which the poet lives is to be bracing and invigorating.

But such bracing and invigorating air is not for everyone to breathe. As the 'lord of the isle' sings, he gathers around him a select audience of lovers of song—'freunde des gesanges'—which recalls unmistakably the George group, the circle of contributors to *Blätter für die Kunst*. From the beginning, George tells us, the poet has lived like this, appreciated only by an *élite*. From the outside world, at most some of the shipwrecked and unfortunate ever caught a glimpse of him. And when his little sacramental plot is invaded by the outside world, when the mainland is brought into contact with the isle, then the lord of the island can do no more than look once more on the domain he loved so well, spread his wings, and die. The poet cannot sing to the crowd.

George's poem—and it is representative—is thus an extreme statement of the division of art and life in the modern world: an extreme development of an attitude already observed in Theodor Storm. The poet, George observes, must keep close to the earth, close to experience (such, at least, seems the implication of 'zu schwerem niedrem flug'); but he must at the same time keep his distance from the garish bustle of modern life. If he cannot keep this distance, cannot remain on his island, then he must, as a poet, perish. Yet this process is inevitable—it is inevitable that the poet's island should be affected by the life of the mainland: and it is precisely because George realized this, that *Der Herr der Insel* becomes what its last line proclaims it to be.

Verscheidend in gedämpften schmerzeslauten.

The whole poem is a muffled cry of pain.

'Gedämpft', muffled, is the keynote. The poet endeavours at all costs to keep his distance, not to admit the reader too far into his confidence. Instead of talking directly about his experiences and problems, he chooses a symbol: the 'lord of the isle' represents the poet. Yet even this symbol is distanced. 'Die Fischer überliefern ...' Instead of looking on the bird, we only learn of it from vague hearsay, from traditions among the fishermen; and this lack of immediate apprehension, this uncertainty, this distance, is emphasized by constant subjunctives.

habe
Er einer dunklen wolke gleichgesehn.
Des tages sei er im gehölz verschwunden.

The many muffling, hushing consonants of the poem—*sch, f*—also increase the force of the 'gedämpft' of the last line, and reinforce the general impression of aristocratic distancing.

It can hardly be denied that there is about George's attitude something debilitating. Either, he seems to suggest to the poet, withdraw from the ugliness of modern life, or—if that is impossible—die in a ritual of self-immolation. And the ritualism of the whole poem may well be felt as unpleasant. The sacerdotal images are obtrusive, some individual touches self-consciously 'beautiful'. Such lines as

> *Im meer voll goldner federn goldner funken*

call too much attention to themselves, suggest a self-adoring pose, just as there is something very near to pose in the later, much-admired park-lyrics:

> *Der rain bereitet aus gesträuch und blüten*
> *Den duft des abends für gedämpften schmerz.*

George still seems to see himself as an Algabal (Heliogabalus), 'born for the purple', whom it does not become 'to be shaken by earthly laments'. The poet muffles his cry because the crowd is not worthy to hear it. Away from the crowd and its bread and circuses, the poet-priest and a few acolytes are at their cult. If the cult is interrupted, the priest must immolate—himself.

George was not to remain satisfied for ever with a priestly cult of poetry. Inspired by Nietzsche, he sought for a new myth, and created such a myth in his odes to *Maximin*, a handsome and intelligent boy with whom he had struck up a friendship. To his chance meeting with Maximin George lent a world-historic significance, and he proclaimed to his contemporaries that the new god had been born:

> *Nun klagt nicht mehr — denn auch ihr wart erkoren —*
> *Dass eure tage unerfüllt entschwebt . . .*
> *Preist eure stadt die einen gott geboren!*
> *Preist eure zeit in der ein gott gelebt!*
> *(Auf das Leben und den Tod Maximins)*

From now on, George saw himself as the prophet of a new order of things.

> *Der mehr denn fürst sich sondernd herrischen blickes traf*
> *Die brüder und ihr werk verwies zum kot —*
> *Wer bist du Fremder? Ich bin nur demütiger sklav*
> *Des der da kommen wird im morgenrot.*
>
> (*Frage*)

Like Hölderlin, whom he much admired, George still felt his distance from the people among whom he had chanced to be born:

> *Wo an entlegnem gestade*
> *Muss ich vor alters entstammt sein*
> *Brüder des volkes?*
> *Dass ich mit euch wohl geniessend*
> *Wein und getreid unsres landes*
> *Fremdling euch bleibe?,*

felt himself more akin to that classical antiquity whose moderation and sense of form he ever extolled; but he set himself henceforth to speak to all who would hear, and not simply a deliberately confined circle. His voice was to be the voice of his people's conscience:

> *Ich euch gewissen, ich euch stimme, dringe*
> *Durch euren unmut, der verwirft und flucht ...*
> (*Das Zeitgedicht*)

He was to guide his people towards that *Neue Reich* of the spirit which is named in the very title of his last collection of poems, a Reich with a new myth, a new aristocracy, and himself as cultural legislator. George steadfastly refused to ally himself with those other prophets of a new myth, or new order, a new Reich, those other advocates of the leader-principle who were, within George's lifetime, to seize power in Germany. Their evil rule he seems to have foreseen, with a shudder, in such poems as *Der Gehenkte*. Yet despite the voluntary exile of his last year of life, it can hardly be denied that George, through his more than normal distrust of the people, unwittingly helped to prepare the ground for the very rulers he despised: and that his later poetry will never achieve abroad the reputation which historical developments have created for it in Germany.

CHAOS AND CONTROL

(d)
HOFMANNSTHAL
MANCHE FREILICH...
AND
BALLADE DES ÄUSSEREN LEBENS

Manche freilich...

Manche freilich müssen drunten sterben,
Wo die schweren Ruder der Schiffe streifen,
Andre wohnen bei dem Steuer droben,
Kennen Vogelflug und die Länder der Sterne.

Manche liegen immer mit schweren Gliedern
Bei den Wurzeln des verworrenen Lebens,
Andern sind die Stühle gerichtet
Bei den Sibyllen, den Königinnen,
Und da sitzen sie wie zu Hause,
Leichten Hauptes und leichter Hände.

Doch ein Schatten fällt von jenen Leben
In die anderen Leben hinüber,
Und die leichten sind an die schweren
Wie an Luft und Erde gebunden:

Ganz vergessener Völker Müdigkeiten
Kann ich nicht abtun von meinen Lidern,
Noch weghalten von der erschrockenen Seele
Stummes Niederfallen ferner Sterne.

Viele Geschicke weben neben dem meinen,
Durcheinander spielt sie alle das Dasein,
Und mein Teil ist mehr als dieses Lebens
Schlanke Flamme oder schmale Leier.

Ballade des äusseren Lebens

Und Kinder wachsen auf mit tiefen Augen,
Die von nichts wissen, wachsen auf und sterben,
Und alle Menschen gehen ihrer Wege.

Und süsse Früchte werden aus den herben
Und fallen nachts wie tote Vögel nieder
Und liegen wenig Tage und verderben.

Und immer weht der Wind, und immer wieder
Vernehmen wir und reden viele Worte
Und spüren Lust und Müdigkeit der Glieder.

Und Strassen laufen durch das Gras, und Orte
Sind da und dort, voll Fackeln, Bäumen, Teichen,
Und drohende, und totenhaft verdorrte . . .

Wozu sind diese aufgebaut und gleichen
Einander nie? und sind unzählig viele?
Was wechselt Lachen, Weinen und Erbleichen?

Was frommt das alles uns und diese Spiele,
Die wir doch gross und ewig einsam sind
Und wandernd nimmer suchen irgend Ziele?

Was frommt's, dergleichen viel gesehen haben?
Und dennoch sagt der viel, der 'Abend' sagt.
Ein Wort, daraus Tiefsinn und Trauer rinnt

Wie schwerer Honig aus den hohlen Waben.

Closely associated with the George of the 90's was another, a younger poet: 'the first person in Germany', as George wrote at the time, 'who, without having been previously associated with me, understood and valued my work—and that at a time when I began to tremble on my lonely rock'. Hugo von Hofmannsthal (1874-1929)—or, to give him the pseudonym he then adopted, *Loris*—should not be judged by his lyric poetry alone, for his best work in that genre was done before he was twenty-five years of age, and before he had abandoned that aestheticism which characterized so much of the literature produced at the end of the last century. Loris never regarded his ivory tower as a last refuge, in the manner of Gérard de Nerval:
'Il ne nous restait pour asile que cette tour d'ivoire des poètes, où nous montions toujours plus hauts pour nous isoler de la foule'; it was to him rather a prison, like Rapunzel's tower in Grimm's fairy-tale, from which he strove vainly to escape. Regretfully he

had to note: 'There is no direct road from poetry into life, or from life into poetry.' 'All my poems', he was to write much later,
'were written at the loneliest time of my life—between my eighteenth and twenty-first year. From out of this loneliness, which was strangely powerful, these poems were created—they lovingly call out to life across this belt of loneliness.'
But when he wrote these lines in a letter to a friend, Hofmannsthal had already stepped, as Richard Alewyn formulates it, from the temple of *l'art pour l'art* into the street of common life.

Manche freilich represents an attempt to heroicize the life of the aesthete, with his subtle and fine sensations. Like Hofmannsthal's fairy-tale, *Das Märchen der 672. Nacht*, the poem begins with the confrontation of two different classes of men: those who must live and die in the holds of the ship of life, where they must labour—cooped up and unable to look upwards or outwards—so that the ship may move: and those who, apparently more fortunate, stay at the helm above, and are thus able to command a larger view of life. It is the image made familiar by Freiligrath in *Von unten auf*, though its tenor is here the very opposite. The one class of men must ever grope about the roots of the tree of life, heavy of limb and dull of understanding: to the others, uninhibited by mechanical labour, knowledge comes easily. 'Leichten Hauptes und leichter Hände' they may sit with the Sibyls. Both images point, not only (like Freiligrath's) to different classes of men living contemporaneously, but to whole generations. The knowledge one generation has to grope towards and work for, becomes to the next easily acceptable.

But—continues the poem—the two kinds of lives are not to be separated. The sorrows and pains of the 'heavier' kind of life throw a shadow on the 'lighter' who depend on them. At this point in the poem narrative gives way to personal statement, and for the first time the poet speaks in the first person, implying that his own is one of those 'leichte Leben' of which the poem speaks. The efforts which have tired out generations of toilers have left their tiredness behind for those who come after them or depend on them. All events in this world, however apparently remote, leave a mark on the sensitive soul.

> *Und mein Teil ist mehr als dieses Lebens*
> *Schlanke Flamme oder schmale Leier.*

As Hofmannsthal puts it in his essay *Der Dichter und die Zeit*: 'Into the poet's present the past is inexplicably woven; he feels in the very pores of his body the life of days long past, of far-off ancestors he has never known, of long forgotten peoples and of times which are no more.'[1]

The heirs of striving and fighting generations have not an easier, but a harder lot than their predecessors. Poets are more unenviable than toilers 'at the tangled roots of life'. Because of their more exquisite consciousness, they have to bear the fate of others as well as their own.

The rhythms of the poem convey to perfection the infinite tiredness of the aesthete, that heaviness of the eyelids increased by every new experience.

> *Ganz vergessener Völker Müdigkeiten*
> *Kann ich nicht abtun von meinen Lidern ...*

Falling cadences predominate, and all the lines end on unaccented syllables, with a tired, dying fall. Frequent alliteration on *sch* and *f* seems to enforce a tired whisper, while echoing assonances—

> *Stummes Niederfallen ferner Sterne*
> *Schlanke Flamme oder schmale Leier* —

and full rich vowels convey alternately cloying richness and monotonous sameness of sensation. Slow movement, magically compelling, with many heavy stresses, makes the reader share those 'Müdigkeiten' of which the poem speaks.

Tiredness, 'Müdigkeit', is not however the only reaction to life conveyed by this poem. The other reaction is *terror*.

> *Noch weghalten von der erschrockenen Seele*
> *Stummes Niederfallen ferner Sterne.*

The stars, as they fall, are dumb, and cannot tell mankind why they are falling. The roots of life are tangled and confused

> (*Bei den Wurzeln des verworrenen Lebens ...*)

---

[1] Hofmannsthal later attempted to account for this by the neo-platonic doctrine of 'pre-existence' (Präexistenz).

beyond the ken even of those who sit with the sibyls and can read the flight of birds. May not life be purposeless, as well as confused? 'Durcheinander spielt sie alle das Dasein.' Existence plays with the lives of men, plays with confusion. Why then live at all, why bear the lot of others as well as your own? That is the question which links *Manche freilich* ... to that *Ballade des äusseren Lebens* which forms its natural complement.

In the *Ballade* the reader looks afresh, through the poet's eyes, at the simplest facts of that outer life he knows so well and has ceased to notice. At first, as end-stopped line follows end-stopped line, he merely looks, and tries to *see* again: to see the puzzled wonderment of blind children never vouchsafed an explanation, growing up in darkness, dying without having ever lived, unnoticed by the hurrying crowds; to see things come to fruition, but then falling like dead birds to the ground and left to rot, since no one regards them. A frightening spectacle of waste, which, in the third tercet, breaks up the even rhythm.

> *Und immer weht der Wind, / und immer wieder*
> *Vernehmen wir und reden viele Worte ...*

What imports our talk and our listening, what imports our joy, our tiredness? We never reach conclusion.

> *Und immer weht der Wind ...*

In rhythms more broken than they had been in the third, the fourth tercet looks afresh at the most common sights of all: at paths through the grass, villages and towns full of lights and trees and ponds: and suddenly, in this new perspective, this whole comfortable, familiar world seems threatening and horrible.

> *Und drohende, und totenhaft verdorrte.*

Harsh consonantal collocations, the long echoing *o* associated with threatening danger, with withering and death (drohen, tot, verdorrt) all bespeak, unmistakably, the poet's *Angst*.

Now, having seen the abyss, the poet can ask the question which had been implicit in *Manche freilich:* a question about the meaning and purpose of all life. Why is there all this variety and multiplicity? Why do we have sensations, why do we laugh, cry, grow pale? Always alone, part of some game we do not understand, always wandering without aim: why should we have sensations at all?

And at once comes the answer, in lines which so delighted Rilke:

> *Und dennoch sagt der viel, der 'Abend' sagt.*
> *Ein Wort, daraus Tiefsinn und Trauer rinnt*
>
> *Wie schwerer Honig aus den hohlen Waben.*

Sensation, experience, is good in itself. There is a heavy sweetness (as honey oozing from the hollow combs) in the concept, in the very word, 'evening', which has real meaning, 'Tief-sinn' as well as 'Trauer'. Alliteration binds 'Tiefsinn' and 'Trauer' together, shows meaning to reside *in* sorrow. To experience to the full the sadness of life, and to express that feeling (der Abend *sagt*), is to give meaning to life. By indulging his sorrow and expressing it the poet can face life with a Baroque 'Dennoch', can help mankind to bear the aimless terror of their existence.

Only now can we appreciate the appropriateness of the mould in which the poem is cast—Hofmannsthal's favourite *terze rime*. The poet speaks of the purposeless, disconnected nature of the 'outer life'; yet the echoes of interlinked rhymes do all the time establish the most subtle connections between the children of the first tercet and the fruits and birds of the second, the winds and words of the third, the streets and towns of the fourth. Disconnected content is counterpoised by interlinked form. It is the poet who can bring order into chaos.

'The poet may not reject any thought that comes into his mind, as though it came from another order of things. For into his order of things every particular thing must fit. In him everything must—and everything yearns to—come together. It is he who assimilates into himself all time. In him, or nowhere, is the present. (*Der Dichter und die Zeit.*)'

Or again, more clearly still:

'Out of past and present, out of animal, man, dream and thing, out of great and small, sublime and unimportant. the poet creates the world of cross-connections ("die Welt der Bezüge").' The very form of Hofmannsthal's poem speaks of the poet's function: to rescue the world from the flux of time and bring meaning and purpose into it.

It is not of course without significance that Hofmannsthal singles out the concept of 'evening' in the consolatory final section of his poem. The word 'Abend' crystallizes the poet's feelings about his own time, about the Vienna of the turn of the century—the evening of a culture, when men no longer act, but reflect on the achievements of the day.

'We are to take leave (writes Hofmannsthal in the essay so often quoted) of a world about to collapse. Many already know this, and an inexpressible feeling turns many into poets. They go their ways with hearts strangely moved, freed already from all bonds and yet, deep down, fast bound to it all ...'

This dying culture the young Hofmannsthal represents as well as chronicles. There is, about his poem, much that is unquestionably decadent: his heavy-lidded cult of sorrow, of sensation, for its own sake; his Byronic–Georgean pose—

Die wir doch gross und ewig einsam sind;

his affectation of 'facing fully' a life he hardly knew.[1] Yet there has seldom been a greater master of the German language, of its rhythms and melodies, than Hofmannsthal; and the German lyric lost a great deal when Hofmannsthal came to realize the futility of the aesthete's life[2] and stepped—to use Alewyn's terms just once again—from the temple into the street.

[1] The *torchlight* introduced into the fourth tercet of *Ballade des äusseru Lebens* is one of the stage-properties beloved by poets of the 90's—it is not an observed phenomenon.

[2] What Henry James said of *l'art pour l'art* in America and England holds good for Germany also: 'The spectacle was strange and finally wearisome, for the simple reason that the principle in question, once it was proclaimed—a principle not easily formulated, but which we may conveniently speak of as that of beauty at any price, beauty appealing alike to the senses and to the mind—was never felt to fall into its place as really adopted and efficient. It remained for us a queer highflavoured fruit from overseas, grown under another sun than ours, passed round and solemnly partaken of at banquets organized to try it, but not found on the whole really to agree with us, not proving thoroughly digestible' (*Notes on Novelists*).

CHAPTER TWELVE

Rilke

(a)

DIE FLAMINGOS

Paris, Jardin des Plantes.
In Spiegelbildern wie von Fragonard
ist doch von ihrem Weiss und ihrer Röte
nicht mehr gegeben, als dir einer böte,
wenn er von seiner Freundin sagt: sie war

noch sanft von Schlaf. Denn steigen sie ins Grüne
und stehn, auf rosa Stielen leicht gedreht,
beisammen, blühend, wie in einem Beet,
verführen sie, verführender als Phryne,

sich selber; bis sie ihres Auges Bleiche
hinhalsend bergen in der eignen Weiche,
in welcher Schwarz und Fruchtrot sich versteckt.

Auf einmal kreischt ein Neid durch die Volière;
sie aber haben sich erstaunt gestreckt
und schreiten einzeln ins Imaginäre.

George, in poems like Der Herr der Insel, showed one way of dealing with the machine-age and its problems of mass-production, standardization and human misery: the way of keeping one's distance, shunning the market-place, creating and living a myth, producing highly-wrought poetry written only for a few 'friends of song'. George also showed one way of dealing with 'things', with the world in which the poet finds himself. He carefully selected certain aspects of that world and made them symbolize something within man. To clasps, birds, islands, shepherds, George says in effect: be I, be myself.

Rainer Maria Rilke (1875–1926) felt no less strongly than his great contemporary the oppressiveness of a machine-civilization. The last section of his early, much-admired *Stundenbuch* (1903) had been full of romantic accusations of the city and city-life:

> *Da wachsen Kinder auf an Fensterstufen*
> *die immer in demselben Schatten sind,*
> *und wissen nicht, dass draussen Blumen rufen*
> *zu einem Tag voll Weite, Glück und Wind, —*
> *und müssen Kind sein und sind traurig Kind.*
>
> *Da blühen Jungfraun auf zum Unbekannten*
> *und sehnen sich nach ihrer Kindheit Ruh;*
> *das aber ist nicht da, wofür sie brannten,*
> *und zitternd schliessen sie sich wieder zu.*
> *Und haben in verhüllten Hinterzimmern*
> *die Tage der enttäuschten Mutterschaft,*
> *der langen Nächte willenloses Wimmern*
> *und kalte Jahre ohne Kampf und Kraft.*
> *Und ganz im Dunkel stehn die Sterbebetten,*
> *und langsam sehnen sie sich dazu hin;*
> *und sterben lange, sterben wie in Ketten*
> *und gehen aus wie eine Bettlerin.*

Such life Rilke rejected as 'untrue', 'unreal':

> *Die grossen Städte sind nicht wahr; sie täuschen*
> *den Tag, die Nacht, die Tiere und das Kind!*
> *ihr Schweigen lügt, sie lügen mit Geräuschen*
> *und mit den Dingen, welche willig sind.*
> *Nichts von dem weiten wirklichen Geschehen,*
> *das sich um dich, du Werdender, bewegt,*
> *geschieht in ihnen. Deiner Winde Wehen*
> *fällt in die Gassen, die es anders drehen,*
> *ihr Rauschen wird im Hin- und Widergehen*
> *verwirrt, gereizt und aufgeregt.*

Yet if the city, the most obtrusive daily reality, were 'unreal', where was truth to be found? It is hardly surprising that some of Rilke's early poems—the famous *Herbstbild*, for instance, beginning: 'Herr, es ist Zeit...'—voiced an autumnal sense of inevitable decline,¹ while others show the poet taking refuge in a religious mysticism somewhat too easily arrived at.

Die Flamingos was written after this early, somewhat sentimental phase. At the time of writing his *Neue Gedichte* (first section published 1907) Rilke was most painfully aware of the extent to which his contemporaries lacked concentration, dissipated their energies, gave to the world of 'things' only the most superficial and utilitarian attention. He therefore set himself to reveal once more the beauty and significance of 'things' even in the 'unreal cities'. He had learnt from Rodin, whose secretary he had been for a time, to look closely at some object (a piece of sculpture, perhaps, or a Cathedral window, a merry-go-round, a black cat, a group of flamingos), to contemplate it for a long time without prejudice or conscious preconception; and then to convey in poetry what G. M. Hopkins called the 'inscape', the 'thisness' of the object—that which made it, for the poet, different from all other objects.² In *Neue Gedichte* Rilke endeavoured to present 'pure evidences of the extent, the multiplicity, the completeness of the world'.

[1] Sidney Keyes can hardly have been thinking of these early poems when he penned his tribute to Rilke:

> *Rilke tenderly*
> *Accepted autumn like a rooted tree.*
> *But I am frightened after every good day*
> *That all my life must change and fall away.*

The acceptance is hardly 'tender', and the terror all too obviously there, despite the easy religiosity.

[2] This is a matter quite as much of resemblance as of difference, as Henry James knew when he strictured Maupassant for suggesting a 'recipe for originality' very similar to that of Rodin: 'On the question of style our author has some excellent remarks; we may be grateful indeed for every one of them, save an odd reflection about the way to "become original" if we do not happen to be so. The recipe for this transformation, it would appear, is to sit down in front of a blazing fire, or a tree, or any object we encounter in the regular way of business, and remain there until the tree, or the fire, or the object, whatever it be, become different for us from all other specimens of the same class. I doubt whether this system would always answer, for surely the resemblance is what we wish to discover, quite as much as the difference, and the best way to preserve it is not to look for something opposed to it.' (*Partial Portraits*, London and New York, 1888.) The justice of James's observation is completely borne out by Rilke's practice, as my analysis of *Die Flamingos* should serve to demonstrate.

The sonnet *Die Flamingos* is the fruit of many visits to the Jardin des Plantes at Paris: the record of a composite experience of these exotic birds at many moments, in many postures. Flamingos in the water (lines 1–4); flamingos standing among the green plants (lines 5–8); flamingos preparing for sleep (lines 8–10); flamingos stalking away (lines 11–14).

Rilke introduces his reader first not to the birds themselves, but to their reflection in the water, reminiscent of the delicate brushwork and colouring of the paintings of Fragonard. But water, we know, cannot completely reflect colours, it can only suggest them: the Fragonard image is therefore at once modified. The tender whites and pinks of these flamingos are not apprehended directly, but at second hand. We can guess at them, as we can guess at the beauty of a woman yet half asleep when her lover speaks of her.

But Fragonard, we know, was the court-painter of Louis XV, who decorated the salons of Mme du Barry and other famous courtesans, whose sensuous southern temperament ran easily to such paintings as *Le Verrou*, *La Chemise Enlevée*, *La Culbute* with which Rilke was familiar. We are conscious, therefore, of suggestions not only of colour, but also of sensuous beauty, voluptuous allure, obviously strengthened by the image of the 'Freundin' awaking from sleep. But the dark *a* sounds (associated with gentleness and sleep, 'sanft' and 'Schlaf') seem to veil this theme, which is here as delicately, shily touched as the rhymeword is delicately, shily touched:

*sie war
noch sanft von Schlaf.*

Enjambment here seems to envelop in a haze the natural division of the octet.

In this first section of the poem, then, everything appears veiled, unclear: the flamingos themselves (seen, not directly, but mirrored in the water) and the voluptuous allure suggested by their colouring and softness. The second sentence, however, brings greater clarity. As the reader looks, not at reflections, but at the birds themselves, colours become richer and fuller, 'blühend' like those of flowers. Half turning on their pink 'stalks', the flamingos stand

beisammen, blühend, wie in einem Beet

(how this line, with its three alliterating parts, seems to clear up the haze, make us look from one defined object to the next!) against a landscape ('das Grüne') strange to them. And just as the physical presence of the flamingos now appears 'unveiled', so also their sensuous allure. Suggestions only faintly perceptible in references to Fragonard and the 'Freundin ... sanft von Schlaf' become now, in the last line of the octet, unmistakable.

> *Verführen sie, verführender als Phryne ...*

The allusion to the Greek courtesan whom the flamingos are said to outdo in powers of seduction, the triple *ü* sound, the flowing movement of the line suggest voluptuous sensations almost excessively sweet. What had before been veiled, only hinted at, is now fully revealed.

But, as, with heavy retarded emphasis, the octet spills over into the sestet, the direction of the sonnet seems to change.

> *Verführen sie, verführender als Phryne,*
> *sích sélber;*

Unlike the beauties of Fragonard's paintings, unlike the friend awaking from sleep, unlike Phryne, the flamingos do not direct their appeal outwards, towards others. With a shock the reader realizes their self-absorption and self-sufficiency. The flamingos of the Jardin des Plantes are like that Narcissus of whom Rilke loved to write: needing neither the outside world nor one another, they are content in the contemplation of their own beauty. Rilke was later to write of Narcissus:

> *Er liebte, was ihm ausging, wieder ein.*

That describes exactly what the verse-movement here tells us about the flamingos: 'they love back into themselves what went out from them'; and it is no accident that the poem which deals with them begins with the image of a watery mirror in which, as we contemplate them, they contemplate themselves.

The impression of self-sufficiency into which the reader is shocked at the very opening of the sestet is reinforced more calmly by the succeeding lines. The verse seems now to come to rest: rhymes (Bleiche: Weiche) immediately follow one another, and are themselves followed by an end-stopped line coinciding with the natural division of the sestet. Such divisions had previously (l. 4, l. 8) been restlessly disregarded. The flamingos are shown burying their heads in their own soft flanks[1]: and it is here, under the wing-feathers, that the richest colours yet mentioned hide themselves. 'Schwarz und Fruchtrot. The very vowel-sounds bespeak their fullness and beauty. Yet these colours are hidden from others, are seen only by the flamingos themselves. To the world they show only their delicate whites and pinks; even their eyes (the 'mirrors of the soul'!) seem all turned inwards, exhibit nothing but 'Bleiche' to the spectator.

In sharp contrast to the liquid softness of the rest of the sonnet comes a dissonant cry of envy from the outside world, from other birds in an aviary.

Auf einmal kreischt ein Neid durch die Volière.

'Kreischt' is the keyword of this deliberately cacophonous line. But the flamingos are as impervious to envy as to admiration. They do not need anyone but themselves. Slowly they stretch their legs—tempo and character of this act of stretching are superbly rendered in the line:

Sie aber haben sich erstaunt gestreckt;

and each, with a step that seems to mock the guardsman's slow march, stalks off—'ins Imaginäre'. Apparently right out of the landscape, into a private, invisible world. Rilke here seems to open up, suddenly, a new dimension, a 'diagonal into infinity'. The Jardin des Plantes does not 'contain' his flamingos as it 'contains' the birds in the aviary. They are in it but not of it, and have power to transcend at any moment its limits of time and space.

In this delicate sonnet Rilke has evoked, to perfection, the 'thisness' of flamingos: their sensuous allure, flower-like beauty, self-sufficiency, self-absorption, stateliness, repose: he has done so through direct statements, images, rhythmic and grammatical deviations from a pattern once established, the sounds of vowels and consonants, all informed by a central purpose. The poem thus

---

[1] The one word 'Weiche' designates both the flanks and their yielding softness.

compels its reader to share Rilke's experience of these particular birds.

But the poem does far more than this. The 'things' of which it speaks are not, as they might have been to Franz Werfel, strange outside objects who avail themselves of the poet to 'say themselves', to 'come into being':

> *Das Fremde ist wohlgelaunt.*
> *Es hat mich erwählt, dass es werde.*
> *Nun grüsst es scheidend mit kalter Gebärde.*
> *Ich starre ihm nach, müd und erstaunt.*
> (WERFEL: *Das Gedicht*)

They are intimately related to the problems of the poet, to our problems. *Die Flamingos* treats (like many of Rilke's poems) the theme of 'Le Narcisse exaucé': the theme of beauty, tender and yet strong in its self-sufficiency, in a hostile world. Yet our sympathies are not all with the flamingos, against the other birds and plants: for we are made conscious of the peculiar problem of the modern poet, whose appeal is only too often turned inward, who only too often leaves 'das Grüne' of contemporary life to stalk off 'into the Imaginary'. Both these themes are present, though unexpressed, and determine the complex attitude of the poet to the 'thing' he contemplates.

Rilke, then, recognized an affinity between himself and 'things' without losing his detachment, or the ability to see the object of his poem steadily and whole. The more clearly he recognized the affinity, the more concretely he saw the object.

> *Immer verwandter werden mir die Dinge*
> *Und alle Bilder immer angeschauter.*
> (*Fortschritt*)

It is this rare combination of objectivity and subjectivity, of foreground of precision and background of suggestion, which makes the *Neue Gedichte* the great and invigorating work which its readers have always felt it to be.

(b)
AUSGESETZT AUF DEN BERGEN...

Ausgesetzt auf den Bergen des Herzens. Siehe, wie klein dort,
siehe: die letzte Ortschaft der Worte, und höher,
aber wie klein auch, noch ein letztes
Gehöft von Gefühl. Erkennst du's? —
Ausgesetzt auf den Bergen des Herzens. Steingrund
unter den Händen. Hier blüht wohl
einiges auf; aus stummem Absturz
blüht ein unwissendes Kraut singend hervor.
Aber der Wissende? Ach, der zu wissen begann,
und schweigt nun, ausgesetzt auf den Bergen des Herzens.
Da geht wohl, heilen Bewusstseins,
manches umher, manches gesicherte Bergtier,
wechselt und weilt. Und der grosse geborgene Vogel
kreist um der Gipfel reine Verweigerung. — Aber
ungeborgen, hier auf den Bergen des Herzens —

. . . .

Two figures, two images, perpetually fascinated Rilke: that of Narcissus and that of St. Francis of Assisi. Narcissus, who loved only himself: St. Francis, who loved only the 'little flowers' of the world. These two tended more and more to coalesce in Rilke's mind. As a poet he had set out to teach his contemporaries to look at the world once again with eyes like those of children; but he came to believe that such work of the eyes was insufficient, that the poet must capture the images of the outside world and then proceed to transform them through introspection. Loving the world like St. Francis was to be only a first step: we must come to love a transformed world *in ourselves*, our own hearts and minds, like Narcissus, like the 'angel' of the *Duino Elegies*. This change from 'work of the eyes' to 'work of the heart' is the theme of a poem of 1914 significantly entitled *Wendung*:

Denn des Anschauns, siehe, ist eine Grenze,
und die geschautere Welt
will in der Liebe gedeihn.
Werk des Gesichts ist getan
Tue nun Herzwerk

AUSGESETZT AUF DEN BERGEN...

an den Bildern in dir, jenen gefangenen. Denn du
überwältigtest sie; aber nun kennst du sie nicht.
Siehe, innerer Mann, dein inneres Mädchen,
Dieses errungene aus
tausend Naturen, dieses
erst nur errungene, nie
noch geliebte Geschöpf.

Such 'heart-work', Rilke grew to believe, was the prime task of man on this earth. Man was to transform the world within himself; to render it 'invisible'.

Erde, ist es nicht dies was du willst: unsichtbar
in uns erstehn? — Ist es dein Traum nicht
einmal unsichtbar zu sein? — Erde! unsichtbar!
Was. wenn Verwandlung nicht, ist dein drängender Auftrag?
(*Ninth Duino Elegy*)

Only through this introspective transformation could mankind hope to achieve that reconciliation of all apparent opposites, of lament and praise, of life and death, which the later Rilke desired above all other things. The poet cannot hope, as *Jung Deutschland* had once dreamed, directly to transform the outside world: he therefore retires within to transform the world in his heart. 'Now accomplish your heart-work on the images captured within you.'

Ausgesetzt auf den Bergen... transports the reader to those 'mountains of mind' with their 'cliffs of fall' familiar already to Gerald Manley Hopkins. It is the world of Kierkegaard, who was just then, in that Age of Anxiety, beginning to be widely known: a world of 'frontier situations' in which the individual, beyond the help of words, is thrown back only on his own 'existence'. Jaspers and Heidegger have since familiarized us with these boundaries of human consciousness. The individual recognizes that he is 'thrown' into a situation not of his own choosing or making (Heidegger's 'Geworfenheit'), and that he stands utterly alone before the abyss of Nothingness; that he is 'hineingehalten in das Nichts'. Only then may he make his choice, the only choice, the 'Either/Or' of reality or unreality, life or death, the Whole or Nothing. *Ausgesetzt auf den Bergen*... shows the terror of such 'heart-work'.

The poem opens with an image which Nietzsche had so often used to convey the isolation of the exceptional individual: the image of a high mountain beyond the cities of men. But Rilke's man, unlike Nietzsche's, has not retired to this mountain of his own free will. He is 'ausgesetzt'—exposed, abandoned, as sailors are abandoned on lonely islands, as children are abandoned in the more frightening fairy-tales. He finds himself, lonely and terrified, on the crags of his own heart. The opening phrase stands by itself, thrown up, not integrated into any sentence. It too is 'exposed'. So is the reader—for he finds himself *with* the poet, who points out to him the landscape of these heart-mountains.

> ... Síehe, wie kleín dórt,
> Síehe ...

From heavy stress to heavy stress we seem, in these short phrases, to be climbing away, higher and higher, from all the words, all the feelings we have ever known. As the mountain traveller leaves behind him the dwellings of men—villages and farms—so the poet here leaves behind all the familiar words and feelings he has in common with other men. Hardly recognizable, they lie far below him ('Erkennst du's?'). He is alone (and now the opening phrase is repeated, with added force), exposed on the mountains of mind.

We no longer glance down, glance back now at the villages of words, the farms of familiar feelings. Under our hands—for the effect is now that of climbing on hands and feet in strange stony regions—is the bare rock. The verse renders unmistakably the effort of climbing in broken lines and difficult passages from one line to the next.

> *Steingr*und
> Unter *den Händen.*

The stressed syllable that ends line 6 is the same as that which begins line 7: we seem to be stumbling over stones. Yet the following lines (with their keywords 'aufblühen', 'hervorblühen) bring a flowering of hope. Though the 'Absturz', the sheer wall of the mountains, is dumb and silent, there is *song* now to compensate for the 'villages of words': the song of the plant which, without consciousness, flowers on the abyss.

AUSGESETZT AUF DEN BERGEN...

> *aus stummem Absturz*
> *blüht ein unwissendes Kraut singend hervor.*

Rising cadences convey directly the relief and release experienced when the dreadful silence is broken by this ethereal song.

But what of man the knower in these regions of unconsciousness? The 'on the one hand' (Wohl) of consolation is now followed by the 'on the other' (aber) of lament, as the ninth line mockingly echoes the eighth.

> *Aber der* Wissende? *Ach, der zu* wissen *begann,*
> *und schweigt nun, ausgesetzt auf den Bergen des Herzens.*

Silence is re-established. Human thought, human consciousness, are here of no avail. A sentence breaks off, unfinished, leaving us with a sense of inadequacy and incompleteness. More and more clearly we come to realize what it means to be 'abandoned on the mountains of the heart': more and more clearly we understand the full import of the opening phrase of the poem, which is now repeated.

There follows another attempt at consolation, again introduced by 'Wohl', again—we surmise uneasily—to be followed by 'Aber'. Even here it is possible to feel safe (gesichert) and sheltered (geborgen): to feel beyond time. 'Wechselt und weilt.' Change and permanence may be—as the very alliteration tells us—identical at this still point of the turning world. It is not man, however, not the poet, who is thus lifted out of the flux of time. Only the mountain beast is safe, the mountain bird sheltered and of hale consciousness, like the animals of the eighth Duino Elegy:

> *Wäre Bewusstsein unserer Art in dem*
> *sicheren Tier, das uns entgegenzieht*
> *in anderer Richtung — riss' es uns herum*
> *in seinem Wandel. Doch sein Sein ist ihm*
> *unendlich, ungefasst und ohne Blick*
> *auf seinen Zustand, rein, so wie sein Ausblick,*
> *und wo wir Zukunft sehn, dort sieht es alles*
> *und sich in allem und geheilt für immer.*

Even if the peaks of these mountains are inviolate, the sheltered bird may at least encircle their 'pure denial'.

> *On a huge hill*
> *Cragged and steep, Truth stands, and he that will*
> *Reach her, about must and about must go . . .*

Donne's lines read curiously like a commentary on Rilke's poem.

In imagination, the reader has identified himself with mountain-beast and bird, safe and sheltered: but the passage from line 14 to line 15 brings him back, with a shock, to reality.

> — Áber
> ungebórgen, híer auf den Bérgen des Hérzens —

The opening phrase, repeated twice before, is now modified. 'Ungeborgen' replaces 'ausgesetzt', contrasting with the 'geborgene Vogel' of line 13, impressing on the reader (not least through its heavy stress) that there is no shelter or hiding-place in this existential situation, itself made vividly concrete by the pointing 'hier'. '*Here*, on these mountains.' There seems no escape.

But now the reader becomes conscious of a curious, characteristically Rilkean, process. Throughout the poem Rilke had established links between the most disparate things through the very sound of the words he employed. He had identified in this way the mountain-landscape with things of the heart and mind:

> *Berge des Herzens*
> *Ortschaft der Worte*
> *Gehöft von Gefühl;*

he had joined the changing to the eternal:

> *Wechselt und weilt.*

By this means, the reader's mind has been prepared to recognize an affinity between 'geborgen' (infinitive: 'bergen') and 'Bergen': between a sense of safety and the utmost degree of exposure. Might not the 'Berge' 'bergen', the mountains shelter? Might not 'Geborgenheit' be found in 'Ungeborgenheit'? The poem here breaks off, as so often, in the middle of a sentence. A definite answer cannot be given, our knowledge cannot help us. Only the poet can suggest the possibility, as on the very crags of those mountains of the heart an unknowing plant could flower, singing.[1]

[1] The reader may here find apposite a passage from Stephen Spender's recently published autobiography, *World within World*: 'Most writers allow

(c)
SONETTE AN ORPHEUS, I, xiii

Voller Apfel, Birne und Banane,
Stachelbeere ... Alles dieses spricht
Tod und Leben in den Mund ... Ich ahne ...
Lest es einem Kind vom Angesicht,

wenn es sie erschmeckt. Dies kommt von weit.
Wird euch langsam namenlos im Munde?
Wo sonst Worte waren, fliessen Funde,
aus dem Fruchtfleisch überrascht befreit.

Wagt zu sagen, was ihr Apfel nennt.
Diese Süsse, die sich erst verdichtet,
um, im Schmecken leise aufgerichtet,

klar zu werden, wach und transparent,
doppeldeutig, sonnig, erdig, hiesig —:
O Erfahrung, Fühlung, Freude —, riesig!

In *Ausgesetzt auf den Bergen* ... Rilke succeeded in communicating experiences apparently beyond the reach of human language. He ascended as high as possible into the remote and terrifying regions of the human mind, experienced to the full the inadequacy of the usual 'consolations', and found that on the highest peak of Despair hope could suddenly be found. Such discovery was known already to Keats (who uses the same mountain-image):

> *Ay, on the shores of darkness there is light*
> *And precipices show untrodden green;*
> *There is a budding morrow in midnight,*
> *There is a triple sight in blindness keen.*

Rilke believed that if the terrifying were not evaded but con-

their ideas to lead them back from terrifying solitude to the consolatory society of approximate and familiar phrases. An experience to them is the beginning of a journey where they soon arrive at already expressed ideas. *The writer who clings to his own metaphor is facing his own loneliness*; in fighting to distinguish a new idea from similar ideas which have already been expressed, he may find that his most hidden experience brings him ... face to face with the terrifying truth of his own isolated existence.' (My italics.)

fronted and realized to the full, it would suddenly be converted into its opposite. As he wrote in his *Requiem* to Count Kalkreuth, reproaching his friend for evading the 'heaviness' of life by committing suicide:

> *Was hast du nicht gewartet, dass die Schwere*
> *ganz unerträglich wird, da schlägt sie um*
> *und ist so schwer, weil sie so echt ist.*

That explains what is, to Rilke, the poet's especial function:
'Art can be of service only in this way: that we artists live through our sufferings with fuller awareness and thereby (sometimes, perhaps) give clearer meaning to our living on. We develop the means of expressing what we suffer and how we conquer suffering, and may therefore express it more clearly and exactly than those who have to expend their powers on other things.[1]
If the sorrows of the world are fully faced, then lament (Klage) will turn to praise (Rühmung). Such 'praise' of all existence is the keynote of the *Sonnets to Orpheus*, written in February 1922.

The sonnet chosen begins by naming some of the most common and familiar objects of our world: apple, pear, banana, gooseberry. These are simply enumerated, placed side by side, only the first of them (*Voller* Apfel) being qualified by an adjective. Then follows a pause for reflection (indicated by '...') and then—unexpectedly—the familiar and ordinary is connected with ultimate things, with death as well as life.

> *Alles dieses spricht*
> *Tod und Leben in den Mund.*

Weightily the stress falls on 'Tód und Lében', of which the fruit can speak to us, not in intellectual concepts, but directly, physically, 'into the mouth'.[2] After a further pause comes the keyword of this opening section of the poem. 'Ich ahne ...' Rilke's sonnet is to convey the gradual approach of intimations of another kind, another order of life: to show the timeless approaching us through the most ordinary and familiar. Hence the slow movement of these

[1] Letter quoted in Dieter Bassermann: *Der späte Rilke*, p. 51.
[2] Cf. the end of the fourth Duino Elegy, in which the same experience is integrated into a different context.

first lines, their many reflective pauses, their breaking off in the middle of a sentence to start on another tack.

Such intimations as these cannot be communicated to the intellect—they must be apprehended through taste and touch. Rilke, like D. H. Lawrence, approaches 'the frontier' through the senses. If mature men cannot 'taste' the Unknown in the fruit they eat, if their perceptions are too blunted by many distractions, then they may 'read' of it in the faces of children. With their as yet unspoiled vividness of sensation, children are nearer to 'things', more 'open' to all influences, than their elders.[1] They surrender themselves more unreservedly and explore more fully the taste of fruit.

Wenn es sie erschmeckt.

The prefix 'er-' suggests this exploration, this tracing back to the origin, in which the child unconsciously engages. What it is that the child finds, what we may read on its face, remains (as yet) unexpressed.

Lest es einem Kind vom Angesicht.
Dies kommt von weit..

It, this—the pronouns point to something definite without indicating its nature. They suggest the approach of the Unknown.

And now we ourselves become—as the early *Stundenbuch* had already insisted we must—as little children. We are once again tasting fruit to the full.

Wird euch langsam namenlos im Munde?

The line makes explicit what the poem has so far only implied. Slowly ('Langsam' characterizes the movement) the reader is passing beyond words, into realms of experience where our ordinary terms and concepts no longer apply. He is once again on the mountains of the heart, beyond the last 'village of words'.

Instead of words, however, he finds realities. The very sound of lines 7 and 8, passing suddenly from soft-voiced to the more energetically pronounced unvoiced fricatives (from *w* to *f*), conveys this surprising *trouvaille*.

[1] Rilke speaks somewhere of 'Das volle Offensein des Kindes', of the 'unbegrenzte Realität' of childhood.

> *Wo sonst Worte waren, fliessen Funde,*
> *aus dem Fruchtfleisch überrascht befreit.*

The word 'überrascht', isolated through sound and stress, is the keyword. The sudden echoing rhyme (Munde—Funde), the sudden change from *w* to *f*, the sudden flow of these lines, all surprise and excite. Vague intimations are becoming certainties.

The sestet makes concrete what had in the octet been only indicated: the process of piercing beyond mere names (nennen) to reality (sagen).

> *Wagt zu sagen, was ihr Apfel nennt* . . . —

assonance assimilates 'wagen' and 'sagen', tells us immediately that it requires courage to 'say' a thing truly instead of affixing a conventional label to it. This courage is the courage of remaining 'open' to all influences.

> *Aber wann, in welchem aller Leben*
> *Sind wir endlich offen und Empfänger?*
> (*Sonette* II, v)

The word 'apple', generally only a husk empty of meaning, is given, once again, the content of real experience.

In the magnificent lines that follow Rilke 'says'—in words which defy paraphrase—his experience of the sweetness of *apple*. At the first bite this sweetness cannot fully enter into the mouth: it is felt as concentrating or condensing itself, as thick and obscure (verdichtet); then, as the juice spreads itself over the palate, a vague shape or outline of taste rears itself up; and at last, startlingly, sweetness becomes real, taste becomes clear, certain, transparent. With retarded emphasis, the main stress falls on 'klar':

> *um, im Schmecken leise aufgerichtet,*
> *klar zu werden* . . .

The taste of the apple, like the poem, like Rilke's apprehension of the totality of life, has passed from obscurity to clarity, from dim intimations to certain knowledge. 'Klar', 'wach', 'transparent' —the very vowel-sounds 'say' 'Apfel'.

The sudden *flow* of which line 7 had spoken now determines the movement of the verse. The slow exploratory movement of the opening is giving way to rapid ejaculation. The taste of the apple, fully experienced, becomes 'transparent', reality may be seen through it, 'Funde' flow from it. We are approaching the frontier, the summit of the mountains of the heart.

What may be felt in and through the taste of this fruit is indicated by the concluding lines of the sonnet. The apple speaks to us, directly, of the unity of life, the divine realm of the Sun and the human realm of the Earth. It points two ways ('doppeldeutig'), for it has drawn its strength from earth and sun alike, has matured on the divinely nourished tree which is itself one of the recurrent symbols of the *Sonette an Orpheus*. Yet though it points to both these realms and is thus a living symbol of their unity, it belongs wholly to our own world, is itself 'hiesig'.

> *O Erfahrung, Fühlung, Freude—riesig!*

To experience this is the highest joy. Experience (*Erfahrung*) exploratory sensation (*Fühlung*) and joy (*Freude*) are now one—as the alliteration tells us directly; they tower gigantic, 'riesig', in the child-like exclamation which ends the poem.

Only now does the reader realize the significance of the opening word of the Sonnet, the adjective which marked off the apple from the other fruit enumerated. It indicated not only the appearance, the roundness of the apple, but also (more especially) Rilke's intention of revealing its true 'fullness', its plenitude of meaning.

'Our eyes need only become a trifle more seeing, our ear more receptive, *we would only have to allow the taste of fruit to enter more deeply into us* . . . to derive immediately from our most common experiences, consolation more convincing, weighty and true than all the sufferings which may shake us.'[1]

No facile consolation, this—behind it is all the weight of the Duino Elegies, and of poems like *Ausgesetzt auf den Bergen* . . . ; but heart-work is triumphantly vindicated, negation conquered, and life seen to be infinitely rich and precious. Lament is necessary and justified—but only in the dimension of Praise:

> *Nur im Raum der Rühmung darf die Klage*
> *Gehn.*
>
> (*Sonette* I, viii)

[1] Letter of October 1918—my italics.

More than any other poet Rilke was able to show his contemporaries that the whole of life, its terror as well as its beauty, could and must be joyfully accepted; and that salvation was to be found, not by flying into the exotic realms of neo-Romanticism, but by experiencing afresh the simplest objects and actions of our everyday lives. To do this men must cultivate what Kierkegaard, in *Sickness unto Death*, called 'Christian heroism': each must 'venture wholly to be himself, as an individual man, this definite individual man, alone in this tremendous exertion and this tremendous responsibility',

so that each may achieve, in the words of another poet, 'a condition of complete simplicity Costing not less than everything'.

Conclusion

What English readers will have missed most in this survey of the German lyric is the continuous development which characterizes the history of their own poetry: a stream of tradition constantly swelled by new tributaries. After the age of Goethe, extreme seems constantly to follow extreme. There was among the German Romantics no Wordsworth, so intimately linked not only to Gray and Thomson but also to Dryden and Pope; no Keats, who has affinities with the metaphysical poets no less than the early Elizabethans and the lesser Milton. Nowhere in English poetry is there so sharp a division as that between the German Romantics and the political poets of the 1830's and 40's; between these and the Poetic Realists; between the Poetic Realists and Stefan George. In Germany, conscious traditionalists proved only too often, like the poets of the Munich school, barren imitators. It is therefore significant that the history of the German lyric culminates, not in an Eliot for whom 'all time is eternally present', aware at every moment of the great tradition in which he stands and which he modifies and enriches, but in a Rilke,[1] who stands (despite his homage to Hölderlin) as if he were author of himself and knew no other kin.

One consequence of this lack of a continuous tradition has been an absence of urbanity, of social grace, in the German lyric. There is no equivalent of that metaphysical 'wit' which characterizes so much that is best in English poetry since the seventeenth century;

[1] Not that the history of the German lyric ends with Rilke. New infernos had to be passed through: the inferno of 'demon city' in the poetry of Georg Heym; that of the First World War, made vividly concrete in one of the greatest as well as most terrifying of all German poems, Georg Trakl's *Grodek*; the clutching at secular faith, be it Communism (Johannes R. Becher) or barbarous National Socialism; the agony of the Second World War, mingled pain and guilt and fear, which has found its most convincing expression so far in Hans von Savigny's *Elegie der getrosten Verzweiflung* (brilliantly analysed in that invaluable survey *German Poetry 1944–1948* by Professor Leonard Forster); and now the search for new values or living traditions to which to return.

neither do we find the great commonplaces of successive ages reiterated with the weight of personal experience. A Ben Jonson, a Pope would be unthinkable in Germany. The German lyric has therefore been constantly beset by two dangers: on the one hand, the excessive 'inwardness' which was the weakness of Klopstock, Novalis, Rilke; on the other (despite constant receptivity to foreign influences) a parochialism from which especially the Poetic Realists were not always free.

Historical reasons may of course be found for this development,[1] and it is a fascinating study to relate the pendulum swings of literary history to their social and political background. Klopstock's attempts to transcend the world in regions of the mind, Goethe's complete acceptance of this earth, be it as it might (sie sei wie sie wolle), Novalis's rejection of the world of light for one of darkness and death, the resignation of Mörike and Storm, George's attempt to create and live a new myth, Rilke's acceptance of the world only when transformed, made 'invisible', in the mind of the poet—all these correspond to phases in the social and political development of Germany, which has also been (notoriously) less smooth than that of England.

Yet that has not been the prime interest of the study attempted in this book. In and through poetry we were able to establish the closest possible contact with a succession of great (even if isolated) men of another time and another language. We were able to share immediately their experience of the world, to 'meet' them in the sense of Martin Buber's: 'All real life is meeting'.

For in lyric poetry, across all divisions of time and space, man calls to man: to enrich his experience and offer him, in turmoil and chaos, the consolation of achieved form.

[1] 'It takes a great deal of history', said Henry James, 'to produce a little literature.'

Biographical Notes

CLEMENS BRENTANO. Born at Ehrenbreitstein 8 September 1778, the son of an Italian father and a German mother. Refused the commercial career for which his father intended him and led, after his student-days at Halle and Jena, an unsettled wandering life. He settled at Heidelberg in 1804, and there made the acquaintance of Achim von Arnim (1781-1831) with whom he edited a collection of German folk-songs, *Des Knaben Wunderhorn* (1806-8). In later life Brentano became increasingly devoted to a mystical Catholicism. His works include, besides a large number of lyric poems, a completed long novel (*Godwi*, 1801) and a number of fragmentary novels; several fairy tales and Novellen (*Geschichte vom braven Kasperl und dem schönen Annerl*, 1817); and a mystical chronicle of the visions of a nun. He died at Aschaffenburg 28 July 1842.

Edition: Gesammelte Werke, ed. Amelung and Vietor, 4 vols., Frankfurt, 1923.

BARTHOLD HEINRICH BROCKES. Born at Hamburg 22 September 1680. A merchant and senator of Hamburg, commander of the Hamburg militia, and one of the most prominent members of an important literary circle, the Deutschübende patriotische Gesellschaft. His main literary achievement is the 9-volume collection: *Irdisches Vergnügen in Gott* (Hamburg, 1721-48). He died at Hamburg 16 January 1747.

Edition: Selection by L. Fulda, Kürschners Deutsche Nationalliteratur, vol. 39.

KARL BRÖGER. Born at Nuremberg 10 March 1886, the son of a factory-worker. Became a factory hand himself at the age of fifteen, then entered journalism and later became a free-lance writer at Nuremberg. Of his lyric poetry, that written during the 1914-18 War (*Kameraden als wir marschiert*, 1916; *Soldaten der Erde*, 1918) attained particular popularity. He also wrote an autobiographical novel (*Der Held im Schatten*, 1920) and a number of other novels and short stories. He died in 1944.

There is no collected edition of his work.

BIOGRAPHICAL NOTES

MATTHIAS CLAUDIUS. Born at Reinfeld 15 August 1740, the son of a pastor. He lived modestly, with his large family, at Wandsbeck near Hamburg, where he edited a journal *Der Wandsbecker Bote* (1771–5). His writings were collected and published under the title: *Asmus omnia sua secum portans oder Sämtliche Werke des Wandsbecker Boten* (1775–83; 1790–1812). He died at Hamburg 21 January 1815.

Edition: Sämtliche Werke, ed. Redlich, 2 vols., Gotha, 1902.

RICHARD DEHMEL. Born at Wendisch-Hermsdorf (Brandenburg) 18 November 1863. Dehmel began his career as editor of a provincial newspaper, then became (in 1887) secretary of the Union of German Insurance Companies, a post he relinquished in 1895 to devote himself to literature. His writings, pervaded by pity for all social outcasts and by the conviction that physical passion was one of the mainsprings of human life and human spirituality, include the following collections of verse: *Aber die Liebe* (1893); *Lebensblätter* (1895); *Weib und Welt* (1896); *Zwei Menschen* (1903); *Die Verwandlungen der Venus* (1907); and *Schöne wilde Welt* (1913). Dehmel served in the First World War as a volunteer, and published an account of his experiences in the trenches (*Zwischen Volk und Menschheit*, 1919). He died at Blankenese 8 February 1920.

Edition: Gesammelte Werke, 10 vols., Berlin, 1906–9.

FELIX DAHN. Born at Hamburg 9 February 1834. Educated at Munich; later Professor of Law at Würzburg, Königsberg and Breslau. A prolific writer, he achieved literary fame with his 4-volume novel *Ein Kampf um Rom* (1876). His chief collection of *Gedichte* was published in 1857. He died at Breslau 3 January 1912.

Edition: Sämtliche Werke poetischen Inhalts, Leipzig, 1898–1903.

ANNETTE VON DROSTE-HÜLSHOFF: Born on her father's estate at Hülshoff near Münster (Westphalia) 14 January 1797. Educated at home, she lived out most of her lonely life on her mother's estate near Münster, until she removed, for reasons of health, to Castle Meersburg on the Bodensee in 1841. Her first major literary achievement was a collection of poems for the Catholic Saints' Days (*Das geistliche Jahr*, 1852) in which she defends her faith against materialist doubts. Her *Gedichte*, the most notable of which deal with the natural scene and the legends of Westphalia, first appeared in 1838; a slim volume of late poems (*Letzte Gaben*) was published posthumously in 1862. Among her prose-works the powerful Novelle *Die Judenbuche* (1842) ranks highest. She died at Meersburg 24 May 1848.

Edition: Sämtliche Werke, ed. Schulte-Kemminghausen, 4 vols., München, 1925–30.

JOSEF VON EICHENDORFF. Born 10 March 1788 in his father's castle at Lubowitz in Silesia. During his student-days at Halle and Heidelberg, Eichendorff came into personal contact with many of the most eminent leaders of the German Romantic movement, and he began to publish Novellen and poems after his return to Lubowitz in 1808. He entered the Prussian army and fought under both Prussian and Austrian command during the Wars of Liberation (1810–15). After the defeat of Napoleon, Eichendorff entered the Prussian civil service, and spent his life (in a 'Philistine' pursuit he loathed) at Breslau and Berlin until he retired in 1844. He is best known for his lyric poems (*Gedichte*, 1837) and his Novelle *Aus dem Leben eines Taugenichts* (1826), while his other works include a novel (*Ahnung und Gegenwart*, 1815) and several volumes of literary criticism. He died at Neisse 26 November 1857.

Edition: Sämtliche Werke, ed. Zeitler, Leipzig, 1929.

FERDINAND FREILIGRATH. Born at Detmold 17 June 1810, the son of a schoolmaster. Became a merchant, but soon devoted all his time to poetry. In the 40's, Freiligrath lived (for political reasons) in Switzerland and England; he returned to Germany in 1848, and became one of the principal contributors to the radical *Neue rheinische Zeitung*. In 1851, political persecution drove Freiligrath once again to London, but he returned to Germany in 1868 and died at Kannstadt 18 March 1876. His principal collections of lyric poetry are: *Gedichte*, 1839; *Zwischen den Garben*, 1849; *Neuere politische und soziale Gedichte*, 1849–51; *Neue Gedichte*, 1876.

Edition: Sämtliche Werke, ed. Schäfer, 10 vols., Leipzig, 1907.

EMANUEL GEIBEL. Born at Lübeck 17 October 1815, the son of a Protestant clergyman. After travelling over half the world with a Russian nobleman whose private tutor he had become in 1838, he returned to Lübeck in 1840 and devoted himself to writing poetry. In 1843 the king of Prussia awarded him a pension, and in 1852 Maximilian II called him to Munich as Professor of Aesthetics. Besides lyrics, he produced a number of book-dramas (*Brünhild*, 1858; *Sophonisbe*, 1868) which are mercifully no longer read. He returned to Lübeck in 1865 and died there 6 April 1884.

Edition: Gesammelte Werke, 8 vols., Stuttgart, 1883.

CHRISTIAN FÜRCHTEGOTT GELLERT. Born 4 July 1715 at Hainichen in Saxony. Studied theology at Leipzig from 1834 onwards, and began publishing reviews and original works in his undergraduate days. He became first a lecturer, then (in 1851) Professor of Moral Philosophy and Rhetoric at Leipzig University. His fame rests chiefly on a collection of *Fabeln und Erzählungen* (1746 and 1748) and *Geistliche Lieder* (1757); but he wrote also a novel (*Das Leben der schwedischen Gräfin von G ...*, 1747–8) as well as a number of plays and a 'Practical Letter Writer' which became a model to his age. Frederick the Great called Gellert 'le plus raisonnable de tous les savants allemands'. He died at Leipzig 13 December 1769.

Edition: Fabeln und geistliche Dichtungen, ed. Muncker, Kürschners Nationalliteratur, vol. 43.

STEFAN GEORGE. Born 12 July 1868 at Büdesheim near Bingen, the son of a wine-merchant. Studied at Paris (where he came under the influence of the French symbolistes), Berlin and Munich, and lived in great seclusion in various German towns, mainly in Berlin, Munich and Bingen. His chief collections of lyric poetry are: Hymnen (1890); Pilgerfahrten (1891); Algabal (1892); Bücher der Hirten und Preisgedichte (1895); Das Jahr der Seele (1897); Der Teppich des Lebens (1900); Der siebente Ring (1907); Der Stern des Bundes (1907); Das neue Reich (1929). George is known also as a translator of Dante, Shakespeare (Sonnets) and Verlaine, and as editor of *Blätter für die Kunst* (Berlin, 1892–1919). In 1933 he refused Goebbels' offer to become the poet laureate of Hitler's Germany. He died at Locarno 4 December 1933.

Edition: Gesamtausgabe der Werke, endgültige Fassung, 18 vols., Berlin, 1927 ff.

JOHANN WILHELM LUDWIG GLEIM. Born at Ermsleben near Halberstadt 2 April 1719. Studied at Halle, then moved to

BIOGRAPHICAL NOTES

Potsdam, where he became secretary to the Prussian general Dessauer, whom he accompanied in the Second Silesian War. In 1747 he was made secretary to the cathedral chapter at Halberstadt; a comfortable situation which enabled him to devote himself to writing his (mediocre) verses and to help needy poets. Became a beloved paternal figure ('Vater Gleim'). Of his innumerable volumes of verse, only *Versuch in scherzhaften Liedern* (1744) and the patriotic collection which made him famous: *Preussische Kriegslieder von einem Grenadier* (1758), need here be listed. Gleim died 18 February 1803.

Edition: Sämtliche Werke, ed. Körte, 8 vols., Halberstadt, 1812–41.

JOHANN WOLFGANG (VON) GOETHE. Born 28 August 1749, son of an imperial councillor and patrician of Frankfort. Studied Law at the University of Leipzig (1765–8), where his earliest poems were written (*Annette; Neue Lieder*, published 1769). As a poet, Goethe found his true voice at Strassburg, where he had gone to continue his studies (1770–1) and where the famous Sesenheim lyrics were written. After his play *Götz von Berlichingen* had appeared in 1773, Goethe published the novel which was to establish his European reputation: *Die Leiden des jungen Werthers* (1774). During these fruitful years, his 'Storm and Stress' period, Goethe also wrote a number of lyric poems (notably such odes as *Ganymed* and *Prometheus* and the love poems addressed to Lili Schönemann at Frankfurt); began his play *Egmont*; and penned the first draft of *Faust*, the work which was to accompany him throughout his life (*Urfaust*, 1775).

In 1775 Goethe went to Weimar as state councillor of the new Duke Karl August. The main literary fruit of these early years at Weimar, besides a number of didactic odes, are the lyrics inspired by Goethe's love for Frau von Stein (e.g. *An den Mond*). From the increasing burden of administrative business and court squabbles Goethe fled, in 1786, to Italy, where he stayed until 1788. From now on the stream of great works is continuous. 1787 and 1790 see the publication of the classic dramas *Iphigenie auf Tauris* and *Torquato Tasso*; in 1795 are published the *Römische Elegien*; and with *Wilhelm Meisters Lehrjahre* (1795–6) Goethe points out new paths to the German novel. Together with Schiller, now living at Weimar in close friendship with Goethe, he published a collection of ballads in the *Balladenalmanach* of 1798.

The principal works of Goethe's later period are: *Faust, Erster Teil* (published 1808); a novel, *Die Wahlverwandtschaften*, 1809; many writings on scientific themes, in which Goethe now became increasingly interested (e.g. *Zur Morphologie*, 1817–24); the oriental lyrics of the *Westöstlicher Divan* (1819); the most tragic lyrics he was ever to write, *Trilogie der Leidenschaft* (1827), inspired by love for a young girl; *Wilhelm Meisters Wanderjahre* (1829); *Faust, Zweiter Teil* (1832); and his autobiography, *Dichtung und Wahrheit*, which Goethe had begun to publish in 1811, and the last volume of which appeared posthumously in 1833. Goethe died on 22 March 1832.

Edition: Gedenkausgabe der Werke, Briefe und Gespräche, ed Beutler, 24 vols., Zürich, 1948 ff. (in progress). Werke, herausgegeben im Auftrage der Grossherzogin Sophie von Sachsen-Weimar, 50 vols., Weimar, 1887–1919.

JOHANN NIKOLAUS GÖTZ. Born at Worms 9 July 1721. He studied at Halle, where he met Uz, with whom he translated the poems of 'Anacreon' in 1746. He began life as a private tutor and pastor, but later entered the civil service at Baden. He died 4 November 1781.

Edition: Vermischte Schriften, ed Ramler, 1785.

FRIEDRICH VON HAGEDORN. Born 23 April 1708 at Hamburg, where he spent practically his whole life. He became secretary to 'the English Court', an English trading company. His poetry (*Fabeln und Erzählungen*, 1738; *Moralische Gedichte*, 1750) betrays the influence of English and French as well as classical models. He died at Hamburg 28 October 1754.

Edition: Poetische Werke, ed. Eschenburg, 5 vols., Hamburg, 1800.

CHRISTIAN FRIEDRICH HEBBEL. Born 18 March 1813 at Wesselburen in Holstein. The son of a bricklayer, he experienced bitterest poverty and humiliation in his youth, until the editor of a fashionable Hamburg journal generously enabled him to study: first at Hamburg, and later at the universities of Heidelberg and Munich. In 1839 Hebbel began writing his first tragedy, *Judith* (published 1841), while his second (*Genoveva*, written 1840) appeared in 1843. On a travelling scholarship obtained from the King of Denmark, Hebbel visited France and Italy, and completed in the course of his travels his sombre 'bourgeois tragedy' *Maria Magdalene* (1844). After these travels he settled in Vienna, broke off (somewhat harshly) his relations with a poor seamstress who had helped him in his dark days at Hamburg and Munich and who had borne him a son, and married the actress Christine Enghaus. During his later years, he wrote (besides other plays of less note) the tragedies *Herodes und Mariamne* (1850), *Agnes Bernauer* (1855), *Gyges und sein Ring* (1856) and the trilogy *Die Nibelungen* (1862). Hebbel's contribution to German lyric poetry too is considerable (*Gedichte*, 1842; *Neue Gedichte*, 1848), though none of his poems has been included in the present book. He died at Vienna 13 December 1863.

Edition: Säkular-Ausgabe, ed. Werner, 19 vols., Berlin, 1911–22.

HEINRICH HEINE. Born at Düsseldorf 13 December 1797. Studied law at Bonn, and then moved to Berlin where he abandoned, for reasons of expediency, the Jewish faith into which he had been born, without, however, obtaining the state-employment he had hoped for. A collection of poems (*Gedichte*, 1822— incorporated in the *Buch der Lieder*, 1827) and a brilliant volume of journalistic prose (*Reisebilder*, 1826) made Heine famous. After the 1830 revolution he left Germany for political and other reasons and settled in Paris, where his greatest works were written. These include two verse-satires (*Atta Troll*, 1843, and the more mordant *Deutschland, ein Wintermärchen*, 1844) and a collection of ballads and lyrics: *Romanzero* (1851). On 17 February 1856 Heine died of the creeping paralysis which had confined him, during the last eight years of his life, to a 'mattress grave'. He is buried at Paris.

Edition: Werke, ed Elster, 7 vols., Leipzig, 1887–90.

WILHELM HERTZ. Born at Stuttgart 24 September 1835. A professor of German Language and Literature at the Munich *Technische Hochschule*, Hertz is now principally remembered for his verse-translations of medieval epics. His own volume of *Gedichte* was published in 1859. He died at Munich 7 January 1902.

Edition: Gesammelte Dichtungen, Leipzig, 1900.

BIOGRAPHICAL NOTES

GEORG HERWEGH. Born at Stuttgart 31 May 1817. Herwegh spent most of his life, despite a temporary friendship with Frederick William IV of Prussia, as a political exile in Switzerland and France. Principal collections of lyric poetry: *Gedichte eines Lebendigen* (Zürich, 1841) and *Neue Gedichte* (published posthumously at Zürich, 1877). Herwegh died at Baden-Baden 7 April 1875.

Edition: Werke, ed. Tardel, Berlin, n.d.

PAUL HEYSE. Born at Berlin 15 March 1830. Studied philology at Berlin and Bonn, travelled through Switzerland and Italy in the early 1850's, and was called to Munich by Maximilian II in 1854. With Geibel he became the centre of the 'Munich School' of poets. Of his voluminous writings a number of lyrics and a Novelle (*L'Arrabbiata*, 1855) still live a shadow-life in anthologies. Heyse died at Munich 2 April 1914.

Edition: Gesammelte Werke, 38 vols., Stuttgart, 1899–1914.

HUGO VON HOFMANNSTHAL. Born at Vienna 1 February 1874, the son of a wealthy *rentier*. He studied Law and Romanic Languages, and then retired to Rodaun near Vienna, where he lived most of his life. Under pseudonyms he published his dramatic fragment *Gestern* in 1891, and the lyrical drama *Der Tor und der Tod* in 1900. He became a contributor to George's *Blätter für die Kunst*, published a number of other dramatic sketches and (in 1905 and 1907) his best lyrics. Among Hofmannsthal's later works, the most notable are the plays set to music by Richard Strauss (*Elektra*, 1903; *Der Rosenkavalier*, 1911; *Ariadne auf Naxos*, 1912); adaptations of medieval mysteries and moralities (*Jedermann*, 1911; *Das Salzburger grosse Welttheater*, 1923); a comedy, *Der Schwierige* (1921); *Der Turm* (1925); and a number of prose-tales and critiques. He died at Rodaun 15 July 1929.

Edition: Gesammelte Werke in Einzelausgaben, Stockholm, 1947 ff.

FRIEDRICH HÖLDERLIN. Born at Lauffen in Württemberg 20 March 1770, the son of the (Protestant) bailiff of a Benedictine convent. Intended for the Church, Hölderlin lost his simple religious beliefs during his years of study at Tübingen, and embarked on the more hazardous life of a private tutor. During his first tutorship at the house of a rich Frankfurt banker,

Hölderlin fell in love with his employer's wife, Susette Gontard, the *Diotima* of his poetry. After the inevitable rupture, Hölderlin returned to his mother's house, stayed with friends, held various tutorships in Switzerland and France, and succumbed in 1802 to the madness which had always menaced him. He had by that time already produced a number of the greatest lyrics in the German language (which had, for a time, attracted the attention of Schiller); a novel *Hyperion, oder der Eremit in Griechenland* (1797-9); and a dramatic fragment *Empedokles*, of which we have several drafts. Hölderlin lived on, in madness and obscurity, until 7 June 1843. Only in the last half century has his greatness been recognized: he is now the most potent influence on modern German poetry.

Edition: Sämtliche Werke, ed. Beissner, Stuttgart, 1943 ff. (in progress). Sämtliche Werke, ed. Hellingrath, Pigenot and Seebass, 6 vols., Munich and Berlin, 1912-23.

LUDWIG CHRISTOPH HEINRICH HÖLTY. Born at Hanover 21 December 1748. Studied at Göttingen, where he was one of the members of the 'Göttinger Hain'. His uneventful life was early wasted by consumption, of which disease he died at Hanover 1 September 1776. His poems were collected after his death and first published 1782-3.

Edition: Sämtliche Werke, ed. Michael, 2 vols., Weimar, 1914-18.

ARNO HOLZ. Born at Rastenburg (East Prussia) 26 April 1863, the son of a chemist. His family moved, in 1875, to Berlin, where Holz was to spend most of his subsequent life. A professional journalist and writer, he helped through his theoretical works (*Die Kunst. Ihr Wesen und ihre Gesetze*, 1890-2; *Revolution der Lyrik*, 1899), his lyrics (notably *Buch der Zeit*, 1886, and *Phantasus*, 1898 ff.), his Novellen (*Papa Hamlet*, in collaboration with Johannes Schlaf, 1890) and his drama (*Die Familie Selicke*, in collaboration with Schlaf, 1890) to found the Naturalist school in Germany. Holz died at Berlin 26 October 1929.

Edition: Das Werk von Arno Holz, 10 vols., Berlin, 1924.

GOTTFRIED KELLER. Born at Zürich 19 July 1819, son of an artisan who died when his son was still a child. In 1840 Keller went to Munich to study painting, but soon found that he had mistaken his vocation. He returned to Zürich in 1842 and

BIOGRAPHICAL NOTES

obtained a state scholarship to study philosophy and history at Heidelberg. From 1850 till 1855 he lived in Berlin, where his first great collection of Novellen (*Die Leute von Seldwyla*, published 1856) and his autobiographical novel *Der Grüne Heinrich* (published 1854–5) were written. In 1855 Keller returned to Zürich where he soon became town-clerk, and remained in the service of the Swiss republic until 1876. He published many Novellen (notably *Züricher Novellen*, 1878) and a new version of *Der grüne Heinrich* (1879). His collected poems appeared in 1883. Keller died at Zürich 17 October 1890.

Edition: Sämtliche Werke, ed. Fränkel, 26 vols., Erlenbach-Bern, 1926 ff.

EWALD CHRISTIAN VON KLEIST. Born at Zeblin (Pomerania) 7 March 1715. Studied Law at Königsberg, and entered the Danish army in 1736; he later served in the Prussian army under Frederick the Great, was wounded at the battle of Kunersdorf and died soon afterwards of his wounds (24 August 1759). His best-known work is *Der Frühling* (published 1749), a descriptive poem in the manner of Thomson's *Seasons*.

Edition: Werke und Briefe, ed. Sauer, Berlin, 1881.

FRIEDRICH GOTTLIEB KLOPSTOCK. Born at Quedlinburg 2 July 1724, the son of a lawyer. While still at school (the famous Schulpforta, which Klopstock attended from 1739 to 1745), he resolved to become the German Milton. Studied theology at Jena and Leipzig, and published, in 1748, the first three cantos of his religious epic *Der Messias* (not completed until 1773). He then became a private tutor at Langensalza, and after a brief stay in Zürich settled in Kopenhagen in 1751, where he found a royal patron in Frederick V of Denmark. In 1770 Klopstock returned to Germany and settled in Hamburg. Two collections of *Geistliche Lieder* had been published in 1758 and 1769; the *Oden*, containing the greatest lyrics, appeared in 1771. Klopstock died at Hamburg 14 March 1803, and was given a state funeral.

Edition: Oden, ed. Merker, 2 vols., Leipzig, 1913.

NIKOLAUS LENAU (pseudonym of Nikolaus Franz Niembsch von Strehlenau). Born at Csatad in Hungary 13 August 1802. Studied at Vienna, and then lived an unsettled life in Hungary, Germany and North America. He made his name with two

BIOGRAPHICAL NOTES

collections of poetry: *Gedichte* (1832) and *Neue Gedichte* (1838–40). In 1844 he became insane, and died at Oberdöbling near Vienna 22 August 1850

Edition: Sämtliche Werke und Briefe, ed. Castle, 6 vols., Leipzig, 1910–23.

HERMANN VON LINGG. Born at Lindau 22 January 1820. Became a doctor, and served as army surgeon in the Bavarian army from 1846 to 1851. He then settled in Munich. A voluminous, now almost forgotten poet and dramatist. His first collection of lyrics (*Gedichte*) was published in 1854, his last (*Schlussrhythmen*) in 1901. He died at Munich 18 June 1905.

Edition: Ausgewählte Gedichte, ed. Heyse, Leipzig, 1905.

CONRAD FERDINAND MEYER. Born at Zürich 11 October 1825. Studied Law; but his studies were interrupted by signs of insanity. He lived at Lausanne and Zürich, and first appeared in public as a translator of French historical works. From 1857 to 1858 he travelled in France and Italy. His first collections of poetry (*Zwanzig Balladen*, 1864; *Romanzen und Bilder*, 1871) went unnoticed. About 1871 began C. F. Meyer's 'Indian Summer', both as man and poet. He wrote a historical novel, *Jürg Jenatsch* (1876), and many Novellen (*Der Heilige*, 1879; *Das Amulet*, 1883; *Angela Borgia*, 1890); and his chief collection of *Gedichte* was published in 1882 (revised edition, 1892). In 1892 Meyer became insane. He died at Kilchberg near Zürich 28 November 1898.

Edition: Sämtliche Werke, 14 vols., Leipzig, 1925.

EDUARD MÖRIKE. Born at Ludwigsburg 8 September 1804; studied theology at Tübingen (1822–6) and became pastor of Cleversulzbach in Swabia, an office he did not administer to the satisfaction of either his congregation or his ecclesiastical superiors. He retired in 1843 and moved to Mergentheim; taught literature at the *Katharinenstift* in Stuttgart from 1851 onwards, married, and lived so unhappily with his wife that he separated from her in 1873. His *Gedichte* were first published in 1838, an augmented edition appeared in 1867. Mörike also wrote a novel in the Romantic tradition (*Maler Nolten*, 1832), and one of the most perfect Novellen of German literature, *Mozart auf der Reise nach Prag* (1856). He died at Stuttgart in 1875.

Edition: Sämtliche Werke, ed. Deibel, Leipzig, 1918.

BIOGRAPHICAL NOTES

FRIEDRICH WILHELM NIETZSCHE. Born 15 October 1844 at Röcken in Saxony, the son of a Lutheran pastor. After passing through the famous Schulpforta grammar-school, Nietzsche studied classical philology at Bonn and Leipzig, and became Professor of Classical Philology at Basle University in 1869. At Leipzig he had met Richard Wagner, whose music-drama he celebrated in his first book, *Die Geburt der Tragödie* (1872). *Unzeitgemässe Betrachtungen* appeared between 1873 and 1876. Notable mainly for his contribution to philosophy (*Menschliches, Allzumenschliches,* 1878–80; *Also sprach Zarathustra,* 1883–5; *Der Wille zur Macht,* 1888–94), Nietzsche is also a lyric poet of great power and scope, though the present book contains no example of his work. In 1879 Nietzsche was forced by ill-health to give up his professorship at Basle; he spent the rest of his life mainly in Italy and Switzerland, and became incurably insane in 1889. He died at Weimar 25 August 1900.

Edition: Musarion-Ausgabe, 23 vols., München, 1920–29.

NOVALIS (pseudonym of Friedrich Leopold von Hardenberg). Born at Oberwiedstädt 2 May 1772. Studied at Jena, where he came under the influence of Schiller, then Jena's most distinguished professor; an influence which he soon shook off, however, on meeting Friedrich Schlegel (1772–1829). Of his vocation as a poet Novalis first became conscious through his love for a thirteen-year-old girl, Sophie von Kühn, who died in 1797. This experience of love and death precipitated Novalis' *Hymnen an die Nacht* (1800). His other works include a collection of religious poems (mainly hymns to the Virgin Mary): *Geistliche Lieder*; and an (incomplete) novel, *Heinrich von Ofterdingen* (1802). He died of consumption 25 March 1801.

Edition: Schriften, ed. Kluckhohn, Leipzig, 1929.

AUGUST VON PLATEN-HALLERMÜNDE. Born at Ansbach 24 October 1796. Platen became an officer cadet in the Bavarian army, but soon resigned from the army to devote himself to writing. *Ghaselen* (1821), written in Persian metres and thus following in the wake of Goethe's *Westöstlicher Divan*, were followed in 1825 by *Sonette aus Venedig*. In 1826, disgusted by the conditions of German literature and politics, Platen settled permanently in Italy. He directed angry dramatic satires against contemporary German writers (*Die verhängnisvolle Gabel*, 1826; *Der romantische Oedipus*, 1829), and drew down on his head the wrath of Heine, whose attack on Platen as man and poet, in *Die Bäder von Lucca*, is one of the most vicious in the history of German literature. Platen's tortured spirit best reveals itself in his diaries, published posthumously. He died at Syracuse 5 December 1835.

Edition: Sämtliche Werke, ed. Koch and Petzet, 12 vols., Leipzig, 1909.

RAINER (RENÉ) MARIA RILKE. Born at Prague 4 December 1875. Intended by his parents for a military career, Rilke entered the officers' academy at Pölten, but left it again in 1890. Journeyed through Russia with his friend Lou Andreas Salomé, then returned to Berlin and lived at Westerwede. His earliest poetry was published in the collections *Larenopfer* (1896), *Traumgekrönt* (1897) and *Mir zur Feier* (1899), followed by *Das Buch der Bilder* in 1902. But it was not until the ever popular *Stundenbuch* (1905) that Rilke began to find his real voice. From 1902 until 1904 Rilke lived in Paris, and acted for a time as secretary to Auguste Rodin, on whom he wrote a monograph (published 1903 and 1907). *Neue Gedichte* appeared in 1907 and 1908; *Requiem*, 1909; while Rilke's chief prose-work, the autobiographical *Aufzeichnungen des Malte Laurids Brigge*, was first published in 1910. *Duineser Elegien*, begun in 1912 at Castle Duino near Trieste, and *Die Sonette an Orpheus* appeared in 1923. Rilke spent his last years at Muzot in Switzerland, and died there 29 December 1926. A great deal of his work is still being prepared for publication.

Edition: Gesammelte Werke, 6 vols., Leipzig, 1927. Gesammelte Gedichte, 4 vols., Leipzig, 1930–3.

JOSEPH VICTOR VON SCHEFFEL. Born at Karlsruhe 16 February 1826. A practising lawyer, Scheffel achieved fame with his (unbearably coy and Philistine) epic *Der Trompeter von Säckingen* (1854). He has written also a historical novel (*Ekkehard*, 1855) and a large number of popular student-songs (*Gaudeamus*, 1868) as well as other lyrics. Scheffel died at Karlsruhe 9 April 1886.

Edition: Gesammelte Werke, ed. Proelss, 7 vols., Stuttgart, 1907–8.

BIOGRAPHICAL NOTES

JOHANN CHRISTOPH FRIEDRICH (VON) SCHILLER. Born at Marbach 10 November 1759, the son of an army-surgeon, Schiller was forced by Duke Karl Eugen of Württemberg to give up his plan of studying theology and to enter instead (in 1773) the Duke's military academy, to study medicine. At the *Karlsschule* Schiller wrote his first play, *Die Räuber*, successfully performed at Mannheim in 1782. In September of the same year Schiller fled from Württemberg to Mannheim, where he offered for stage-presentation his second play *Fiesko* (1783) and began his third, *Kabale und Liebe* (1784). After an unhappy stay at Mannheim, Schiller found friends at Leipzig and Dresden who helped him morally, socially and financially, and in these years one of Schiller's best-known lyrics (*An die Freude*, 1785) and his first Blank Verse drama (*Don Carlos*, 1787) were written. In 1787 Schiller moved to Weimar, and became in 1789, on Goethe's recommendation, professor of History at Jena. In the 1790's appeared a number of Schiller's reflective and philosophical poems, and also his most important essays on ethics, aesthetics and education (*Ueber Anmut und Würde*, 1793; *Briefe über die ästhetische Erziehung des Menschen* and *Ueber naive und sentimentalische Dichtung*, 1795). From 1794 dates Schiller's close friendship and collaboration with Goethe. The major works of his last years are: the three parts of the tragedy *Wallenstein* (1798–9); a large number of ballads ('Balladenalmanach', 1798); *Maria Stuart* (1800), *Die Jungfrau von Orleans* (1801), *Die Braut von Messina* (1803), *Wilhelm Tell* (1804), and the dramatic torso *Demetrius* (1805). Schiller died 9 May 1805.

Edition: Werke, Nationalausgabe, 33 vols., Weimar, 1943 ff. (in progress). Sämtlich Werke, Horen-Ausgabe, 16 vols., Munich, 1910 ff.

THEODOR WOLDSEN STORM. Born at Husum (Schleswig) 14 September 1817. Studied law and settled in Husum, where he married in 1846. In 1853 Storm left Husum in protest against Danish policy in Schleswig-Holstein. Settled in Prussia, where he became a county-court judge at Heiligenstadt. In 1864 Storm returned to Husum, rose high in the legal hierarchy there, until he retired from office in 1880. He died at Hademarschen in Holstein 4 July 1888. Known chiefly as a writer of Novellen (*Immensee*, 1850; *Viola Tricolor*, 1873; *Der Schimmelreiter*, 1888),

BIOGRAPHICAL NOTES

Storm published a slender volume of *Gedichte* in 1852 which appeared in revised and augmented form in 1885.

Edition: Sämtliche Werke, ed. Köster, Leipzig, 1919–20.

JOHANN LUDWIG TIECK. Born at Berlin 31 May 1773, the son of a ropemaker. From the first, Tieck devoted himself to literature and the theatre. His writings include dramatic satires (*Der gestiefelte Kater*, 1797) and romantic dramas glorifying the Middle Ages (*Franz Sternbalds Walderungen*, 1793); and a large number of fairy-tales, Novellen and lyrics. Tieck collaborated with A. W. Schlegel (1767–1845) in producing a magnificent German translation of Shakespeare's plays. He died at Berlin 28 April 1853.

Edition: Ausgewählte Werke, ed. Berend, 6 vols., Berlin, 1908.

JOHANN PETER UZ. Born at Ansbach 3 October 1720. Studied Law at Halle. Translated Horace (rather badly) into German prose in 1775; composed an imitation of Pope's *Rape of the Lock* in 1853, and issued a rhymed philosophical poem, *Theodicee*, in 1755. Herder and other eminent critics thought highly of Uz during his life-time, but he is now forgotten. He died at Ansbach 12 May 1796.

Edition: Sämtliche poetische Werke, Deutsche Literatur-Denkmale des 18. und 19. Jahrhunderts in Neudrucken, Heilbronn, 1881 ff. (vols. 33–8).

JOHANN HEINRICH VOSS. Born at Sommersdorf (Mecklenburg) 20 February 1751, the son of a poor schoolmaster. Friends enabled him to study classical philology at Göttingen; he then became a schoolmaster, and was later (after a stay at Jena and Weimar) appointed professor at the University of Heidelberg, where he died 29 March 1826. Voss is best known for his hexameter translations of Homer (*Odyssee*, 1781; *Iliad*, 1793), and for a number of hexameter idylls of which only *Luise* (1795) is still occasionally read.

Edition: Sämtliche Gedichte, 6 vols., Königsberg, 1892.

Select Bibliography

A. APPRECIATION OF LYRIC POETRY

S. BEHN: *Rhythmus und Ausdruck in deutscher Kunstsprache* (Bonn, 1921).
L. BERIGER: *Die literarische Wertung* (Halle, 1938).
M. BODKIN: *Archetypal Patterns in Poetry* (London, 1934).
C. BROOKS: *The Well-Wrought Urn* (English edition, London, 1949).
C. BROOKS and A. WARREN: *Understanding Poetry* (New York, 1938).
K. BÜCHER: *Arbeit und Rhythmus* (Leipzig, 1896).
H. BURGER (ed.): *Gedicht und Gedanke* (Halle, 1942).
K. BURKE: 'Freud and the Analysis of Poetry' (in *Philosophy of Literary Form*', New York, 1941).
W. DILTHEY: *Das Erlebnis und die Dichtung* (Berlin, 1905).
T. S. ELIOT: *Selected Essays* (London, 1932).
W. EMPSON: *Seven Types of Ambiguity* (revised edition, London, 1947).
N. FOERSTER: 'The Teaching of Great Literature' (*Journal of General Education*, I, 1947).
R. GRAVES: *The Common Asphodel* (London, 1949).
E. HIRT: *Das Formgesetz der epischen, dramatischen und lyrischen Dichtung* (Leipzig, 1923).
R. IMMERWAHR: 'German Lyric Theory since 1890' (*Germanic Review*, January 1937).
W. KAYSER: *Das sprachliche Kunstwerk* (Bern, 1948).
W. KAYSER: *Kleine deutsche Versschule* (Bern, 1946).
M. KOMMERELL: *Gedanken über Gedichte* (Frankfurt, 1933).
M. KOMMERELL: *Geist und Buchstabe der Dichtung* (3rd edition, Frankfurt, 1944).
G. LANSON: 'Quelques mots sur l'explication de textes' (in *Methodes de l'histoire litteraire*, Paris, 1925).
F. R. LEAVIS: *Education and the University* (London, 1943).

SELECT BIBLIOGRAPHY

C. DAY LEWIS: *The Poetic Image* (London, 1947).
J. PFEIFFER: *Das lyrische Gedicht als aesthetisches Gebilde* (Halle, 1931).
J. PFEIFFER: 'Ton und Gebärde in der Lyrik' (*Dichtung und Volkstum*, xxxvii, 1936).
J. PFEIFFER: *Umgang mit Dichtung* (6th edition, Hamburg, 1949).
H. READ: *Collected Essays in Literary Criticism* (London, 1938).
I. A. RICHARDS: *Practical Criticism; a Study of Literary Judgment* (London, 1929).
I. A. RICHARDS: *Principles of Literary Criticism* (London, 1925).
R. A. SCHRÖDER: 'On the Vocation of the Poet in the World of Time' (*German Life and Letters*, Jan. 1949).
E. SNYDER: *Hypnotic Poetry* (Philadelphia, 1930).
E. STAIGER: *Grundbegriffe der Poetik* (Zürich, 1946).
E. STAIGER: *Meisterwerke deutscher Sprache* (Zürich, 1943).
F. STRICH: *Der Dichter und die Zeit* (Bern, 1947).
E. M. W. TILLYARD: *Five Poems* (London, 1948).
E. M. W. TILLYARD: *Poetry Direct and Oblique* (London, 1945).
R. VIGNERON: *Explication de textes* (Chicago, 1928).
O. WALZEL: *Gehalt und Gestalt im Kunstwerk des Dichters* (Potsdam, 1927).
O. WALZEL: *Das Wortkunstwerk* (Leipzig, 1926).
H. WERNER: *Die Ursprünge der Lyrik* (München, 1924).
W. WITTE: 'The Sociological Approach to Literature' (*Mod. Lang. Rev.*, xxxvi, 1941).
The Letters of KEATS, G. M. HOPKINS, D. H. LAWRENCE, EZRA POUND, RILKE and W. B. YEATS.

B. HISTORY OF THE GERMAN LYRIC

F. BEISSNER: *Geschichte der deutschen Elegie* (Berlin, 1941).
E. BÜCKEN: *Das deutsche Lied. Probleme und Gestalten* (Hamburg, 1939).
A. CLOSS: *The Genius of the German Lyric* (London, 1938).
A. CLOSS: *Die freien Rhythmen in der deutschen Lyrik* (Bern, 1947).
E. ERMATINGER: *Die deutsche Lyrik seit Herder* (3 vols., 2nd edition, Leipzig and Berlin, 1925).

SELECT BIBLIOGRAPHY

R. FINDEIS: *Geschichte der deutschen Lyrik* (2 vols., Sammlung Göschen, Berlin, 1914).

A. GÖTZE: *Das deutsche Volkslied* (Leipzig, 1929).

R. IBEL: *Weltschau deutscher Dichter* (2 vols., Hamburg, 1943-8).

W. KAYSER: *Geschichte der deutschen Ballade* (Berlin, 1936).

A. H. KOBER: *Geschichte der religiösen Dichtung in Deutschland* (Essen, 1919).

I. LEES: *The German Lyric* (London, 1914).

N. MACLEOD: *German Lyric Poetry* (London, 1930).

G. MÜLLER: *Geschichte des deutschen Liedes* (München, 1925).

H. M. MUSTARD: *The Lyric Cycle in German Literature* (New York, 1946).

W. NELLE: *Geschichte des deutschen evangelischen Kirchenliedes* (3rd edition, Hamburg, 1928).

J. SCHOPP: *Das deutsche Arbeitslied* (Heidelberg, 1935).

E. SCHURÉ: *Histoire du Lied* (Paris, 1903).

H. SPIERO: *Geschichte der deutschen Lyrik seit Claudius* (2nd edition, Leipzig and Berlin, 1915).

CH. STRASSER: *Arbeiterdichtung* (Zürich, 1931).

H. WELTI: *Geschichte des Sonetts in der deutschen Dichtung* (Leipzig, 1884).

R. M. WERNER: *Lyrik und Lyriker* (Hamburg, 1890).

PH. WITKOP: *Die deutschen Lyriker von Luther bis Nietzsche* (2 vols., Berlin, 1925).

B. V. WIESE: *Politische Dichtung Deutschlands* (Berlin, 1931).

K. VIETOR: *Geschichte der deutschen Ode* (München, 1923).

C. OTHER WORKS

CHAPTER 2

F. KÄMMERER: *Studien zur Geschichte des Landschaftsgefühls in der deutschen Dichtung des frühen 18. Jahrhunderts* (Berlin, 1910).

M. DURACH: *Chr. Fr. Gellert, Dichter und Erzieher* (Dresden, 1938).

K. MAY: *Das Weltbild in Gellerts Dichtung* (Frankfurt, 1928).

A. BRANDL: *B. H. Brockes* (Innsbruck, 1878).

A. MANIKOWSKI: *Die Welt- und Lebensanschauung in dem 'Irdischen Vergnügen' von Brockes* (Greifswald, 1944).

SELECT BIBLIOGRAPHY

H. SCHUSTER: *Hagedorn und seine Bedeutung für die deutsche Literatur* (Leipzig, 1882).
E. KOZLOWSKI: *Gleim und die Klassiker* (Halle, 1906).
G. KOCH: *Gleims Scherzhafte Lieder* (Jena, 1894).
E. PETZET: *J. P. Uz* (2nd edition, Berlin, 1930).

CHAPTER 3

E. BUSCH: 'Die Form von Klopstocks Oden' (*Germ. Rom. Monatsschrift*, January 1949).
E. KAUSSMANN: *Der Stil der Oden Klopstocks* (Leipzig, 1931).
M. H. JELLINEK: *Bemerkungen über Klopstocks Dichtersprache* (Walzel Festschrift, Potsdam, 1924).
K. KINDT: *Klopstock* (Berlin, 1941).
F. MUNCKER: *F. G. Klopstock* (Stuttgart, 1888).
O. WALZEL: *Klopstock*. (*Jahrbuch des freien deutschen Hochstifts* Frankfurt, 1926).
H. RUETTE: *Hölty, sein Leben und Dichten* (Guben, 1883).
E. ALBERT: *Höltys Naturgefühl* (Dortmund, 1910).
J. PFEIFFER: *Matthias Claudius, der Wandsbecker Bote* (Bremen, 1947).
U. ROEDE: *Matthias Claudius. Sein Weg und seine Welt* (Berlin, 1934).
W. STAMMLER: *Matthias Claudius* (Halle, 1915).

CHAPTER 4

H. A. KORFF: *Geist der Goethezeit* (3 vols., Leipzig, 1923-40).
M. KOMMERELL: *Der Dichter als Führer in der deutschen Klassik* (Berlin, 1928).
W. REHM: *Griechentum und Goethezeit* (Leipzig, 1936).
F. SCHULZ: *Klassik und Romantik der Deutschen* (2 vols., Stuttgart, 1935-40).
F. STRICH: *Deutsche Klassik und Romantik* (3rd edition), (München, 1928).
L. A. WILLOUGHBY: *The Classical Age of German Literature* (1748-1805) (Oxford, 1926).

SELECT BIBLIOGRAPHY

E. KIRCHNER: *Volkslieder und Volkspoesie in der Sturm- und Drangzeit* (Strassburg, 1902).
H. BAUMGART: *Goethes lyrische Dichtung* (3 vols., Heidelberg, 1931–9).
J. BOYD: *Notes to Goethe's Poems* (2 vols., Oxford, 1944–9).
B. FAIRLEY: *Goethe as Revealed in his Poetry* (London–Toronto, 1932).
B. FAIRLEY: *A Study of Goethe* (London, 1948).
V. HEHN: *Ueber Goethes Gedichte* (Stuttgart, 1911).
A. HÜBNER: 'Goethe und die deutsche Sprache' (*Goethe*, II, Weimar, 1937).
R. IBEL: *Der junge Goethe* (Bremen, 1949).
H. KEIPERT: *Die Wandlung Goethescher Gedichte zum klassischen Stil* (Jena, 1933).
A. KÖSTER: 'Ganymed' (*Goethe-Jahrbuch*, xix, Weimar, 1908).
W. F. OTTO: *Der griechische Göttermythos bei Goethe und Hölderlin* (Berlin, 1939).
H. H. SCHAEDER: *Goethes Erlebnis des Ostens* (Leipzig, 1938).
E. TRUNZ: 'Goethes späte Lyrik' (*Deutsche Vierteljahrsschrift*, xxiii, 1949).
K. VIETOR: *Goethes Altersgedichte: Euphorion xxxiii* (1932).
E. M. WILKINSON: 'Goethe's Poetry' (*German Life and Letters*, July 1949).

CHAPTER 5

K. BERGER: *Schiller, sein Leben und seine Werke* (2 vols., Berlin 1890.)
H. H. BORCHERDT: *Schiller und seine geistige und künstlerische Entwicklung* (Leipzig, 1929).
H. CYSARZ: *Schiller* (Halle, 1934).
H. B. GARLAND: *Schiller* (London, 1949).
M. GERHARD: *Schiller* (Bern, 1950).
E. KÜHNEMANN: *Schiller und seine Welt* (Leipzig, 1934).
G. ROSENTHAL: Schillers Gedicht 'Das Ideal und das Leben' (*Bergs Jahrbücher*, xxxix, 1917).
W. WITTE: *Schiller* (Oxford, 1949).

SELECT BIBLIOGRAPHY

CHAPTER 6

F. BEISSNER: *Hölderlins Uebersetzungen aus dem Griechischen* (Stuttgart, 1933).
F. BEISSNER: 'Vom Baugesetz der späteren Hymnen Hölderlins' (in *Hölderlin Jahrbuch*, Tübingen, 1950).
P. BERTAUX: *Hölderlin* (Paris, 1936).
P. BÖCKMANN: *Hölderlin und seine Götter* (München, 1935).
W. BOEHM: *Hölderlin* (Halle, 1928).
R. GUARDINI: *Hölderlin. Weltbild und Frömmigkeit* (Leipzig, 1939).
M. HEIDEGGER: *Erläuterungen zu Hölderlins Dichtung* (Frankfurt, 1944).
N. V. HELLINGRATH: *Hölderlin-Vermächtnis* (Frankfurt, 1936).
M. MONTGOMERY: *F. Hölderlin and the German Neo-Hellenic Movement* (London, 1923).
E. MÜLLER: *Hölderlin* (Stuttgart-Berlin, 1944).
R. PEACOCK: *Hölderlin* (London, 1938).
D. SEKEL: *Hölderlins Sprachrhythmus* (Leipzig, 1937).
E. L. STAHL: 'Hölderlin's Poetic Mission' (*German Life and Letters*, October, 1948).
E. L. STAHL: *Hölderlin's Symbolism* (Oxford, 1945).
K. VIETOR: *Die Lyrik Hölderlins* (Frankfurt, 1921).
E. G. WINKLER: *Der späte Hölderlin* (Dessau, 1943).

CHAPTER 7

R. BENZ: *Die deutsche Romantik* (Leipzig, 1937).
F. GUNDOLF: *Romantiker* (2 vols., Berlin, 1930-1).
R. HUCH: *Die Romantik* (2 vols., 3rd edition, Leipzig, 1908).
P. KLUCKHOHN: *Die deutsche Romantik* (Leipzig, 1924).
S. V. LEMPICKI: 'Bücherwelt und wirkliche Welt' (*Deutsche Vierteljahrsschrift*, III, 1925).
H. LEVIN: *Die Heidelberger Romantik* (München, 1922).
J. NADLER: *Die Berliner Romantik* (Berlin, 1921).
J. PETERSEN: *Die Wesensbestimmung der deutschen Romantik* (Leipzig, 1926).
T. STEINBÜCHEL (ed): *Romantik. Ein Zyklus Tübinger Vorlesungen* (Tübingen, 1948).

SELECT BIBLIOGRAPHY

R. ULLMANN und H. GOTTHARD: *Geschichte des Begriffs 'romantisch' in Deutschland* (Berlin, 1926).

L. A. WILLOUGHBY: *The Romantic Movement in Germany* (Oxford, 1930).

H. LICHTENBERGER: *Novalis* (Paris, 1912).

R. PEACOCK: 'The Poetry of Novalis' (in *German Studies presented to H. G. Fiedler*, Oxford, 1938).

H. RITTER: *Novalis' Hymnen an die Nacht* (Heidelberg, 1930).

H. GUMBEL: *Ludwig Tiecks dichterischer Weg* (Halle, 1929).

E. H. ZEYDEL: *Ludwig Tieck the German Romanticist* (Princetown, 1935).

H. JÄGER: *Cl. Brentanos frühe Lyrik* (Frankfurt, 1926).

K. SCHUBERT: *Cl. Brentanos weltliche Lyrik* (Breslau, 1910).

W. SCHELLBERG: *Cl. Brentano* (München-Gladbach, 1922).

I. SEIDEL: *Brentano* (Stuttgart, 1944).

H. BRANDENBURG: *J. v. Eichendorff, sein Leben und Werk* (München, 1922).

J. HOFFMEISTER: *Nachgoethesche Lyrik* (Bonn, 1948).

J. NADLER: *Eichendorffs Lyrik* (Cologne, 1911).

B. V. WIESE: 'Rede über Eichendorff' (*Zeitschrift für deutsche Bildung*, 1933, pp. 71–8).

CHAPTER 8

H. H. HOUBEN: *Jungdeutscher Sturm und Drang* (Leipzig, 1911).

H. V. KLEINMAYR: *Welt- und Kunstanschauung des jungen Deutschland* (Wien, 1930).

CHR. PETZET: *Die Blütezeit der deutschen politischen Lyrik* (München, 1903).

H. G. ATKINS: *Heine* (London, 1929).

E. ELSTER: *Das Vorbild der freien Rhythmen Heinrich Heines*. '*Euphorion*' xxv (1924).

H. HERRMANN: *Studien zu Heines Romanzero* (Berlin, 1922).

J. LEGRAS: *Henri Heine, Poète* (Paris, 1897).

C. F. REINHOLD: *Heinrich Heine* (Berlin, 1920).

A. STRODTMANN: *Heines Leben und Werke* (2nd revised edition, 2 vols., Berlin, 1873).

H. WALTER: *Heinrich Heine* (London and Toronto, 1930).

SELECT BIBLIOGRAPHY

E. BALDINGER: *Die Gedankenwelt der 'Gedichte eines Lebendigen'* (Tübingen, 1917).

A. TRAMPE: *Georg Herwegh. Sein Leben und sein Schaffen* (München, 1910).

P. BESSON: *Freiligrath* (Paris, 1899).

E. G. GUDDE: *Freiligraths Entwicklung als politischer Dichter* (Berlin, 1922).

M. F. LIDDELL: *Poems by Ferdinand Freiligrath* (Oxford, 1949).

THOMAS MANN: 'Platen' (in *Adel des Geistes*, Stockholm, 1945).

R. SCHLÖSSER: *August von Platen. Ein Bild seines geistigen Schaffens* (2 vols., München, 1910–13).

R. UNGER: *Platen in seinem Verhältnis zu Goethe* (Berlin, 1909).

CHAPTER 9

H. BIEBER: *Der Kampf um die Tradition. Die deutsche Dichtung im europäischen Geistesleben 1830–80* (Stuttgart, 1928).

R. M. MEYER: *Die deutsche Literatur des 19. Jahrhunderts* (Berlin, 1900).

G. FRÜHBRODT: *Der Impressionismus in der Lyrik der A. v. Droste-Hülshoff* (Berlin, 1930).

C. HESELHAUS: *Annette von Droste-Hülshoff* (Halle, 1943).

C. HESELHAUS: 'Die späten Gedichte der Droste' (*Zeitschrift für deutsche Philologie*, LXX, 1947).

H. HÜFFER: *A. v. Droste-Hülshoff und ihre Werke* (3rd edition, Gotha, 1911).

E. STAIGER: *A. v. Droste-Hülshoff* (Zürich, 1933).

A. GOES: *Mörike* (Stuttgart, 1944).

W. EIGENBROD: *Mörike Studien I. 'Euphorion' xiv* (1907).

H. HESSE: *Eduard Mörike* (Leipzig, 1911).

H. MAYNC: *E. Mörike, sein Leben und Dichten* (4th edition, Stuttgart, 1927).

B. V. WIESE: *Eduard Mörike* (Tübingen und Stuttgart, 1950).

H. BOESCHENSTEIN: *Gottfried Keller. Grundzüge seines Lebens und Werkes* (Bern, 1948).

F. HEYDEN: 'Gottfried Kellers "Abendlied"', *Zeitschrift für Deutschkunde* XLII (1928).

A. KÖSTER: *Keller. Sieben Vorlesungen* (4th edition, Leipzig, 1923).

SELECT BIBLIOGRAPHY

H. MAYNC: *Gottfried Keller. Sein Bildnis und seine Werke* (Frauenfeld, 1923).
G. MÜLLER-GSCHWEND: *Keller als lyrischer Dichter* (Wien, 1910).
A. WEYMANN-BISCHOFF: *Keller und die Romantik* (München, 1917).
H. BINDER: *Theodor Storm. Ein deutscher Lyriker* (Leipzig, 1914).
H. HEITMANN: *Theodor Storm* (Stuttgart, 1943).
W. HERRMANN: *Th. Storms Lyrik* (Leipzig, 1911).
H. E. KNOTH: *Th. Storm als Lyriker* (Leipzig, 1906).
P. SCHÜTZE und E. LANGE: *Th. Storms Leben und Dichtungen* (4th edition, Berlin, 1925).

CHAPTER 10

E. PETZET: *Paul Heyse, ein deutscher Lyriker* (Leipzig, 1914).
H. SPIERO: *Heyse, der Dichter und sein Werk* (Stuttgart, 1910).
L. FISCHER: *Der Kampf um den Naturalismus* (Borna, 1930).
W. MAHRHOLZ: *Deutsche Literatur der Gegenwart* (Berlin, 1931).
H. NAUMANN: *Die Dichtung der Gegenwart* (Stuttgart, 1923).
A. SOERGEL: *Dichtung und Dichter der Zeit I* (Leipzig, 1911).
H. W. FISCHER: *Arno Holz. Eine Einführung in sein Werk* (Berlin, 1924).
K. TURLEY: *Arno Holz. Der Weg eines Künstlers* (Leipzig, 1935).

CHAPTER 11

W. BRECHT: *C. F. Meyer und das Kunstwerk seiner Gedichtsammlung* (Wien, 1918).
A. FREY: *C. F. Meyer, sein Leben und seine Werke* (4th edition, Stuttgart, 1925).
H. V. LERBER: *C. F. Meyer. Der Mensch in der Spannung* (Basel, 1949).
H. MAYNE: *C. F. Meyer und sein Werk* (Frauenfeld, 1925).
A. SCHRÖDER: *Kritische Studien zu den Gedichten C. F. Meyers* (Cologne, 1928).
J. BITHELL: *Modern German Literature* (London, 1939).
F. LENNARTZ: *Die Dichter unserer Zeit* (Leipzig, 1938).

SELECT BIBLIOGRAPHY

J. M. M. ALER: *Im Spiegel der Form* (Amsterdam, 1947).
C. M. BOWRA: *The Heritage of Symbolism* (London, 1943).
F. GUNDOLF: *George* (Berlin, 1920).
F. HERMANN: *George und Hofmannsthal* (Zürich, 1947).
W. KOCH: *Stefan George. Weltbild — Naturbild — Menschenbild* (Halle, 1933).
E. MORWITZ: *Die Dichtung Stefan Georges* (Godesberg, 1949).
H. RÖSSNER: *Georgekreis und Literaturwissenschaft* (Frankfurt, 1938).
F. WOLTERS: *Stefan George und die Blätter für die Kunst* (Berlin, 1930).
R. ALEWYN: *Hofmannsthals Wandlung* (Frankfurt, 1949).
W. H. BERENDSOHN: *Der Impressionismus Hofmannsthals* (Hamburg, 1920).
M. KOMMERELL: *H. v. Hofmannsthal* (Frankfurt, 1930).
K. J. NAEF: *H. v. Hofmannsthals Wesen und Werk* (Zürich-Leipzig, 1938).
W. PERL: *Das lyrische Jugendwerk H. v. Hofmannsthals* (Berlin, 1936).

CHAPTER 12

J. F. ANGELLOZ: *R. M. Rilke, Évolution spirituelle d'un poète* (Paris, 1936).
D. BASSERMANN: *Am Rande des Unsagbaren* (Buxtehude, 1948).
D. BASSERMANN: *Der späte Rilke* (München, 1946).
E. M. BUTLER: *R. M. Rilke* (London, 1946).
F. DEHN: *R. M. Rilke und sein Werk. Eine Deutung* (Leipzig, 1934).
R. GUARDINI: *Zu R. M. Rilkes Deutung des Daseins* (Berlin, 1941).
H. E. HOLTHUSEN: *Der späte Rilke* (Zurich, 1949).
H. E. HOLTHUSEN: *Die Sonette an Orpheus* (München, 1937).
W. KOHLSCHMIDT: *R. M. Rilke* (Lübeck, 1948).
E. KRETSCHMAR: *Goethe und Rilke* (Dresden, 1937).
J. B. LEISHMAN: Introduction and Notes to his translations of Rilke's poems, published in London by the Hogarth Press.
E. C. MASON: *Lebenshaltung und Symbolik bei R. M. Rilke* (Weimar, 1939).
H. PONGS: *Rilkes Umschlag und das Erlebnis der Frontgeneration.* 'Dichtung und Volkstum' (1936).

SELECT BIBLIOGRAPHY

W. ROSE and R. CRAIG HOUSTON (ed.): *Rainer Maria Rilke. Aspects of his Mind and Poetry* (London, 1938).
P. ZECH: *R. M. Rilke* (Dresden, 1930).

D. SOME ENGLISH TRANSLATIONS OF GERMAN LYRIC POETRY

(Only twentieth-century translations are here listed; for the rest, the reader is referred to B. Q. Morgan's admirable *Critical Bibliography of German Literature in English Translation*, 2nd edition, Stanford University Press, 1938.)

N. MACLEOD: *German Lyric Poetry* (Contains specimens of nearly all the poets mentioned in this book) (London, 1930).
A. MÜNSTERBERG: *A Harvest of German Verse* (Most of the poets mentioned in this book) (New York, 1916).
K. FRANCKE and W. G. HOWARD (ed.): *The German Classics of the 19th and 20th Centuries* (Most of the poets mentioned in chapters 6-12) (New York, 1913-15).
D. BROICHER: *German Lyrics and Ballads done into English Verse* (Goethe, Brentano, Eichendorff, Hölderlin, Lenau, Meyer, Mörike, Platen, Storm) (London, 1912).
A. DAVIDSON: *Anthology of German Songs and Lyrics* (Claudius, Goethe, Schiller, Eichendorff, Heine, Lenau) (London, 1949).
A. H. FOX-STRANGWAYS and ST. WILSON (ed.): *Schubert's Songs* (Claudius, Hölty, Goethe, Schiller, Heine) (London, 1924).
L. YOUNG: *German Lyrics for English Singers* (Goethe, Heine, Mörike, and others) (Oxford, 1928).
G. F. CUNNINGHAM: *Translations from Goethe*[1] (Edinburgh and London, 1949).
G. CLARKE: *The Ballads and Shorter Poems of Schiller*[2] (London, 1901).
J. B. LEISHMAN: *Selected Poems of Friedrich Hölderlin.* (London, 1944).

[1] For a full list of earlier translations of Goethe, see S. M. Hinz: *Goethe's Poems in England translated after 1860* (Univ. of Wisconsin Studies, 1928).
[2] A list of other translations of Schiller's poetry will be found in T. Rea: *Schiller's Dramas and Poems in England* (London, 1906).

SELECT BIBLIOGRAPHY

M. HAMBURGER: *Poems of Friedrich Hölderlin* (London, 1943).
F. PROKOSCH: *Some Poems of Friedrich Hölderlin* (Norfolk, Conn., 1943).
M. COTTERELL: *Novalis. Hymns to Night* (London, 1948).
M. ROSSI: *J. v. Eichendorff: The Happy Wanderer, and Other Poems* (Boston, 1925).
F. EWEN (ed.): *Heinrich Heine. Poetry and Prose* (New York, 1948).
A. GRAY: *Songs from Heine* (London, 1928).
H. M. JONES: *Heine's Poem: The North Sea* (Chicago, 1916).
R. B. LEVY: *Heinrich Heine. Poems and Ballads* (London, 1914).
H. WOLFE: *Heine: Selected Lyrics* (London, 1935).
Heine's Prose and Poetry (Everyman's Library) (London, 1934).
R. B. COOK: *August von Platen-Hallermünde: Sonnets from Venice* (Boston, 1923).
W. and C. A. PHILLIPS: *Eduard Mörike: Mozart on the Way to Prague* (contains: *Denk es, o Seele* ...) (Oxford, 1934).
B. DEUTSCH and A. YARMOLINSKY: *Contemporary German Poetry* (Holz, Dehmel, George, Rilke) (New York, 1923).
B. Q. MORGAN: *Modern German Poets in English Translation* (Dehmel, George, Hofmannsthal, Rilke) (New York, 1937).
J. BITHELL: *Contemporary German Poetry* (Hofmannsthal, Rilke) (London, 1909).
D. BROICHER: *German Lyrists of To-day* (George, Hofmannsthal) (London, 1909).
C. SCOTT: *Selections from Stefan George* (London, 1910).
C. N. VALHOPE and E. MORWITZ: *Stefan George: Poems* (London, 1944).
C. W. STARK: *Hugo von Hofmannsthal: Lyrical Poems* (Yale, 1918).
J. B. LEISHMAN: *Rainer Maria Rilke: Requiem and other Poems* (London, 1935).
J. B. LEISHMAN: *Rainer Maria Rilke: Sonnets to Orpheus* (London, 1936).
J. B. LEISHMAN: *Rainer Maria Rilke: Later Poems* (London, 1938).
J. B. LEISHMAN and STEPHEN SPENDER: *R. M. Rilke: Duino Elegies* (London, 1939).
J. B. LEISHMAN: *Rainer Maria Rilke: Selected Poems* (London, 1941).

SELECT BIBLIOGRAPHY

J. LEMONT: *Rainer Maria Rilke: Poems* (New York, 1943).

C. F. MACINTYRE: *R. M. Rilke: Fifty Selected Poems* (Berkeley, Calif., 1940).

V. and E. SACKVILLE-WEST: *R. M. Rilke: Elegies from the Castle of Duino*[1] (London, 1931).

[1]For a fuller bibliography of Rilke translations, see R. v. Mises: *Rilke in English*, Cambridge, Mass., 1947.

General Index

Alewyn, Richard, 206, 210
Anacreontic Poetry, 34, 38, 41, 55, 236
'Anastasius Grün', 145
'Angelus Silesius', 27
Aristophanes, 61
Arnim, Achim von, 127, 231
Arnold, Matthew, 152
Atkinson, Margaret, 125
Aufklärung, 26-35, 52

Baroque, 27-8, 31, 32, 52
Bassermann, Dieter, 224
Becher, Johannes R., 229
Biedermeier, 167, 173
Blake, William, 72
Blätter für die Kunst, 195, 201
Bodmer, J. J., 28
Boisserée, Sulpice, 81, 125
Börne, Ludwig, 148
Breitinger, J. J., 28
Brentano, Clemens, 24, 121-6, 127, 140, 163, 231
Brockes, Barthold H., 32, 33, 39, 231
Bröger, Karl, 18-20, 231
Buber, Martin, 230
Bürger, Gottfried A., 18
Byron, Lord, 75, 152, 210

Catullus, 74
Chaucer, Geoffrey, 152
Claudius, Matthias, 9, 47-53, 232
Closs, August, 49, 190
Coleridge, Samuel Taylor, 4, 6, 11, 111
Collings, E., 188
Conrad, Joseph, 9

Dahn, Felix, 186-8, 232
Dante, 169

Dehmel, Richard, 190, 232
Donne, John, 222
Droste-Hülshoff, Annette von, 161-7, 174, 177, 178, 232
Dryden, John, 229
Dubarry, Marie Jeanne de, 214

Eckermann, Johann P., 71, 75
Eichendorff, Josef von, 21-3, 126-37, 140, 163, 233
Eliot, T. S., 5, 18, 30, 126, 229
Empson, William, 72
Esenbeck, Nees von, 81
Estienne, Henri, 34

Feuerbach, Ludwig, 175
Fleming, Paul, 27
Forster, Leonard, 229
Fragonard, Jean Honoré, 214, 215
Frederick William III, 145
Frederick William IV, 145
Freiligrath, Ferdinand, 145, 149, 206, 233

Geibel, Emanuel, 183, 184, 188, 233
Gellert, Christian F., 26-30, 33, 38, 39, 41, 43, 52, 234
George, Stefan, 126, 194-203, 210, 211, 229, 230, 234
Gessner, Salomon, 35
Gleim, Johann W. L., 34, 54, 234
Goethe, Johann Wolfgang von, 34, 35, 44, 53, 54-82, 89, 92, 94, 99, 100, 116, 121, 123-5, 132, 135-6, 144, 163, 169, 172, 174, 176, 229, 230, 235
Goldschnittlyriker, 183
Gontard, Susette, 95
Görres, Josef von, 128

259

GENERAL INDEX

Göttinger Hain, 44-5, 49, 239
Gottsched, Johann Christoph, 34
Götz, Nikolaus, 34, 54, 236
Gray, Thomas, 229
Grierson, Sir Herbert, 77
Grimm, Brothers, 128, 205
Gryphius, Andreas, 28
Gutzkow, Karl, 148

Hafiz, 78
Hagedorn, Friedrich von, 30-5, 38, 39, 41, 43, 52, 236
Haller, Albrecht von, 32, 35, 39, 41
Hamann, Johann Georg, 55, 61
Hart, Heinrich and Julius, 186, 189, 190
Hauptmann, Gerhart, 190
Hebbel, Friedrich, 236
Hegel, Georg W. F., 6
Heidegger, Martin, 219
Heine, Heinrich, 10-11, 20, 30, 138-56, 157, 163, 186, 237, 243
Henckell, Karl, 190
Herder, Johann Gottfried von, 43, 55, 56, 57, 60, 61, 127
Hertz, Wilhelm, 184-5, 186, 237
Herwegh, Georg, 145, 149, 153, 238
Heym, Georg, 229
Heyse, Paul, 182, 184, 188-9, 238
Hoffmann, E. T. A., 136
Hofmannsthal, Hugo von, 204-10, 238
Hölderlin, Friedrich, 6, 14-18, 42, 66, 89, 92, 93-111, 113-14, 115, 117, 229, 238
Hölty, Ludwig, 43-7, 49, 51, 52, 71, 163, 239
Holz, Arno, 189-90, 239
Homer, 94
Hopkins, Gerard Manley, 78, 165, 188-9, 213, 219
Horace, 34, 35
Huysmans, J. K., 200

Immermann, Karl, 59
Insel, Die, 200

James, Henry, 210, 213, 230
Jaspers, Karl, 219
Jefferies, Richard, 63
Jonson, Ben, 230
Jungdeutschland, 148, 162, 163, 166, 219

Kalkreuth, Graf E. von, 244
Keats, John, 223, 229
Keller, Gottfried, 163, 174-7, 178, 239
Keyes, Sidney, 213
Kierkegaard, Sören, 219, 228
Kleist, Ewald von, 32, 35, 39, 41, 240
Klopstock, Friedrich G., 34, 36-43, 44, 45, 46, 49, 51, 52, 61, 63, 66, 71, 92, 100, 163, 230, 240
Knights, L. C., 46
Körner, Theodor, 145
Köster, Albert, 63

Lafontaine, Jean de, 30
Laube, Heinrich, 148
Lawrence, D. H., 7, 14, 186, 188, 225
Lenau, Nikolaus, 14-17, 18, 158, 240
Lessing, Gotthold E., 28, 34
Lewis, C. Day, 159
Lingg, Hermann, 185-6, 241
Louis XV, 214
Lowes, Livingston, 195
Ludwig, Otto, 162

Maltitz, 153
Mann, Thomas, 160, 178, 181
Marsh, Sir Edward, 14
Maupassant, Guy de, 213
Maximilian II, 183
Meyer, Conrad F., 191-4, 199, 241
Milton, John, 229
Mittelachsenverse, 190
Mommsen, Theodor, 162
Mörike, Eduard, 7, 9, 12-14, 92, 163, 164-5, 167-74, 177, 178, 230, 241
Moser, Moses, 152
Mozart, Wolfgang A., 14
Mundt, Theodor, 148

GENERAL INDEX

Munich School, 183-9, 191, 196, 229, 238

Naturalism, 189-90, 195, 239
Neo-Platonism, 207
Nerval, Gérard de, 205
Neuffer, 42
Nietzsche, Friedrich, 159, 182-3, 198, 199, 202, 220, 242
'Novalis', 9, 81, 100, 112-20, 122, 129, 132, 140, 144, 173, 230, 242

Opitz, Martin, 27

Peacock, Thomas L., 1
Pfeiffer, Johannes, 9
Platen, August von, 9, 143, 145, 153, 156-60, 183, 191, 242
Plato, 61
Poetic Realism, 161-81, 184, 194, 229, 230
Pope, Alexander, 229, 230
Propertius, 75

Richards, I. A., 6
Rilke, Rainer Maria, 1-5, 17, 209, 211-28, 229, 230, 243
Rococo, 56, 60
Rodin, Auguste, 213
Romanticism, 46, 58, 89, 98, 100, 112-37, 140, 142-3, 157, 159, 162, 166, 173, 186, 229

Saadi, 78
St. Francis of Assisi, 218
St. John of the Cross, 118
Saint-Simonianism, 149
Savigny, Hans von, 229
Scheffel, Viktor von, 186, 188, 189, 243
Schenkendorf, Max von, 145
Schiller, Friedrich von, 18, 28, 42, 60, 83-92, 94, 144, 156, 239, 244
Schlegel, August W. von, 114, 115, 126
Schlegel, Friedrich von, 58, 114, 127
Schlosser, Friedrich, 82

Schottel, J. G., 27
Schubert, Franz, 124
Shakespeare, William, 94
Shelley, Percy Bysshe, 6, 7
Sophocles, 94
Southey, Robert, 152
Spender, Stephen, 222
Spenser, Edmund, 45, 71
Spinoza, Baruch, 60
Stein, Charlotte von, 68
Sterne, Laurence, 49
Stifter, Adalbert, 167
Stolberg, Christian and Friedrich, 45
Storm, Theodor, 23-4, 30, 163, 177-81, 230, 244
Sturm und Drang, 61, 62, 74, 76
Symbolism, 192, 195

Themistocles, 95, 99
Thomson, James, 229
Tibullus, 75
Tieck, Ludwig, 46, 114, 115, 122, 140, 245
Trakl, Georg, 229

Uz, Johann P., 34, 245

Verlaine, Paul, 192
Vischer, Friedrich Th., 169
Volkslied, 127-9, 186, 231
Voss, Johann H., 45, 245

Wagner, Richard, 120
Waller, Edmund, 175
Weimar Classicism, 76-7, 94
Werfel, Franz, 217
Wieland, Christoph M., 45
Wienbarg, Ludwig, 148
Wilde, Oscar, 200
Wilkinson, Elisabeth M., 135
Wilson, John, 7
Wolf, Hugo, 184
Wordsworth, William, 7, 142, 171-2, 229

Yeats, W. B., 50
Young, Edward, 55

Index of First Lines

An des Balkones Gitter lehnte ich...	161
Augen, meine lieben Fensterlein,...	174
Ausgesetzt auf den Bergen des Herzens. Siehe, wie klein dort,...	218
Dämmrung senkte sich von oben...	135
Dämmrung will die Flügel spreiten...	131
Der Nachtigall reizende Lieder...	30
Die fischer überliefern dass im süden...	199
Ein Bruder und eine Schwester...	182
Ein Tännlein grünet wo,...	12
Erschlagen lag mit seinem Heer...	187
Es ging Maria in den Morgen hinein...	126
Es sang vor langen Jahren...	121
Es schlug mein Herz. Geschwind, zu Pferde!...	54
Ewigklar und spiegelrein und eben...	83
Fern hallt Musik; doch hier ist stille Nacht...	177
Grössers wolltest auch du, aber die Liebe zwingt...	14
Hinunter in der Erde Schoss...	112
Holder Lenz, du bist dahin!...	14
Ich aber lag am Rande des Schiffes...	138
Im düstern Auge keine Träne...	143
Im wunderschönen Monat Mai...	10
Immer leiser wird mein Schlummer...	185
In Spiegelbildern wie von Fragonard...	211
Krapülinski und Waschlapski...	150
Manche freilich müssen drunten sterben...	204
Meine Ruh' ist hin,...	123
Mit gelben Birnen hänget...	17
Mühle lass die arme still...	194
O Fluss, mein Fluss im Morgenstrahl!...	167
O Täler weit, o Höhen...	20
O wie fühl' ich in Rom mich so froh! Gedenk' ich der Zeiten,...	73

INDEX OF FIRST LINES

Sagt es niemand, nur den Weisen...	77
Schliesse mir die Augen beide...	23
Schön ist, Mutter Natur, deiner Erfindung Pracht...	36
Schwarzschattende Kastanie,...	191
So schlafe nun, du Kleine!...	47
Trennen wollten wir uns? Wähnten es gut und klug?...	93
Und frische Nahrung, neues Blut...	63
Und Kinder wachsen auf mit tiefen Augen...	204
Ungezählte Hände sind bereit...	19
Unter blühenden Bäumen...	184
Venedig liegt nur noch im Land der Träume...	156
Verlangst du ein zufriednes Herz...	26
Voller Apfel, Birne und Banane...	223
Warum gabst du uns die tiefen Blicke...	67
Wenn der silberne Mond durch die Gesträuche blickt...	43
Wer kennt ihn, diesen, welcher sein Gesicht...	1
Wie im Morgenrot...	59
Wie wenn am Feiertage, das Feld zu sehn...	100

For Product Safety Concerns and Information please contact our EU
representative GPSR@taylorandfrancis.com
Taylor & Francis Verlag GmbH, Kaufingerstraße 24, 80331 München, Germany

www.ingramcontent.com/pod-product-compliance
Lightning Source LLC
Chambersburg PA
CBHW071813300426
44116CB00009B/1303